A sketch of Erroll Bruce, aged 27, drawn in 1940 by his cousin Peter Scott, the naturalist.

FROM DUCK POND TO DEEP OCEAN
– a life of adventure

Erroll Bruce

Boldre Marine
Kestrel Cottage, Shirley Holms, Lymington,
Hampshire, SO41 8NH.
Tel & Fax (01590)683106

Page layout by *Dragonfly*, 117 Portland Road, Bournemouth BH9 1NG.

Contents

CHAPTER ONE

A Parson's Son 1913-1930

Born in Birmingham, 4 November 1913, about as far from the coast as anywhere in Britain, it seems odd that so much of my life was associated with the sea. My mother, born Rachel Gurney, was ill at my birth, so we did not see each other for several weeks, but that did not stop her being the main influence in my life for the first few years.

Indeed longer than that, as we spent a month or more each summer at her mother's home in Norfolk, Northrepps Hall, a large country estate surrounded by the estates of other Gurneys, besides Buxton and Barclay kinsmen, who seemed often to marry each other's cousins.

My mother did not conform in that way. While walking on the farm at threshing time, a Buxton cousin came by with a young parson, Rosslyn Bruce, on crutches after a hunting accident. When a rat ran out the cousin missed it with his stick, while the parson hurled one of his crutches, scoring a direct hit, but leaving himself sprawled on the ground. Her sporting instincts were roused by the accurate shot while her sympathies were inspired by the need to help him to his feet. Romance followed.

By the time I, their third child, was born, my father was busy as a vicar of a large Birmingham parish. He was also a Territorial Army chaplain and, as the Great War broke out soon after my birth, this added to his work and for a short time took him to France, later going to America to visit President Roosevelt over a diplomatic affair.

Northrepps Hall stood in its estate beside the Norfolk Coast.

Though Norfolk was far closer to the path of a Zeppelin than Birmingham, I was sent to Northrepps for a long period of recuperation after a major abdominal operation when only four years old. It was then that I first went to sea. A Gurney uncle, on leave from the Western Front, drove me in a pony trap to nearby Overstrand where an elderly fisherman launched a boat from the beach and took us for a short sail in the North Sea.

The horrors of the Great War seemed very far away and were only dimly sensed by a small child. Yet the memory of the Armistice a few days after my fifth birthday is still vivid. By that time I was attending an infant class, walking a mile or so with my elder sister Rhalou, who attended a junior class at the same school. One morning I had gone to the cloakroom when there was much shouting and noise of children running. By the time I could get my trousers on there was not a sign of anyone in the classroom, and through the windows came peals of church bells. I peeped into the next classroom - no-one there either. Could it be a Zeppelin raid I wondered? But I had no idea what to do.

It really was an anxious wait all by myself, before my Mother arrived. She told me that the war was over, so everyone had rushed to give thanks in church, and only when that was over did she realise that I was missing. She searched the house before running to the school only to find it locked. At last she found the caretaker who opened it up to disclose a very frightened little boy.

At the age of seven I was sent to boarding school. My brother Merlin, four years older than me, escorted me by train to Oxford and introduced me to Summerfields, a school well known for its classical education. Maybe it also taught me some self dependence. At the start of the second term I was unwell, so could not return with Merlin. A week later I was allowed to travel on my own by train to Oxford with my school trunk, and from the station it meant hiring a hansom cab, as taxis were still rather few.

Certainly I enjoyed Summerfields, right from the start. Apart from Merlin at the top of the school, there were some cousins from Norfolk of about my age. Only one point annoyed me. The woman who coached the very young at cricket insisted we bat and bowl right-handed, while I had previously made some progress left-handed. This put me off cricket. Yet for rugger and soccer the male coaches accepted the left foot, but of course encouraged the use of both. So in time I played in the first teams.

Yet one is sent to school for more than games and learning to swim in the River Cherwell, which bordered the school grounds. I liked all the masters, some of whom came our way in the holidays. So I made quite reasonable progress with lessons, except for Greek, despite having a Greek princess in my ancestry. Dr. Allington, the headmaster, who expected a high proportion of his boys to gain scholarships to Public Schools, stressed that Greek was essential for this but, if I insisted on the Modern Side, there would still be a chance of an Exhibition at Dartmouth with a naval career to follow.

Until that time, my Mother had hinted in terms of a career for me in her family bank of Barclays, as I was top of the form in what she called 'sums'. With Merlin already at Dartmouth, she felt that having both her sons in the Navy was going too far. However my Father pointed out that on his side of the family there was my uncle, Captain Robert Falcon Scott, who had died coming back from the South Pole and also another uncle, Wilfred Bruce, who had been on Scott's expedition, although not in the final team which was lost. The choice was left to me. Although banking was in my blood from my Mother's side, I felt drawn to the instincts that ran on my Father's side for sea and discovery. I firmly opted for the Navy, although my Father pointed out that if I failed to gain an exhibition, he could probably not afford to send me to Dartmouth.

By then he had moved on from Birmingham to a fine country parish in Sussex. Herstmonceux is a farming district four or five miles inland from the English Channel. It was a widespread parish twenty-seven miles around with three churches of which All Saints dated back to the fourteenth century and stood beside an ancient moated castle. But it

The ancient moated Castle of Herstmonceux was beside the 14th Century All Saints Church of which my father was Rector.

was a couple of miles from the rectory while only a mile away, in the village, was a corrugated iron church. A third church, in the hamlet of Cowbeech, was a couple of miles in the other direction.

The rectory was a spacious house with ample room for the family which, at times, had one or two honorary members whose parents had careers in the East. At first my sisters, Rhalou and Verily, were educated at home by a governess. Miss Fortescue was recommended by a close university friend of my Father's, Neville Chamberlain, who was by then the Chancellor of the Exchequer. She came straight to the country rectory from 11 Downing Street. Often during the holidays there was an au pair, a girl to teach us some French as well as helping my Mother generally. On the domestic side, Mother had as a wedding present the wages for two Norfolk girls, who were still living with the family as cook and parlour maid.

We children each had domestic holiday tasks. My main one was pumping water from two hand pumps. One sucked up drinking water from a well in the park to a roof tank, while the other provided bath water from an underground tank fed by rainwater from the gutters. Another task was filling the lamps with paraffin, there being no electricity in the house. The garden was extensive. It included tennis and croquet lawns, a good acre of brick-walled kitchen garden, a paddock with a couple of duck ponds and the park scattered with fine forest trees screening the house from a main road. The coach-house had loose boxes and stall, besides living accommodation for a groom; a large thatched barn housed a couple of pig sties with its own wooden walled yard.

For me it was one of the duck ponds that gave most pleasure of all, although the ducks really had more right to it. A disused wooden door and some odd scraps of timber created a raft, which gave me my first experience of boat building and perhaps seamanship too. When an elderly umbrella was thrown away in the house, that brought sailing into it too, and added to the experience of capsizing. Merlin had made a boat of Meccano covered in canvas, which put him a long way ahead of me in technique. Yet my raft gave me every bit as much pleasure.

Beyond all of this was the glebe farm of well over one hundred acres, most of which were well cultivated fields, besides marshland fields of ten acres which flooded in winter. The farm was rented to two families, the Elphicks and the Walkers, who with ten siblings also provided the parish verger, the organist, some of the choir and the grave-digger.

In no time Merlin, Rhalou and I knew every field and also each tree on the estate, although Verily was more of a town child. There was vast

Teaching Lorema seamanship on my duckpond raft.

scope for Father's vigorous love of animals. Certainly the pig sties soon housed a pig, to which he gave the name Soul, explaining that it's body was obvious. However the other buildings took on new uses; thus the coach house, stalls and loose boxes became kennels, while the groom's room had guinea pigs, rabbits, a monkey and, at one time, a kinkajou. The barn became home for ponies, as Rhalou, and later our baby sister Lorema, were very keen riders especially to hounds.

Yet dogs were Father's main hobby, indeed perhaps more than a hobby as the canine books and articles he wrote certainly helped the family budget. Later he once told me that writing until midnight paid for some of the family's education, but that mine came from sex. He saw how astonished I looked, so explained that one of his fox terriers was so much in demand that the ration of one bitch a week was sent for mating from all over Britain, providing the funds for my education.

Father also taught me to shoot when I was thirteen, especially stressing the needs of safety, but also helping Merlin and I to stock the larder with rabbits, pigeon, partridges, mallard, teal and a very occasional wild goose.

For the demanding parish work, Mother learned to drive the car presented as a farewell gift by the parishioners of Edgbaston, and this also served for the many Sunday services. Yet for everyday parish visiting, Father preferred his bicycle and, as I enjoyed that too, he frequently took me with him. He and I often went on bicycles to visit one of his sisters living at Battle just ten miles away. My aunt Gwen came in the middle of Father's family of eleven children, which included two sets of twins and three parsons, the fourth boy making the sea his profession. Father used to tell me that he was the third son and the seventh child, and that it had some mystic significance. As a Doctor of Divinity his proper title was not Rev. but Doctor Bruce. Thus, unlike nursery days, he came to have a very large influence upon my life.

During one of the school holidays Father took Merlin and me to visit some of the battlefields of Flanders. Especially we went to Ypres, which he would call Wipers, as that is how the soldiers had referred to it when he was there as an Army chaplain during the Third Battle of Ypres in 1917. Perhaps few cities have ever suffered more from wars than it has: not only from three long battles in the Great War, it was also sacked by the Normans about a thousand years earlier. We were told of the hundreds of thousands of soldiers who died there in the mud. I came back with immense respect for such bravery, coupled with the feeling that, if wars there had to be, I would prefer to be a sailor.

Another year, when I was eleven, Father took Merlin and I to Zeebrugge on the Belgian coast. There we saw the scene of the famous British naval attack in 1918, which blocked the German submarine base. I returned with more interest than ever in a naval career.

On another school holiday Mother took Rhalou, Verily and I to Paris, where she took us to all the right places for our cultural education. Certainly the girls knew a great deal more about pictures than I did, and my lack of architectural taste was shown by my diary giving most attention to the Eiffel Tower. That may have been because at the top an Englishman spoke to me, and I recognised him as Uffa Fox, a distinguished yachtsman and yacht designer.

Photography was one of my hobbies, but it was limited at home. There was no electricity until much later, and my dark room in the cellars was usually flooded in winter. However, an easy three mile bicycle ride away in Hailsham was a photographic shop, whose owner not only sometimes allowed me to use his enlarging equipment but, when his assistant was ill, took me on as a temporary help in exchange for free films and processing. He also took me out to help on one or two photographic jobs, teaching me much about taking pictures. Best of all he suggested that one or two of my photos would sell to the Press, and advised me how to set about it.

By then I had moved from Summerfields to Dartmouth College and at once began to enjoy playing with boats on the River Dart. Play it needed to be as far as pleasure was concerned, as instructional boating

Photography became a hobby which still at school brought pocket money from the Press.

became dull. This was before the days of sailing dinghies in which later cadets were free to sail themselves. At that time, sailing meant a dozen cadets sitting in a naval cutter while the instructor steered and occasionally shouted orders for the cadets to pull the ropes. For recreation a pair of us could take out a rowing skiff to explore the creeks and river banks, besides learning for ourselves the effect of tidal streams.

The hilly countryside of Devon was also a great joy as we were free to go as far as we could walk or run, except that the town was out of bounds. I had joined for the summer term when cricket was the main game; as rather a dud, I played a little of it, but there was squash, tennis and cross-country running which appealed to me more. The lessons seemed quite easy to me, so in exams at the end of term I was first in maths, and well up overall.

We had already begun to talk in naval phraseology so it was leave instead of holidays. Merlin was also on leave from his battleship, and having acquired an elderly two seater car, offered to drive Rhalou and I the 160 odd miles to Northrepps. When the time came to return I had a cold, but of course my seat was the dickey, fully exposed to the rain and wind. Thus it was more than a cold when we reached home and a day or two later the doctor was called and pronounced it to be double pneumonia, soon leading to other complications. The word tuberculosis was not mentioned to me, but years later some old letters to my father from my Aunt Dorothy in Switzerland came to me. She told of the benefit to those with TB from living in Haute Savoie, and offered to squeeze me into her chalet. However I was determined to stick to Dartmouth and persuaded our kindly family doctor to leave my fitness for a naval career to the naval doctors.

Back at the college it was explained that with an absence of over half a term it would normally mean going down to the term below, which would mean separation from my first term friends. The headmaster checked my records and said that the results had been good enough for me to keep my original term if confident of making up for lost time. My enthusiasm was far greater than my thirteen year old wisdom, and I had no idea how much the fairly serious illness had sapped my strength. Indeed I did not catch up in the remaining three years at Dartmouth, and I was not allowed to play games for some time.

Yet there was much else to do, and one obvious direction for a country boy was to follow the College pack of beagles, which led in time to becoming a whipper-in. One took turns with the other whips to take charge of the pack and honorary whips for exercising. My very good friend Roly Boddy and I competed with each other as whips, over who could take the hounds the furthest in the two hours allowed.

With the summer term there was also bird photography, as Mr Nickols, a science master, guided a few keen cadets in this hobby; perhaps even more than a hobby as one of my photos of a whitethroat perched on the head of a baby cuckoo was published in the magazine The Field, which paid for photographic plates over at least a year. A

Dartmouth College parade ground also served for the opening meet of the College beagles.

French master, Mr Bashford, took on Roly Boddy and I as hands in his sailing sloop *Jay*. Not only did he race her in the summer term, but his wife also invited me to stay at their home for the Tor Bay regatta during the leave period. As he was also master of the beagles, he had much influence on Roly and I. As it happened the college masters had stronger influence on me than our naval term officers. The latter acted in the same capacity as house masters in a normal public school, and could order us to be caned, while the masters used more positive methods of control, which appealed to me more.

Dartmouth is 250 miles from Herstmonceux, which cost Father some £2 by train via London, so I set myself the challenge of getting home each leave without involving any money. The first time it was my bicycle which Mother brought in her car for my confirmation service. With the first 100 miles hilly, this proved my limit for a day, but the lee of a haystack made a reasonable bed. Another time it was walking, with the advice from Mr Bashford to accept lifts in daylight hours only; thus when darkness was approaching I asked the lorry driver to put me down, but could not find a suitable haystack, so walked on through the summer night. Certainly an early lorry driver offering me a lift soon after dawn was very welcome, and he dropped me scarcely a mile from home in time for breakfast. Most of all I longed to get home by sea, but Brixham trawlers did not go that way. However Mr Bashford helped by introducing me to a yachtsman sailing eastwards, who agreed to take me to Newhaven, only twelve miles from home. Perhaps I was some use to him on the passage, as his wife gave me the bus fare to Herstmonceux.

In 1930 the fifty cadets of our term passed out of Dartmouth and were promoted to Seagoing Cadets. Looking back from the time when the last of us left the Navy, thirteen were killed in action, three more died and of the remaining thirty-four, Michael Le Fanu reached the highest naval position as First Sea Lord, two more became Admirals of various degrees, six reached the rank of Captain and a further nine retired as Commanders, while some of those who retired as Lieutenant Commanders had commanded warships. So that particular Dartmouth term, named after Admiral Benbow, had served the Navy well.

CHAPTER TWO

Out Into The World 1931

In February 1931 six of us Seagoing Cadets aged 17 joined *HMS Royal Sovereign* at Malta. Our pay was £6 a month, of which the gun room mess bill would need about half. However none of us had selected a naval career in order to amass a great wealth; at that time, the basic pay of an Admiral of the Fleet was no more than £5 a day. Yet we were certainly going to be offered an interesting life, without wasting any time either, as the great battleship set out from harbour an hour after we joined. That first night the main armament of 15 inch guns, the secondary armament of 6 inch weapons, and the 4 inch anti-aircraft guns were all fired for practice, as were the guns of the other four battleships of His Majesty's First Battle Squadron. Early next morning, with the ship steaming at 20 knots, we fired torpedoes from submerged tubes.

By then we had been shown where to sling our hammocks each night in the passages outside the officers' cabins, as those of the rank of sub-lieutenant or above normally had cabins. We had also by then been given our action stations. Mine went by the name of Captain's

Aged 17, I set off as Seagoing Cadet in the 15 inch gun H.M.S. Royal Sovereign.

Doggie, which meant that I would be on the bridge, within call of him and immediately available to run messages, bring his overcoat or perhaps carry out some simple task. Certainly it meant that I was well placed to see and hear all that was going on.

The exercises at sea completed, the ship returned to Grand Harbour, and we settled into harbour routine. That meant, for midshipmen and cadets, physical training on the quarter-deck at 6 am then, after cleaning, into day uniform, a semaphore exercise before breakfast. After that we attended Both Watches for Exercise, when the seaman branch were given their work for the morning. For us that usually meant instruction, each group learning navigation, gunnery, torpedo, signals, seamanship or perhaps the normal school subjects of maths, science, English and so forth. This was all controlled by an officer normally known as Snotties' Nurse, usually a Lieutenant-Commander, and in our case a very live wire Lieutenant, St. John Cronyn who was also responsible for all our life on board, stressing character and leadership.

We also had ship's duties from 5.30 am to 10 pm in harbour. These were mostly running the ship's boats and keeping watch on the quarter-deck as understudy to the midshipman of the watch, who was assistant to the Officer of the Watch. These eventually came under the Executive Officer, normally known as The Commander, as he co-ordinated all departments, with a Commander heading the Engineers, the Pay and Supply Branch, besides the Principal Medical Officer. Lieutenant Cronyn stressed to us the importance of sport, both playing and refereeing. There was unrivalled opportunity for so many types of sport in Malta, and I found that early morning riding was acceptable instead of the 6.00 am physical training. It was very good fortune that a lieutenant from the fleet flagship invited me to exercise some of his ponies, and went on to help me play polo. I did not know his name at first, but it was Mountbatten, and this meeting affected my later life.

Onboard even Captain Pipon, soon to be an Admiral, himself took a personal part in our training to be officers. He read the journals which had to give a day to day description of our lives and work. He insisted on the inclusion of sketches or diagrams, and sometimes pencilled notes if the descriptions were muddled. Certainly in *Royal Sovereign* a vast amount of effort went into training us to officer ships in the future.

Before long the whole Mediterranean Fleet set out through the Straits of Gibraltar for a combined exercise with the Atlantic Fleet, in which each side was trying to attack the other's trade routes, while protecting its own. At sea all formal instruction gave way to ship's duties day and night; from the back of a battleship's bridge these duties displayed a mighty token of Imperial Britain's sea power.

Following a visit to Gibraltar, the Mediterranean Fleet had its own exercises on the way to splitting up, with each ship visiting different places. There was intense drama as the fleet aircraft carrier *HMS Glorious* had some 20 aircraft airborne when thick fog came down without warning. She increased to full speed aiming to get out of the fog for the planes to land on, but she ran into the French liner *SS Florida* also at speed, which was damaged with many people killed. Most of the aircraft were diverted to shore airfields, but some of the fighters had too little fuel left, so circled round until a patch of clear air gave them a good chance of being seen as they crashed into the sea. The Captain told me to find the Principal Medical Officer to warn him that we might have to deal with many casualties. It turned out that our help was not needed, but it made me feel important to have taken a part in the whole affair, sad though it was.

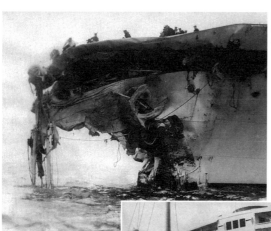

H.M.S. Glorious after steaming fast to get out of fog so her planes could land on her flight deck.

S.S. Florida after being hit by H.M.S. Glorious in fog.

When we visited the French Riviera, two days leave was granted to anyone who wanted it, but I felt that four shillings a day hardly lent itself to such luxuries. However, to my surprise, Captain Pipon asked me if I was visiting my cousins, as I had no idea that he would be concerned with the family affairs of such a nonentity as me. The fact was that his home was Jersey, and Lord Trent also had a house there as well as one in Cannes; some of his grandchildren were my first cousins. Captain Pipon happened to know they would be visiting Cannes; so he gave me a lift, as he was being picked up by friends in Cannes.

I was put in the nursery wing with my Bruce cousins, as the main guest rooms of Lord Trent's house were occupied by important officers from the Fleet Flagship. It was fun to be with Nancy, Cherry and Rosemary, who were not much younger than me.

Then back in the ship to Malta for normal exercises and routine. A complete surprise greeted me there in the form of a cheque for £15 as payment for one of my bird photographs. I had already heard that a small sailing boat was for sale at that price, so I set off with my close friend Roly Boddy, bought the boat and sailed straight back to the ship. Clearly I was not yet used to her, and came alongside badly, which provoked a just reprimand from the Officer of the Watch, who went on to ask who on earth had trusted a mere cadet with a boat. "She's mine, Sir. I've just bought her" somehow changed the picture. It seemed that ownership of one's own craft, whatever one's lowly rank, gave a certain standing. But I quickly put in some intensive

My first seagoing boat, brought from the sale of a bird photo to the Press, cruised around the Mediterranean Sea onboard the battleship.

practice to handle her worthily. After that I was allowed a corner of the deck for her, with permission to use an electric derrick for hoisting her in and out. She was much used on the next fleet cruise which took us to many Greek islands, where we often accompanied one of the ship's whalers for gun room picnics.

Towards the end of that cruise the fleet gathered off Corfu for a rowing regatta and, for several mornings before that, our early morning physical training gave way to regatta practice, in which the gun room crew struggled hard. By then I was the only one left on board of our original term at Dartmouth, and perhaps the strain of life in the high temperature was somewhat intense; certainly I was the youngest in that regatta crew and still only seventeen. Back in Malta I had to report sick and was sent to hospital, where the main treatment seemed to be rest in bed for a couple of weeks.

Soon after returning on board, news came from the Admiralty that all the junior midshipmen and cadets had been appointed to the China Station. The very next day we had stimulating talks about China by the Captain, the Commander and our Snotties Nurse. All stressed that we had before us an amazingly interesting time doing really valuable work, with the possibility of hunting pirates, being on the flank of local wars, and rescuing somebody from something. I was to join up with a group from the term above us, who were all a few months older than me; by then we were all midshipmen, earning no less than five shillings a day and allowed to smoke, although I never had any taste for this. We could also drink beer, but had to wait until coming of age before taking spirits.

We joined the cruiser *HMS Kent* which called at Malta on her way to China. Her gun room was already full, so the dozen of us passenger midshipmen were stuffed into a room intended for meetings when she became flagship. There were already ample midshipmen for ship's duties, so we joined the engine-room department for valuable training in that subject, including taking watches in the engine room, a boiler room and other machinery compartments. This was interesting, but I could have preferred cooler duties in the Suez Canal, the Indian Ocean on the equator and Singapore. It certainly taught me what men of that department have to endure.

Combined with this physical discomfort came news from the Admiralty of large reductions to the pay of naval personnel, owing to Britain's financial crisis. We heard that all the Atlantic Fleet ships had been recalled to their home ports, while we received a signal urging everyone on board to reduce expenditure in any possible way; the Stoker Petty Officer I was working under in the desperately hot boiler room commented "What about those seamen rigging the awnings as sails, think of the fuel that would save."

It was exciting to sail into Hong Kong for the first time and also a great relief for five of us midshipmen to transfer to *HMS Berwick*, a sister cruiser to *Kent*, in which we had taken passage. Very soon afterwards we had our first experience of typhoons, tropical revolving storms which crop up in their season around the world, but best known, perhaps, as the hurricanes of the West Indies. Number One

Sailing into Hong Kong harbour in H.M.S. Kent.

warning was hoisted, meaning that one had formed some 200 miles away. Ships in harbour were all moved to special typhoon berths, awnings furled and ships' boats hoisted or sent to a special typhoon shelter. By next day the typhoon had turned to miss us, so normal routine could be resumed.

Then followed another drama as a signal was received that the despatch vessel *HMS Petersfield* had run aground with the Commander-in-Chief, his wife and daughter all on board. She was some sixty miles from the port of Foochow, on rocks fully exposed to the prevailing wind, so not long afterwards a signal was received that she was a total loss, but all lives had been saved.

A week or so later I happened to be drawn in a minor squash competition against an officer not known to me, and walking back after the game, he began talking to himself as though questioning someone very awkward, and only then did I realise that he was the Captain of the lost ship. Another midshipmen and I were instructed to attend the court-marshal to learn how these affairs were handled. Commander Lang conducted his own defence and, when the lunch break came, we felt he was having a very difficult time. We two midshipmen remained in the court having our sandwiches, as we expected the officers' mess to be crowded. To our surprise the court reconvened half way through the lunch break, and the doors were firmly locked until the next witness had finished. He turned out to be the Commander-in-Chief, who had been on the bridge when the ship struck. Thus the two of us were the only spectators to hear his evidence and cross-examination. Soon it became clear that what I had heard after the squash game was a rehearsal for his cross-examination of this very special witness. No wonder he had lost his game of squash. However, the Admiral was certainly embarrassed when questioned about every word he had said on the bridge, with the suggestion that he had given detailed orders about the pilotage of the ship which in effect had prevented the Captain using his own discretion, and thereby depriving him of responsibility. Before the next witness was called and the door unlocked a warning was given that members of the public present should be very wary of attempting to answer any questions from the Press about what went on in its absence.

The Captain was found not guilty of losing his ship, but received a lesser punishment for hazarding her. The Press suggested that he got away amazingly lightly, but we two members of the public had taken the advice, and kept quiet.

Another subject for our instruction came about when a British steamer was captured by pirates, taken to a sheltered anchorage where some of the cargo was removed. A British destroyer on anti-piracy patrol rushed off at high speed to the scene, but by then the pirates and loot had got ashore. This reminded our Snotties' Nurse that later we would be attached to destroyers, probably on anti-piracy patrol, so we should keep in good practice at revolver shooting, which was easily done with a short course on Stonecutters Island.

When *Berwick* left, other than for local exercises, we were bound for Shanghai, the main international trading port on the China coast. An International Settlement formed a large area off an array of warships in their special berths, so *Berwick* took up her buoys at the head of a line of French, Japanese and Italian ships, which each paid formal visits on our arrival, and our Officer of the Guard returned them with full ceremony. In turn our Captain paid his official call on the French and American Admirals. Indeed it seemed quite a League of Nations and, even at our lowly level, we from the gun room exchanged calls with the junior officers of the other nations.

We also exchanged junior officer visits with a Japanese training squadron, where our hosts were keen to show us every detail of their elderly armoured cruisers, which had been built in England 30 years before. On return they hoped to see as much of our very much more modern ship. I noticed that they were much more interested in domestic than armament matters. We also exchanged visits with Chinese Customs cadets, but as their instructor was a former British Navy Gunner's Mate, they had no need for intelligence tasks.

Suddenly there was a call for help when a British merchant ship on the Yangtze River was boarded by men who held up the Captain with a pistol and beat up some of the crew. However one of the British gunboats was nearer so answered this call; yet three days later another

Japanese officers were keen to show us every detail of their elderly cruiser besides giving me a photo of their battleship, but hoped in return for details of our modern cruisers.

British river steamer was held up, so off we went in a hurry, leaving several of our men ashore shopping. *HMS Cricket,* a British Naval gunboat, had already arrested four armed men, but did not know whether they were some quasi-military body or even the Chinese Customs. So they were transferred to us as hostages while this was sorted out. The British Minister signalled that he did not approve of hostages, so a British Vice-Consul was found who arranged for the prisoners to be handed over to Chinese authorities. Quite clearly they had enjoyed their time on board, even if under arrest, as the sailors treated them with kindness.

These policing activities in support of British trade were at that time the normal way of life on the China Station, and some might have questioned that we quite often sent armed men ashore. Some were not even in uniform, and I was usually one of these, as wild fowl shooting was good sport. One of the jokes was that the ship's gunnery officer seldom hit a thing with his 12-bore, but I was much more fortunate with my lighter 16-bore gun, and once or twice brought back enough to feed the whole gun room on fresh meat.

In early 1932 came a more serious matter than the normal policing operations, when fighting broke out in Shanghai between the Japanese and the Chinese. A fellow cruiser, *Suffolk,* sailed from Hong Kong at

H.M.S. Berwick setting off for Shanghai with 850 Army troops onboard.

once, and when China announced her intention of declaring war on Japan, we were ordered to embark a battalion of the Argyll and Sutherland Highlanders, besides a Mounted Battery of Yats, then proceed at speed from Hong Kong to Shanghai. Fast steaming in winter conditions was always stimulating when on the bridge as Midshipman of the Watch, but it was certainly uncomfortable for soldiers on board, crowded and often seasick; but some who had enjoyed yachting fared much better. The Yats accepted that they could leave their mules behind, but insisted on bringing their goats, and these were definitely not rough sea sailors. Even as we approached Shanghai, three Japanese destroyers passed near us firing at Woosung Fort, which guarded the entrance to Shanghai's river.

As the Japanese soldiers had attacked from the International Settlement, this would have given an excuse for the Chinese 19th Army, whose political control was not too certain, to attack the Settlement. So barricades were set up round it, also round the separate French Settlement, and the soldiers we brought were to man these barricades. An intriguing complication was that if the Mayor declared a State of Emergency, the existing treaties entailed that overall command would be conferred on the senior international officer present, and that was Japanese Admiral Shiosewa, who would be defending the Settlement from attack by the Japanese. There were complications on the other side too, as the Chinese 19th Army defending that area seemed fairly independent from Generalissimo Chiang Kai Shek at Nanking, who sent no reinforcements, but from time to time announced that Japanese warships had been sunk by the fort at Woosung. These kept in tune with Japanese announcements that the same fort had been destroyed. From Shanghai we could watch a great deal of the firing and bombing, but when more British and American warships arrived *Berwick* was ordered to anchor in the Yangtze River off Woosung, to ensure no merchant ships were molested.

From there we were in the front row of the stalls, watching ships and planes attacking the fort, with much noise from its defenders. The nearest to a hit seemed to be some anti-aircraft shells landing in the sea quite close to us. We midshipmen continued our normal instructional programme in the mornings - my group were studying mathematics under an instructor officer with a degree in English - but after lunch we could join the gathering of officers on the quarter-deck, the senior ones relaxing in easy chairs, while we sat on the deck.

One night, flashing was seen from the fort and a message was eventually made out that three intelligence officers had been stranded. At dawn a motor boat was sent in, towing a whaler, in which I had been ordered to hoist a large white ensign from the mast. On landing, a Chinese army officer announced that he was second-in-command of the fort, so I introduced myself as Midshipman Bruce of *HMS Berwick*. He replied in excellent English, "Perhaps you are Scottish, and is King Robert Bruce your ancestor ?" I told him that we had come to pick up some people who had signalled, whereupon he said that they had been put in a special guest room for safety, as it was not known who they were. "But they are still asleep, so can we show you round the fort?" He piloted me round the many land mines planted around the fort, and was specially proud of some ancient muzzle loading cannons, but there was also a good number of modern small calibre weapons. I mentioned that during the night we had seen quite a large fire, apparently in the fort. "Very careless, some young soldiers. A fag end thrown into a corner set fire to bedding."

Japanese destroyer bombarding Woosung fort at the entrance to Shanghai's river.

Perhaps. But certainly there seemed very little damage from all the shells and bombs we had seen aimed at the fort, which various Japanese announcements claimed to have destroyed. When the "guests" turned up, they had increased to four and appeared to be British; but I avoided getting into conversation with them assuming them to be journalists, and feeling there were officers on board better suited to answer questions. I hurried them into the boat, as three Japanese destroyers were approaching, and we did not want to foul the range for either side, or indeed prove to be the unintentional target. The quartet was soon transferred to a vessel going up to Shanghai, and we never knew who they were. We saw no press story published, so it seemed that they were not journalists. In Shanghai a Japanese attack was going on to a Chinese sector of the city and a few stray shells fell on the International Settlement, which sadly killed two seamen from our sister ship *Suffolk.*

A large convoy of Japanese transport ships arrived, crowded with soldiers, and the announcement that a major assault was to start on the fort seemed likely, in spite of the previous announcements that it had been destroyed. Meanwhile we had a problem, as a Japanese destroyer sneaking up behind us to bombard the fort, came too close and cut our anchor chain. Another anchor was promptly let go, and in the next few days we midshipman had ample practice in the boats dragging for the lost anchor and cable, but only succeeded in catching the cable the ship was lying to.

A Japanese Officer of the Guard, in full finery, came on board to request the Captain to move further off as the assault was about to begin. The Captain, equally resplendent, returned the call on the Japanese Admiral and arranged where best we could protect merchant shipping bound for or leaving Shanghai, while also keeping clear of the assault.

Soon after that word came that our sister cruiser *HMS Cornwall* was to relieve *Berwick*, which was due to go home. Our batch of four midshipmen were to be transferred to *Cornwall*, as we were not due to go home for well over a year. I was sorry to leave such a happy ship, in which I had learnt so much and experienced a great deal of interest. Captain Reyne said a formal farewell to us, giving generous praise for our service to the ship. He suggested that we had now been out into the world long enough to gain a good idea of what was going on; we had also been tried and tested, so he was confident that each of us would be really valuable in our next ships

CHAPTER THREE

Tried and Tested 1932

Onboard *Cornwall* it seemed that everyone was too busy to notice our arrival, except the gun room Sub-Lieutenant, who arranged where we would sling our hammocks. Search for the missing anchor continued, but that was left to the more senior midshipmen already in the ship. The next day we were given gunnery stations, so I kept watch in a gunnery control position, which gave an excellent view of any attack on the fort; but that remained fairly quiet, except for one morning when a truce had been arranged to evacuate the wounded. It then seemed that bombardment became more vigorous. The actual assault did not take place until after we had moved up to Shanghai but the defenders had already left except for a Chinese general who had decided to fight single-handed to his death.

After securing to a wharf in Shanghai, a new Commander joined the ship as Executive Officer, and ordered one of the motor boats to be hoisted as it had been damaged. Its own midshipman was badly needed for the ship's hockey team, which was to play a match with shells flying overhead, so he invited me to take charge of the boat just for hoisting, as I was quite used to that. He told me that the coxswain, Leading Seaman Kirkby was a first rate man and would know all about their normal system. Indeed when I climbed down to the boat, he told me that apart from the damaged stem one of the falls, the ropes which hoist her, were badly worn. He advised that it was more vital than ever that no one should go outside the falls until the boat was secured; he also mentioned that their normal practice was for him to go forward to help the bowman pass the life line, and the midshipman usually went aft to help the stern sheetsman with that life line.

To my surprise it was the new Commander who hailed me from the ship's deck 30 feet above me, as normally the motor boat would be hoisted by a Lieutenant-Commander, with the title of Mate of the Upper Deck. "All ready in the boat?" was the hail, and unexpectedly, as a junior newcomer to the ship, I found myself answering "The after fall is badly worn, Sir."

The Mate of the Upper Deck told the Commander that of course he knew all about this and was going to replace it when the boat was hoisted, but stressed it was perfectly safe. The Commander repeated the

Coxswain's warning that everyone must keep inside the falls. Then "Hoist away" was his order with some 150 men running along the ship's upper deck with the falls in their hands. "Handsomely" came the order to slow right down and with another two feet to go I moved from the steering wheel towards helping the stern sheetsman.

The next I knew was flying through the air and landing in the river, which was devilish cold. The crew all wore life jackets, so at least we would not sink, but the tide was running really fast. As I was swept past the bows of the ship, with the stern sheetsman beside me, there was a hail from a senior Midshipman, who had reacted very quickly and hurled a heaving line right over me. Then came another nasty shock as holding the line gave me a violent pain, and only then did I realise that my left wrist was broken. The sailor in the water was as quick to act as that bright Midshipman, and wound one arm round me while holding onto the heaving line with the other.

Yet another Midshipman was quick to act as he shouted "Away lifeboat's crew" and swarmed down into the pinnace, lying at the lower boom, to rescue the pair of us; but it was not easy to get a man with a broken wrist into the boat. "Is there anyone else?", I asked, thinking of the coxswain. "I'm afraid not", came the answer. When we got back against the tide we passed the motor boat hanging with her stern in the water and her bow at the davit head. I was horrified to see the body of the Coxswain, crushed between the falls and the stem, with a stream of blood all down the deck. My rescuer explained that when the after fall broke, the strain also broke the forward davit's guy, so Kirby was thrown into the fatal position, while the two of us were thrown into the river; the bowman clung onto some part of the boat and was unhurt.

My guardian took me for medical attention, and still new to the ship besides being in a very distressed state, I was only vaguely aware that it was not the doctor who was dealing with my wrist. Indeed it was the dentist, who had been called by that helpful Midshipman as the doctor was out of the ship. Yet even more immediate treatment came from Commander Middleton, who said firmly to me "You are in no way responsible." He added that he was in charge of hoisting the boat so was fully responsible. However the Court of Enquiry a few days later put no blame on him, as many people had heard him told, by the man actually responsible, that the rope was perfectly safe.

Before then the British Minister to China had arrived in another warship and soon managed to negotiate a cessation of hostilities, which certainly benefited the many countries trading with China. But the world press seemed to give more attention to the news that in Germany

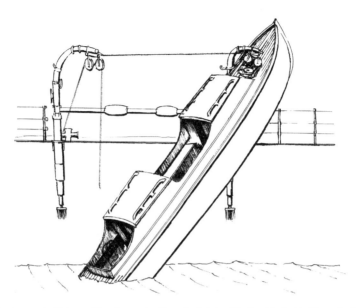

The davits are held in position by a wire from their tops. The boat is hoisted by rope falls, fore and aft, led to the ships upper deck where a large number of seamen walk away with them.

When the after fall broke the stern of the boat fell hurling us into the fast running river except the unfortunate coxswain who was jammed between the forward davit and the boat's deck.

Marshal Von Hindenburg had gained a large majority over Herr Hitler to remain President.

Later *Cornwall* returned to Hong Kong for a refit, so with no cooking facilities on board the midshipmen were sent to live under canvas on the rifle range for a couple of weeks. That was followed by a week's cruise in the elderly 10-ton yacht *Tavy*, commanded on this occasion by one of our lieutenants. I certainly enjoyed this, perhaps more than any of the others did, and was told at the end by the lieutenant that he had recommended I should be skipper on any future such cruise.

With the whole ship's side painted, and ammunition brought back on board, in both of which we played a part, *Cornwall* set off for Wei-Hai-Wei, the fleet's summer base in North China. It was on a small island with splendid facilities for many forms of sport, an excellent summer climate and none of the distractions of a town. Around the base the Gulf of Chili offered good waters for every sort of seagoing exercise.

The rowing regatta reached the height of sporting life, as there were so many classes for competition that a very high proportion of the ship's company not only raced, but practised for weeks beforehand. Sadly, *Cornwall* came well after the other big ships in total points, and one soon realised that she was practically never near the top in any of the sports. Nor did she excel in gunnery and similar work contests. I got a hint of what may have contributed to this when we were fortunate to win the fleet midshipman's obstacle whaler race. This started with the boats at anchor, so the first step was weighing anchor, then hoisting the mast and setting sails, next picking up a buoy thrown over as though man overboard; on passing a moored mark it was down mast and sails to row back to the finish. Great fun and cheered by most of the fleet. As helmsman I was fortunate to benefit from a wind shift so we won. On return I was congratulated by two junior lieutenants, whilst at the prize giving, the Captain of another cruiser also said well done. However, neither our snotties nurse, in general charge of the midshipmen, nor any senior officer of our ship, appeared to have noticed it. The atmosphere on board was different from *Berwick*, and perhaps those at the top were not the most likely candidates to become Admirals.

After the regatta the fleet set out for cruises. We were fortunate to have Ching-wan-tao as our main destination, as from there we could visit Peking by train. Fifty men and a dozen officers set out for the first helping, and the three midshipmen in the party were honoured with an invitation to stay in the British legation with the Minister's private secretary, while the others had to find hotels. Our host was the perfect guide, advising which of the historic temples, palaces and other buildings to see; he often accompanied us as interpreter as well. We also had the privilege of meeting the British Minister and hearing in simple terms, suited to those unable to speak the language and without even a degree in Asiatic Studies, some of the problems of China at that time.

On return to the ship some of us had another intriguing treat when we were given leave to visit the Great Wall of China. We hired some reasonably good ponies and rode for two or three hours over flat cultivated country to the Wall, and then along it to the foot of the hills. That section of the Wall was largely in ruins, but the thought that it stretched for 1,400 miles and was built around 200 B.C. made it truly memorable.

After more exercising at sea off Wei-Hai-Wei came a spell of duty 600 miles up the Yang-tzi river to Hankow, an important trading port. Our training as soldiers was called upon to help guard the city, as a section of the Red Army, driven back from somewhere else by Marshal

We hired ponies and rode to the Great Wall of China and along a very small length of its 1,400 miles, said to be built over 2,000 years ago.

Chiang-Kai-Shek, was believed to be approaching the city. However the Marshal himself arrived aboard one of his seaplane carriers, and the threat faded. So we could get back to instruction, as well as cricket, polo and golf.

With as many as 18 warships of many nations at Hankow on occasions, there was much protocol, besides social calling to meet other officers. This meant ample boat work, which I certainly enjoyed as much as any other duties. Sometimes it added to the interest when the engine failed, which was not surprising when one check disclosed that it had not been maintained for 500 hours. However it was embarrassing when I was taking an Admiral on some official business and the engine failed in a part of the river where the anchor would not hold against the strength of the water coming down from the mountains of Tibet. After that it seemed suitable that my group should do a two week engineering course to see for ourselves how the work of that department piled up, with so much machinery to maintain, and with more illness among the stokers than the seamen.

Back in Wei-Hai-Wei the normal intensive exercises continued. One which particularly interested me, as I had been invited on board was when all the submarines went out to compete for their special shoot, was *Orpheus*. Each submarine in turn submerged to periscope depth, keeping half a mile from the target, then at a signal surfaced as fast as possible and fired 12 shells from her 4 inch gun. It was a change for me to be in a ship which won a competition, and that day I began to think that submarines would be the career for me, when I qualified for the rank of lieutenant.

In the Fleet sports, for once among sporting events *Cornwall* was not last, although a long way behind the aircraft carrier *Hermes*. Most of our points actually came from midshipmen, which certainly encouraged the gun room. Many British soldiers from Shanghai spent a rest visit aboard ships at Wei-Hai-Wei and in a match between those embarked in different ships ours proved the winners. I noticed that the senior army officer present came over to congratulate them.

With the north-east monsoon blowing in winter months the seas can become rough off the China coast, but still we were surprised to hear that a Japanese destroyer, less than ten years old, had been lost at sea off Formosa, when she turned over running before the seas. It seemed that such weather benefited the submarines exercising with us on the way to Hong Kong, as we never sighted their periscopes and the Asdic gear of that date failed to locate them in those conditions; yet the submarines achieved excellent dummy torpedo attacks.

Back in Hong Kong, Lieutenant Stileman, one of the few officers on board I aimed to emulate, was sent home suffering general ill health. Several other people from the fleet were also invalided home, which was then normal, as life on board ships of the China Fleet was a strain; but *Cornwall* was the winner in numbers sent home for health reasons.

Midshipman Boyle and myself joined *HMS Wishart* for a three month destroyer course. She was about one tenth the size of *Cornwall*, so living conditions were restricted: yet I began to feel well as soon as I joined her. The First Lieutenant, who was especially responsible for our training and everything we did, was Lieutenant Fisher. Here indeed was an officer on whom I could hope to model myself; this proved a sound judgement as he went on to have a brilliant war career and to become an Admiral.

An important task of the China flotilla of nine destroyers was anti-piracy patrol; this was very interesting and sometimes exciting too. The usual method then employed by these pirates was for one or two to travel as normal deck passengers in the selected merchant ship and become familiar with her layout and routine, besides her officers. Then the whole gang of seven or eight went aboard as deck passengers, heavily armed but disguised. At the moment selected by their leader, they took possession of the ship and forced one of the junior officers to take her to the place arranged to rendezvous which was usually Bias Bay, with craft from ashore. They not only took a small amount of cargo but also kidnapped some wealthy passenger, sending a ransom note. If no answer was received, the next ransom note put up the price, and perhaps included a finger or ear to prove identification.

To protect against such piracy a form of convoy had been established by which ships would be advised to arrive off some headland at a certain time, and then to pass through the main danger area within sight of one another. They were also advised to send their positions by radio every six hours; but the pirates also had radios, so knew that after every such signal, they had six hours before the absence of the next signal would give an alarm. There was always a destroyer or sloop on patrol, keeping in sight the main group, while ready to rush off at top speed if a piracy was suspected elsewhere. On one of our patrols the Captain suspected such a piracy, so speeded off to intercept the ship as she was entering Bias Bay. The destroyer's main guns were trained on her and she was ordered to stop. Then the whaler was lowered with an armed boarding party under the Sub-Lieutenant. As the destroyer fired a machine gun burst over the ship, the whaler's crew threw a grapnel to catch on her guard rail. As I carried just a revolver, lighter and more handy than a rifle carried by the rest of the party, I was ordered to climb up the grapnel with a rope ladder over my shoulder. It was a lively excitement to be part of the boarding party and, after further experience, when the Sub-Lieutenant was ill, I was actually put in charge of the boarding party.

A lost torpedo fired from the destroyer H.M.S. Wishart was salvaged by a junk and carried inland. A party of us landed and hired a team to carry it down to the sea.

Another interesting venture for *Wishart* followed the loss of a submarine's torpedo, when word got through that it had been salvaged many miles from where it was fired and taken three miles inland. The Chinese authorities gave permission for a British naval armed party to land and attempt to recover it, so *Wishart* was sent off with a Chinese interpreter and a portable radio set. The Captain found his way into an anchorage off the small village of Tien Pak, which had little shelter, so the ship rolled heavily while we transferred to the boats. In the motor boat went the Captain, the Torpedo Gunner, the interpreter and Midshipman Boyle, with a store of Chinese money strapped in his belt. Aboard the whaler Lieutenant Fisher took a crew of torpedo-men, with gear for handling a torpedo weighting over a ton, and myself.

It was intriguing to enter the small harbour full of junks, mostly employed in the salt trade. The village consisted of wooden huts built on stakes 10 feet above the ground, but only just above the sea at high water. To our surprise we found the torpedo had been brought back and was lying in a battered condition some 100 yards from the sea. Much negotiating was going on through the interpreter, but meantime Lieutenant Fisher's personality was such that he was able to collect some 30 coolies, then rig ropes and bamboo to carry the torpedo down to the sea, surrounded by the entire population of the village. There was some reluctance to let us proceed into the sea before the money had been paid, but the expression "Scout's honour" seemed to be understood and was accepted. So while the Captain and his party, with the money, remained negotiating, we were allowed to put the torpedo into the sea, where it floated with the help of strapped on buoyancy bags, and at once set off towing it behind the motor boat.

After the torpedo was back on board, it was planned that we should take the motor boat back for the Captain's party and the whaler. Then Lieutenant Fisher said to me "You know they have got something worth a great deal more than the torpedo, and we don't want to have the Captain's ear included with the ransom note. I should remain in charge of the ship, with her guns, but you go in the motor boat, taking a machine gun as well as your pistol."

So off we went again, having a few practice shots at a rock to ensure I was tuned to my pistol. But all was well, with the price agreed within the bundle of notes round Boyle's tummy, allowing just enough to pay the 30 coolies. Back on board an officer who had remained very anxiously on board throughout commented that with the oil fuel used, besides the money paid out, the Admiralty could have bought at least two new torpedoes. Lieutenant Fisher would have none of that "This little exploit has been worth a whole salvo of torpedoes to all of us who took part", and even a very junior officer like me felt emboldened to add "Here, here, Sir."

Back in Hong Kong Boggy Fisher, as by then I felt I could refer to him by his nickname, although of course I still addressed him as" Sir", whether on board or ashore, took me in his crew racing in an H-class sailing boat. He won, which was fairly normal for him, but quite a change for me to be involved in a sporting success. Midshipman Boyle was admitted to hospital for an operation with no chance of re-joining the ship in China. Thus the original group of five young officers sent to China had been reduced by accidents and illnesses to just me.

On another anti-piracy patrol a Danish ship was attacked in the usual way, but when the Chief Officer put up some resistance he was shot. In the hands of the pirates that ship actually passed in the dark, without lights, some three miles from *Wishart*, but it was some hours later before we knew of this and within eight minutes we were at top speed to the rescue. However the Danish ship was by then safely on her way to Hong Kong, so we anchored where the pirates had landed close to Bias Bay, and the Captain took me in his party to investigate ashore. We found a Chinese Customs Officer who pointed out that there was no duty to be paid on kidnapped men, so it was not his business. We discovered that there was a private telephone network between villages near Bias Bay, which must have been better served by phone than any other part of the coast at that date. We also came across another official

On piracy patrol armed with my revolver. I was put aboard a suspected junk but there were no hostages that time.

of some sort who agreed that he might help, but it soon became clear that we would have to put up more money for this than the pirates would give him to keep quiet. We made no progress.

However *Wishart's* activities had perhaps warned the pirates to keep clear of Bias Bay, as the next piracy was in a new area further north, where four officers and a wife were kidnapped. Chinese piracy normally attracted no attention in the British press, but this time a London daily offered £10,000 ransom for the lady. Some of us pirate hunters felt that this would make kidnapping an even more profitable business.

My interesting destroyer time finished with a verbal examination conducted by destroyer officers from other ships. It said much for the instruction I had been given, mainly by Boggy Fisher, that a first class certificate was awarded.

Back to *Cornwall*, and the ship seemed much more alive than when I left her. Captain Bell Davis V.C., D.S.O. had taken command. Our next passage was mostly in fog and, as we had no electronic aids then, the navigator asked to be lowered by crane to near the waterline, where his horizon was close enough to be seen in the fog; from there he took a sun sight with his sextant, changing his wet trousers before working it out. A couple of years later, describing this earned lively interest even if not actual marks, when being examined in navigation, which led to a first class certificate.

Shanghai was renowned for crime, so it was particularly interesting on arrival off the International Settlement to be sent on an anti-riot course with the police. It was explained how their much practised methods were put into effect, and we were told that if all these failed the nearest warship might be asked to land sailors for the job!

The next time *Cornwall* went to Hong Kong for a short refit, the midshipmen were again sent on a local cruise in the 10-ton yacht *Tavy*. This time the recommendation of our lieutenant from the previous cruise was acted on, which meant that I was skipper. On the second day we were sailing quietly some ten miles from the land, when a destroyer approached at speed. "Midshipman Bruce," came a hail from the bridge, "Typhoon warning No. 1 has been hoisted." It amazed me that the Captain should present an order in such a conciliatory manner; but commanding even a small yacht seemed to give one special status.

However, the immediate thing was to make for Lymun Pass, the main entrance to Hong Kong harbour; fortunately that put the wind on the beam, at a reasonable strength. Yet it soon began to increase, so reefs were taken in the mainsail, and that done the wind became stronger still and also veered to almost astern. I steered to get some shelter from the land as soon as possible, and close in there was a steep breaking sea, which is often the case off a headland. Before long we were pooped, with a ton or two of water sweeping forward on the deck, jamming the steering wheel with a loose end of the mainsheet, whose boom had been hauled aft for the gybe. It also overturned a can of paraffin to start a lively blaze. Then finally it snarled all the halyards round the main mast into a dreadful tangle. The fire flared under the main boom, jammed aft by its sheet in the steering wheel, and lapped up the foot of the sail. Someone made a quick decision to bring down the spray-sodden mainsail to put out the fire. He himself was hot and in a smoky position to the lee of the fire, so he sawed at what seemed to be the main halyard with his knife. It was the wrong rope, and so brought down the jib. His next alarmed slashes brought down a confusion of mainsail, gaff and boom, which certainly exterminated the fire, but nearly did the same to two of the crew.

Someone else, seeing angry breakers not far ahead, hurled a sea anchor over the side, complete with its tripping line in a tight coil. The warp stampeded out but the tripping line took the engine starting handle with it. The end of the warp was secured in time for the sea anchor to check the way of the yacht, which allowed me to recover control of myself and the crew. Thus we were able to clear the steering wheel, rig another jib halyard and steer clear of the rocks.

Soon afterwards we saw the typhoon warning flag lowered, so anchored in a quiet corner. Finding no damage beyond the cut halyards, and that there was a spare engine starting handle tucked away below, we considered ourselves fine seamen to have weathered such a situation, and quite wrongly blamed the pooping on poor design. We also talked in terms of saying as little as possible about it, in case authority should forbid further sailing without a more mature skipper. Yet by the next morning I had come to the much more reasonable conclusion that the whole thing was entirely my fault. I had steered into the most broken water close to Tathong Point; I had completely failed to take charge of my crew, and had panicked.

We sailed gently round Hong Kong Island to Repulse Bay, with its excellent bathing beach. Soon we saw someone swimming our way: it was Captain Bell Davis, who had heard that someone ashore had seen the yacht having problems off Tathong Point. He asked me what had happened in such a cool and friendly manner that I had no hesitation in telling him all, including that it was a failure by me. I quite expected that he would relieve me as skipper, and once again put a lieutenant in charge. To my surprise he took it calmly and said that this was just the

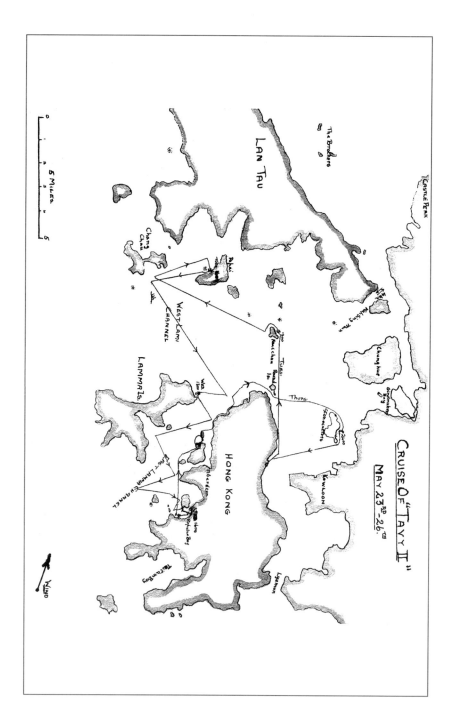

sort of exercise which should prove valuable when one day I commanded my own ship. "Indeed," he added, "as you have realised the mistakes you made, the lessons have been learnt." He suggested that I should pay for the halyards that had been cut and the lost starting handle. Finally came "The ship's programme has been delayed, so you can extend your cruise for a further two days." Not long afterwards the Captain showed me a cutting from the local paper. It told how *Tavy* had needed help after running onto a rock while in the charge of a Commander, and with a qualified navigating officer on board. "So seamanship is not always a matter of seniority," he commented.

That summer, 1933, back in Wei-Hai-Wei, *Cornwall* was second in the Fleet rowing regatta, a sure sign of much improved morale. No wonder the Captain was to become in time a highly respected Admiral. After the regatta the gun room was closed and I was transferred to the sister cruiser *Kent* in which, two years before, I had joined the China Fleet from Malta. This time it was not as a passenger, but as one of the senior Midshipmen. The very next day I was sent away in charge of a boat to rescue three Chinese fishermen hanging to a waterlogged sampan. We took in a good deal of water, and it was too rough to get back to the ship, so I went on to the harbour of Chinwantao to await the ship. She was the Fleet Flagship, so I earned a personal "Well done" from the Commander-in-Chief, as he happened to be on the quarter-deck when we rejoined the ship.

Next the chance cropped up to transfer to the Fleet Aircraft Carrier *Eagle* for some flying experience. Part of this was practising a peel off dive, which is the same as the Hell Dive of American films. The pilot was my brother Merlin, which helped my nerves, although my stomach found it worse than seasickness. "Do it a dozen times and you'll get over those problems" said Merlin.

Once again back in Wei Hai Wei there was the Midshipman's obstacle whaler race. This time I skippered the boat for *Kent* and we won the same trophy as the year before in *Cornwall.*

Then came another change of ships. I joined *HMS Bruce*, a flotilla leader normally working with submarines. There were many extra officers for passage, including eight Midshipmen, so our duties were not heavy, until we transferred back to my own ship *Cornwall*, which was ready to leave for England. Thus in three years since first going to sea I had served in nine different warships - a battleship, two aircraft carriers, three cruisers, a flotilla leader, a destroyer and a submarine. Obviously I had gained a good deal of experience of technical matters, such as seamanship, organisation, gunnery and so forth; but surely the most valuable lessons of all were on leadership, with so many officers using such diverse methods to lead their men.

Arriving at Portsmouth towards the end of 1933 the ship flew a very long paying off pendant; but I had been away even longer than her - nearly three years. However I could not relax as there was still the seamanship examination, normally held before leaving China. Fortunately the Board of Examiners seemed to find China type seamanship acceptable, as they awarded me a first class certificate which was an improvement on the certificates awarded to the candidates coming from the Home Fleet.

CHAPTER FOUR

Higher Education 1934-1935

I made it back to Hertmonceux just in time for my 20th birthday; it was 1933 and it was three years since I left home, but strangely the house, garden and farm seemed quite unchanged. I had prepared myself for great changes in my parents, but they too seemed just the same as I had left them. My brother Merlin introduced me to his wife, Joan and their baby, Euslin, but otherwise he did not seem very different. However, my sisters had changed a great deal. Rhalou was still essentially a country girl with a great love of animals, but was definitely more mature than the teenager who I had last seen. Lorema at 13 was quite different from the crying child of 9 I had left three years earlier. In the years before leaving, I had seen most of Verily when Mother took a family party to Paris. I clearly remember Verily in Paris as shy, but on my return in 1933 she had transformed into an assured young woman of 18, who loved parties and took great delight in mixing with the opposite sex, whatever their age.

Back at Herstmonceux Rectory in 1934. In front our Mother and Father with sister-in-law Joan and Euslin: behind them his father Merlin, then Rhalou and her fiancé Kay Peace, next my sisters Verily and Lorema with me in between.

At first Verily found me a bit of a disappointment. In three years away, I had spent my time almost exclusively with men. Verily interpreted my inexperience with women as indifference and soon started to refer to me as a misogynist. There were British families in Hong Kong, but daughters of my age would be away at school or college. Very few of the officers in my ships had wives in China, and for those that had, normally of captain's rank, it usually meant a formal call, often just leaving a visiting card. I felt no special wish to meet ladies, there were ample activities to keep a young officer occupied. After games or sailing, we often went to the Junior Officers Club, perhaps for a glass of beer. Certainly I was no dancer, so would not have dreamed of visiting a dance hall to sport the local ladies. My sisters took it upon themselves to cure all this, as did my Mother who was always happy to entertain young people at the rectory. My Father celebrated my return with the gift of a car, well suited to my needs and good value for the £10 it cost him. It was a two seater, but another pair could squeeze into the dickey, fully exposed to wind and rain. Rhalou managed to fit her favourite terrier in front with her when we set off for a round of visits to Norfolk relations.

The next step of a Naval career was education ashore. First I went to Greenwich College, which is often referred to as the Navy's university. We were back together with the same group as when cadets at Dartmouth, but we had now become Acting Sub-Lieutenants, with the right to drink spirits, although personally, I did not like them. We were entitled to weekend leave, except for the few occasions when each was on duty. Those of us whose homes were reasonably close could regularly go home. We would often take fellow officers whose homes were too far away to make a weekend trip. Thus one of my special friends from Dartmouth days was John Kennard, who lived in Scotland and so regularly came home to Hertmonceux at weekends. Dick Beckwith, whose real home was in Devon, was also a regular visitor. My sisters were always delighted by their visits. The addition of John's sister, Susan, and Dick's sister, Bridget made weekends great fun, and helped me cast off my mantle as a misogynist. For the longer leave periods, exchange of home visits were often reversed. On one visit to Dick's house in Barnstaple, I met a cousin of his, Francis Chichester, who later became a longstanding friend.

One summer leave the Kennard family invited Rhalou and I to spend a week at their grouse moor. When packing up to leave, Rhalou came to my bedroom looking very serious. "Look here Brucie, when we say goodbye its the right thing to kiss your hostess, and the daughter of

Family and friends afloat on the Norfolk Broads. A party of 12 in 3 chartered sailing yachts.

the house too", "But I've never kissed anyone outside of the family" I protested. "Well it's time you started" she insisted. I adapted to this further intimacy with women, and soon felt less self-conscious.

For the Easter leave break we usually went sailing, not on the open sea, because many of our friends were quite unaccustomed to boats, but on the Norfolk Broads. Organising it was great fun, working with Rhalou who planned the provisions. Together we chose and invited the party. I remember one year particularly clearly. The party numbered 12. I chartered three cabin sailing yachts. The first issue was who would go in which craft. Rhalou insisted only that her dog must go with her. Thus I decided that Kirby Peace, her friend who was training as a vet, would be a good companion for her and the dog. Verily's choice was to go in the boat with the most boys. I added Joan, Merlin's wife, to this yacht to act as a chaperone for Verily. The rest was easily arranged. The main task left for me was to make the numerous introductions.

A young man from Herstmonceux called Peter Cook who owned a car had the responsibility of bringing Verily and a large sack of potatoes. When the car broke down, he abandoned the potatoes and brought Verily on by train. On arrival he was teased for his choice in bringing the girl and not the provisions.

Our 'fleet' of three yachts and three sailing dinghies set off under quant power down the river Bure. We found a convenient stretch of bank to secure the fleet and to create a bonfire for cooking the supper. The next day Joseph Gurney, one of our Norfolk cousins, arrived in answer to Verily's telephone request for a replacement sack of potatoes. Meantime Rhalou's dog, Minnie, had caught a rabbit to be added to the provisions. Verily fell in, probably purposely in spite of the frost, and surfaced to say there were many fish down there; so the fishing gear was brought out, and Lawrence Kettle caught one rather small fish to add to the evening stew.

Kirby Peace, the trainee vet and admirer of Rhalou's, was an experienced point-to-point rider, but definitely a novice in boats. "They're not the same as horses" he wailed after getting caught up in a rope. Certainly one of his fellow crew proved sympathetic, and his engagement to Rhalou was clearly maturing by the end of the week. The week's cruise was a great success, even if not much seamanship had been learnt. All of those introductions at the start of week became firm friendships by the end of the trip.

Back at Greenwich College work was intensive, especially for those of us who as midshipmen had spent more time chasing pirates than feeding the brain with mathematics, chemistry and French grammar. So I was pleased enough to gain a fairly good certificate when the examinations were completed.

Our group of fifty acting sub-lieutenants was next divided up to study courses in navigation, gunnery and torpedo at the various naval technical schools; I gained a first class certificate only in navigation, but I at least qualified in the other two subjects. There was also a short course on leadership. As I asked so many critical questions it was fortunate that it was not marked. Much of the course was squad drill, so that we could get practise in shouting orders to a line of anonymous bodies. I got no credit for insisting that, in my experience, a good leader needed to know his crew as individuals and therefore sport was more important than drills. The training staff were not impressed by the argument that instead of squad drill they should teach us to referee soccer, rugger and hockey.

However, my sea time as a midshipman and the various courses were satisfactory enough to lead to a very formal document confirming me as a Sub-Lieutenant in His Majesty's Fleet. It carried the signature of George R.I., the King himself, beside that of two Sea Lords and the Secretary of the Admiralty. Making full use of capital letters it directed me to see the "Officers and Men subordinate to you behave themselves with all due Respect and Obedience to their Superior Officer."

I volunteered for the submarine service and this was accepted, but there was a month to fill before the special training began. This me gave the opportunity for some ocean racing in *Tai-mo-shan*, a 29-ton ketch which a group of British submarine officers had built in Hong Kong and then sailed home.

The three month submarine course was based in *HMS Dolphin* at Gosport, and impressed me most of all in my Further Education. Our course officer was Mervyn Wingfield, an inspiring lecturer and obvious leader; he later won the V.C. before being lost at sea in his submarine. The course included a good deal of practical work, largely in the elderly submarine L.27, where we carried out each of the tasks that the men serving under us would have to do.

With the course completed and examinations successfully passed, the next appointment was announced as the China flotilla of sixteen modern submarines, first going to the depot ship *HMS Medway* until a vacancy came in one of the submarines. Before that I could have three weeks leave.

This fitted in very well with an invitation from my Mother's elder brother Quentin Gurney to join his family on a grouse moor in Scotland. Driving up in my two-seater, I gathered with the rest of the party at the foot of a long and narrow loch, where we loaded into the motor boat belonging to the shoot and set off for the lodge half way up the loch. The gillie told us that there was no easy access over the mountain on the lodge side, but there was a path along the other side of the loch. He described how, with no telephone, an urgent message would mean that someone would have to walk the three miles along this rough path, then light a bonfire to attract attention for the boat to come over.

The shooting was excellent, with hares and grouse providing us with all the fresh meat. Towards the end of the week we were especially looking forward to a grouse drive high up above the loch. It was satisfying to find that I was hitting quite a few of the grouse flying fast down wind. Then I noticed far down below, some smoke across the loch, which diverted my attention enough to miss the next few birds. I pointed out the smoke to my uncle, who at once asked two of us to go down to the loch and take a boat across.

On the shore we found a postman with two telegrams, one for an Army officer and the other one for me. Mine ordered me to join *Swordfish* at Portsmouth with despatch, and the other ordered my fellow guest back to his regiment forthwith. As a Director of a major bank, my uncle wanted complete relaxation from world affairs, and so had no radio in the lodge. Thus we had no idea that there was a crisis over Abyssinia which threatened peace in the Mediterranean. For the two of us rushing to leave it was certainly a romantic way to be called to the needs of our country.

*Setting off for Gibraltar in
Submarine Swordfish with a
crisis threatening peace in
the Mediterranean.*

*A visit to Egypt with
fellow passengers from
the liner taking us to
Hong Kong.*

*Navigator of H.M.S.
Odin, one of the 16
submarines of the
China station.*

*I shared a car with Hugh Mackenzie, later to become
an Admiral, often going out to shoot snipe and ride my
polo ponies.*

CHAPTER FIVE

Submarines 1936-1939

It was a rush to get down from the grouse moor in Scotland to collect my uniforms and then join the submarine *Swordfish*. Within days we sailed for Gibraltar. There a large British fleet was gathering in case it was needed to deal with the Italian fleet. Aboard the British cruiser Galatea was my brother Merlin, serving as pilot of her only aircraft.

We were all kept busy, but the threat was soon over and I was ordered to take passage in a liner bound for Hong Kong, so as to take up my original appointment. It was fun to enjoy the company of fellow passengers of both sexes, landing for visits ashore in Egypt and Ceylon, and then to arrive in Hong Kong once again. There I joined the submarine depot ship *Medway*, whose Captain Coltart, in charge of all 16 submarines as well as the depot ship, was known to us young officers as Uncle Cyril, while his friendly wife was Aunty Francis. Actually one the group really was their nephew, but that hospitable couple treated us all as nephews - that is until someone made some mistake in his work, when he faced a very firm Captain indeed. As spare third hand I would be sent to sea in any submarine that had a temporary vacancy, so gained experience from *Parthian, Rainbow AND Olympus*, submarines of the three classes included in the flotilla. To my mind, the standard of leadership was very high, compared to some surface ships I had served in, and each Captain knew his men and their abilities.

Soon a permanent berth came available to me in *Odin*, whose Captain, Lieutenant Commander King, had a fine reputation for skill in submerged torpedo attacks. He was relieved soon afterwards by Ronald Jonas, who became a friend of everyone. *Odin* was unique in the flotilla in that all her four commissioned officers were bachelors. In most of the other submarines both Captain and First Lieutenant were married, and most had their wives in China. At that time there was no marriage allowance for naval officers, unlike the army, but extra pay on becoming a Captain or Second-in-Command, besides that for submarine service, fully made up for this.

My sister's training had taught me how to talk to young women, so unlike my midshipman's time of only male company, I now enjoyed the company of some of the girls whose families worked in China. I shared an elderly car with a fellow submarine officer called Hugh Mackenzie, in which we could search out snipe and duck in the New Territory opposite Hong Kong Island. The car also came in useful as we were mutually befriended by the hospitable Hance family, living on the Peak, whose daughters Heather and Barbara proved delightful partners in various activities; I was even persuaded to dance. Yet for me best of all was cruising in the old yacht *Tavy*, which I had commanded as a midshipman; fortunately the girls liked sailing too.

The same yacht TAVY 2 previously I had skippered with fellow midshipmen, now very often included girls in the crew. My bachelor captain was visited in China when his sister and her friend left school.

There was also riding, and I bought a pair of polo ponies, one called 'Perhaps' and the other 'Maybe', to play elementary chukkas at Fanling. The ponies also needed exercising and there were always volunteers to hack them when my ship was elsewhere. Polo may sound like sport for the wealthy, but it was not necessarily so then in Hong Kong. I was fortunate because on my arrival there was a shortage of players, so the prices of ponies were modest; then when it was time to go home pony prices had more than doubled, due to the new regiment having many keen players.

When the fleet sailed North for the summer base at Wei-Hai-Wei we had to say good bye to the Hong Kong ladies, but the Admiralty gave special permission for the wives of the flotilla to take passage on board *Medway*, using the vacant cabins of all the officers now in our submarines. When I got back to my depot ship cabin I found a charming gift of an embroidered handkerchief from my guest, whose identity I never discovered. Up north we no longer had the use of the yacht *Tavy*, but in partnership with another officer I bought a 16 foot half-decked sloop.

Later we bachelors in *Odin* had quite a change in our affairs when my Captain, Ronald Jonas, heard that his 18 year old sister had got parental approval to visit her brother in China. She was to be accompanied by another girl who had been at school with her. Ronald was well on in his thirties, so during a friendly chat when we were shooting snipe together, he suggested that as I was the youngest officer of his ship and had a sister of about their age, I should be Divisional Officer Girls. Laughingly I asked what the duties involved. "Well, see that the girls always stick together for safety, and they should not get closely involved with anyone of the opposite sex until handed back to their mothers."

So Pam and Doreen arrived, and I soon thought of them as sisters. There was no need for my suggested duties as several of the young wives became their close friends, while Aunty Francis could be a kindly chaperone. We bachelors found them good company. One day when they were sailing with me in my boat Pam admitted that she especially wanted to go to sea in the submarine, but knew that Ronald would not allow this. She put pressure on me, saying that I was renowned for adventures. I then committed what must have been a court-martial offence. The submarine was going out for a day exercise and it was quite normal for a spare crew sailor to come for the day, so why not disguise her as one. I only agreed to help if she cut her hair to look like a man and of course dressed in sailor's working rig.

When she arrived on board, we were secured alongside the depot ship, I guided her to the torpedo compartment forward, and briefed her not to speak under any circumstances. I told the Petty Officer in charge that this was a rather immature and shy young person coming for experience. After the dummy periscope attack on a destroyer, when I was helping with some of the detailed calculations on a device called the IsWas, the Petty Officer came from forward and whispered to me that the spare crew man was being a bit awkward as he would not answer when spoken to. I nipped forward and found that one of the real sailors was becoming suspicious. Fortunately it turned out to be a short day at sea, and all went well. Luck was with us. When I went to make my report to the submarine's First Lieutenant - an extremely competent and strong minded officer we called Bick - he mentioned that before diving he looked into the forward compartment. "Of course I recognised Pam, and presumed Ronald did not know about it. Anyway I had a stowaway on board too - my pet monkey, Spud." That evening ashore in the club I heard Ronald expressing surprise that his sister had cut her hair so short, and he suggested it might be because she had recently caught her hair in the rigging aboard my little sloop. Not too far off the mark perhaps.

Certainly *Odin* was a very happy ship, even if perhaps unconventional. For me it was good to have an old friend on board: Mike Harvey, who had been one of the outstanding cadets in my term at Dartmouth. He certainly showed great ability in the ship's work, besides the sporting life ashore.

As a rest from exercises the submarine flotilla went to Ching-wang-tao, so that leave could be given to visit Peking, just as *Cornwall* had done two or three years before. The wives, with the two girls, took a coastal steamer to another port from which they could get a train to Peking. Unfortunately some local warlord started a campaign to capture Peking, where we were all to meet, so there was no train for us from Ching-wang-tao. The women set off by train but were halted half way, where they were instructed to turn back. Pam and Doreen were not easily put off and considered that they had definite orders from Ronald to meet in Peking. So they went ahead and somehow reached the walls of Peking, which had been closed by the Chinese garrison. Word got through to the British Embassy, which negotiated their entry into the city. Fortunately that particular uprising did not last for long, so things soon got back to normal. Thus the girls saw some of the most interesting historic sights of China, besides an adventure or two, before they went home. Their mothers' wish that they should not get too involved with any man had been obeyed, but feelings had been stirred and two or three years later Doreen married Pam's brother, our Captain, Ronald Jonas.

Odin went south to Hong Kong before the main fleet because she was due for a minor refit. She was berthed in the dockyard with engines stripped down, and her main batteries, which were used when dived and sometimes when manoeuvring in confined areas, unshipped. When No 1 typhoon warning was issued, she was towed out to a typhoon berth, leaving one officer and a token crew on board. It was my turn to be on duty for 24 hours, with Mike Harvey due to relieve me at noon next day. That night the barometer remained steady and no further warnings were issued, but with the dawn came No 6 warning "Gale expected from the south west", quickly followed by No 9 "Gale

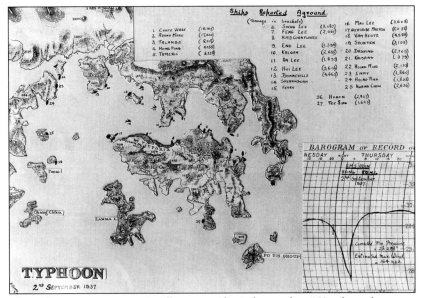

That typhoon was quite exceptionally strong with winds exceeding 150 miles an hour, then 4 minutes of dead calm before striking just as hard in the opposite direction.

expected to increase." Not long after that the Duty Petty Officer and I, standing in the conning tower, heard a gun fire, with No 10 warning hoisted "Winds of typhoon force imminent." I ordered all watertight doors to be closed and the rest of the crew on board to be gathered in the control room beneath the conning tower.

The submarine was very firmly secured by two chain cables to the special typhoon buoy; so there was nothing I could do, except to confirm that a couple of rockets were handy. In the extremely unlikely event of the submarine breaking adrift I knew that there was a special typhoon tug handy, designed to answer a distress call in even the worst conditions.

Very soon afterwards the typhoon hit, blowing very much harder than anything I had ever experienced before. Spray was driven up above the height of the conning tower, but it was hard to know what was spray and what was rain. Certainly I could not see very far and, as the wind screeched alarmingly, ships secured to buoys nearby were seldom visible.

Then through the driving spray and wind the dim shape of a vessel's bow appeared. It was not the typhoon tug and every other ship was supposed to be at a safe typhoon mooring. The moving shape was not immediately to windward of us, but appeared part of a big ship. I

45

was anxious that some part of her might strike *Odin* and so gave orders for those below to don lifejackets, really just to relieve the feeling that I must do something. That threatening ship just missed us, but soon afterwards I saw another ship moving just clear of us; she was HMS *Cornflower*, the Royal Naval Reserve harbour drill ship.

Suddenly the storm ceased. It was clear enough to see a mile or two. Time stands still in such conditions, but records showed afterwards that it was only 4 minutes before the storm hit again, from the opposite direction. It was blowing just a hard as before, and purely guessing, as I had no experience of such conditions, I told the Petty Officer beside me that I reckoned it was over a hundred miles an hour. Gradually it eased, but it seemed ages before the wind was down to the sort of gale I knew quite well. I had really done nothing, but felt as exhausted as if I had been fighting the storm with all my physical strength. My Petty Officer was more relaxed than me, and as visibility improved he pointed out nearby a ship aground and partly under water. That brought me back to my senses, and looking around through my binoculars gave me some idea of the damage to ships in the harbour, but only after we had been towed safely back to the dockyard berth, did I know that the ship which seemed to threaten us was the *AnnaLee* of 2,000 tons which had hit and damaged the cruiser *Sheffield* and a destroyer. Later came the full report with the Hong Kong harbour authority naming 25 ships of over 1,000 tons aground, damaged or even sunk. The list included the Japanese liner *Asama Maru* of 17, 000 tons

One of the 27 ships driven ashore in Hong Kong.

Wives of submarine officers in Honk Kong, whose husbands were our senior submarines officers, entertained by the bachelors.

and the Italian liner *Conte Verde* of over 18,000 tons. The local meteorological office recorded the maximum wind speed as 164 miles an hour.

I was sad to leave *Odin* and the China Station, even to go home after two and a half years abroad, with a crisis in the Mediterranean and quite a few adventures in China, besides a great deal of fun. I was more convinced than ever that the submarine service was the life for me. Indeed my report stated that I was ready for advance to submarine First Lieutenant and added "has shown initiative and ability."

So I went back to Herstmonceux for a good period of foreign service leave. My father, then 67, seemed unchanged as he set off on his bicycle for the parish rounds; my mother had added intense pride in her grandchildren to her many other interests. Lorema had left school, Verily was more in London than Herstmonceux, while Rhalou had married Kirkby Peace, who had been with us on the Norfolk Broads trip, and was settled as a vet near Dorking, with already the start of what was to be a large family of boys. My love of the countryside was no less, and on the Glebe farm pheasants scratched around in just the same spots as their parents and grandparents, the birds I had shot at when last at home.

My next appointment was as spare First Lieutenant with the submarine flotilla at Portland, living in the elderly depot ship *Titania*. Until a vacancy came, I was acting as Staff Officer Operations to Commander Jock Bethell, who commanded the flotilla. Its main task was providing targets for the anti-submarine school nearby, but after each day's session in that capacity the submarine had her turn to practice a periscope attack on one of her hunters. My job included attending a conference each week in the anti-submarine school to work out the programme for the following week, and from then on to be ready to make immediate changes. Mostly it was day exercises going out at 8.30am each morning. Thus an easy task, which allowed me to go out in each of the submarines to gain experience, for I would become First Lieutenant of one, perhaps at half an hour's notice. They were mostly small elderly vessels of the H and L class, but there were also two larger modern ones.

Except for some special exercises, which included a couple of weeks in Scottish waters, the submarines stayed in harbour over the weekends. So soon after joining I was determined to show to myself that I was physically fit after a rather debilitating service in China. Having previously measured in my car a course of 25 miles, I set off on foot to a lovely dawn. With a five minute rest every other hour, I continued at a lively pace until five miles from home a fellow officer came by in his car and stopped to offer me a lift. "No thanks, "I replied, "I'm having a stroll."

Further walks of this type lead me to know and love the Dorset countryside. On my strolls I met several of the local farmers. This led to taking the shooting rights over two adjoining farms, subject to me raising a few pheasants. This meant more money than I had available, so I formed a shoot syndicate with several of my fellow officers.

By then I had taken over as First Lieutenant of *HMS Sturgeon*, so on weekdays I was getting the ship ready for sea at 7.30 a.m. and then after the day at sea often charging the main batteries until supper time. A steady job, but it became lively when David Gregory took over as his first command. He was a superb man at the periscope, manoeuvring in a way when he was attacking that made it very difficult to detect the submarine, and his dummy torpedo attack was always a hit. No wonder he won a pair of D.S.O.'s when war came, and later went on to become an Admiral.

David was also very good with his shot gun, so naturally he was invited to join the shooting syndicate, where the pheasants were coming on well. One of the woods was right on the boundary, so before shooting began I traced the owner of the neighbouring shoot, living in the nearby village of Langton Herring. Colonel Sylvester Bradley invited me to tea on the next Sunday and was extremely helpful over the boundary problem, solving it by joining our syndicate. His wife suggested that I look in to tea when ever coming over to deal with the young pheasants. A month later she asked me to make a point of coming one weekend because her daughter was coming down from art school in London for the weekend.

On my arrival at Langton Herring, my hostess told me that her daughter had insisted that she did not want to meet any young man, least of all a naval officer who slaughtered birds. So she had gone off for a walk with her much loved dog. Her Mother hinted at which wood I might find her and to tell her tea was ready. Indeed, in that wood I noticed someone high up a tree. I chanced to climb that same tree, knocking off my hat in the process. The hat proved an attraction to the dog waiting at the bottom of the tree and was soon in tatters. Naval officer or not, the dog's owner, still up the tree, felt bound to apologise. Thus, my introduction to Daphne was not through her Mother but through her dog, which made it more acceptable. That is how I met my future wife.

Daphne came down from London quite often, and I was becoming increasingly fond of her. So I suggested that she came for a weekend with my parents. Their meeting with Daphne was about as unconventional as had been my first meeting with her. We arrived by car rather late for supper, and my Mother was in bed with a cold. She heard my hail from the front door and shouted back from her bedroom upstairs, "The maids are out, so don't go to the larder, Erroll. They've left cold supper for you both in the dining room." We sat down to this and had just started eating when Father came in from the stables and by way of introduction placed a large white rat on Daphne's lap. Fortunately she loved all animals and responded with enthusiasm much endearing her to Father, which encouraged me in my affection.

Like Susan Kennard, who my sisters had considered my girl friend, and other Chelsea art students I came across, Daphne claimed to be a communist. Party politics were beyond me, but our numerous courting letters were at first mostly philosophical, discussing subjects like ultimate reality. David Gregory, my Captain, also encouraged me over my feelings about Daphne; indeed after she and I had become engaged, he suggested that in his view war with Hitler could not be far away and weddings in peace time were likely to be more stable than wartime weddings. Anyhow, he stressed "You deserve to enjoy some peace time

*With my submarine based in Portland, I became very fond of the Dorset countryside,
which soon led to deep love for a girl whose parents lived in the countryside and who often
came down from her art school in London.*

together as man and wife." So it was in April 1939 that we were married
in the village church of Langton Herring by a squad of clergy including
my father, with the rectors of Langton Herring and of Eton. Bridesmaids
were Daphne's cousins and my sisters, while a guard of honour-cocked
hats, swords and all, was mounted by my fellow officers.

David Gregory's forecast about war proved right; we enjoyed three
months of married life in peace time. A couple of weeks before war was
actually declared *Sturgeon* moved out to a front row position. Five
submarines from different flotillas formed a patrol line off Heligoland,
where we could sight any German warship coming out into the North
Sea, and if war had actually been declared we were to attack it.
Navigation was difficult, as we then had none of the electronic devices
now normally used at sea to show a precise position. We had to remain
dived in daylight, except perhaps for a minute or two on the surface at
dawn or dusk to take sextant angles of stars above the horizon. Once
dark we could remain on the surface to charge the main batteries, but
then could not see the horizon.

After our marriage we raised £200 to buy a delightful thatched Dorset cottage, quite far from any other house. Fresh water came by bucket from our well, and by night an oil lamp lit us.

When war was declared we were all even more on the alert, and very sadly one of our neighbouring submarines was sunk in the dark, mistaken for a German U-boat by another neighbour. Further out into the North Sea, the patrol was kept by R.A.F. planes, mainly the same ones well known to us from anti-submarine exercises off Portland. To help us find our position before making the coast of Scotland when coming home, a safe area had been declared extending some 20 miles from Dundee, which was to be our port. This would enable submarines to surface in daylight, and when sextant angles between the sun and the horizon confirmed that we were well within this safe area, David Gregory went below to study the charts for entering harbour, leaving me on the conning tower.

I was in this position happily motoring under the diesel engines in a calm sea and rather poor visibility. With me was a signal man as lookout. Simultaneously we sighted an aircraft some two miles off, and both of us at once recognised it as one of the R.A.F. planes which had exercised with us. So I was not surprised when it turned, presumably

51

to identify us. Yet when closer, it went into a steep dive straight at us. I pressed the diving hooter, closed the hatch and started down the conning tower ladder with the signal man a few steps below me. I had to close the lower conning tower hatch, and I was using both hands for this purpose when the first depth charge exploded. I was thrown off the ladder, landing with my back thrown heavily against a diving lever, and I was partially stunned. All lights on board went out with the explosion, but this was something David had frequently drilled, and his voice showed no anxiety as he calmly took control and had the submarine on the way to a deep dive when the second charge exploded above us.

The lights were on again by the time I sat up, but I was in much pain and unable to stand, and I was assisted by the signalman back to my bunk. David Gregory and Michael Lumby, who automatically took my place as First Lieutenant, quickly established that neither depth charge had done any real damage to the submarine. But the first one had done a lot of damage to me, although this was not appreciated for a long time.

Back at periscope depth, a search showed no aircraft in sight, so the submarine surfaced and signalled by radio "Expect to arrive 20.00 hundred hours, friendly aircraft permitting." The aircraft had signalled that it had probably sunk a U-boat, so our depot ship in harbour guessed what had happened. Even I, who suffered from this incident for a long time ahead, could not possibly blame the aircraft, as it could not know exactly where it was with the equipment fitted to her. It was just a very unlucky chance that both of my hands were doing something else when I needed to cling on at the moment a depth charge shook the submarine.

CHAPTER SIX

Hospitals in Plenty 1939-1944

Daphne was waiting ashore. Somehow word had been sent to her where *Sturgeon* would be coming, so at 5.00 a.m. she set out in our rickety old car, and drove without stopping, except for petrol and emergency repairs, all the way to Dundee. At least the name Bruce proved helpful in Scotland; when the car gave up on the outskirts of a town, a garage informed her that they were too busy to do anything for days. When she gave her name they suddenly found that the repair could be done at once. Also waiting for me was news of an appointment to a bigger submarine, which I was to join at Portsmouth.

We set off in the car two days later for Portsmouth. By the time we got there I certainly no longer thought my damage was mere bruising, and the doctor sent me straight to Haslar, the naval hospital. By then I was feeling really ill and, without even looking at my back, the doctor there diagnosed me as suffering from a nervous breakdown; this might well have been so after the rough handling my back had suffered since it was damaged. The psychiatrist tried to convince me that it was the nervous strain of submarine service; but I persisted that my naval life was in submarines and I certainly did not want to leave them, having made what my reports suggested was a good start. Anyhow what could be quieter than a dived submarine on patrol? He then tried to make me believe that the trouble was the strain of being newly married with a wartime seagoing career. Again he found me an awkward patient whose worry was that he had severe pains extending from his back to most of his body. It turned out to be very much later before a doctor diagnosed a damaged spine as the culprit, and once his treatment was completed I was able to resume my career at sea.

Meantime I parted from the hospital with the stricture "Unfit for sea service for 3 months." My next job was therefore changed to take command of the large submarine *Triumph* which was undergoing a refit likely to last 3 months. Even a rather junior temporary Captain had very considerable legal powers, as came to light when one night during an air raid I went on board to find an Able Seaman sentry, the only man on board, was fast asleep. At the formal hearing next day I knew it was my duty to treat this seriously, as a minor fire not extinguished straight away might have led to serious damage. So I made out a punishment warrant which awarded him special disciplinary treatment in the detention quarters. This seemed to me a fierce punishment for a man who had never put a foot wrong before, so I asked to see the Commander-in-Chief, who would have to authorise the warrant. It was Admiral Dunbar-Nasmith, who had been my Captain at Dartmouth and as Lieutenant had won the Victoria Cross in submarines. He listened carefully to my concern, then answered "Command is a very heavy responsibility, and what you have awarded is what your training tells you is correct." On leaving, the Admiral's secretary told me that when the Admiral was my age he took his submarine to the sea bottom for a rest, leaving just one man on duty, but woke to find the man asleep, which could have lost the lives of all on board. He awarded the man the death sentence, conforming with naval regulations, but on return to his depot ship persuaded the flotilla Captain to commute it to a lesser punishment. The secretary added that the Commander-in-Chief might do the same in this case; he did.

Besides looking after my ship's company, most of the work was following up every item in the submarine's defect list, encouraging the dockyard staff to give full attention to it as soon as possible. It was a busy time and I felt pleased that the reduced naval complement on board had given such support that we were running two days ahead of schedule.

An experienced Lieutenant-Commander was appointed in command, so I would become his First Lieutenant. I assumed it a mere formality to be passed medically fit for sea and was thus surprised when the verdict was another period fit for shore duty only, and for this offence there was no appeal to my Commander-in-Chief. So I was appointed in command of *H.M.S. Severn*, another fine big submarine, and she was refitting at Chatham.

By then Daphne was expecting our first baby, due the following month, so she stayed in our Dorset cottage. My younger sister Lorema came to care for me in a small rented house near Chatham. A baby boy was born on 13th May 1940 and we called him Peregrine, the pseudonym of my published articles. "Perhaps he will do the writing when he grows up" commented my father when christening him. For a month or so, other than an odd weekend at home, I could give no more help with the baby than an exchange of letters with Daphne, which seemed mostly concerned with breast feeding.

After that Daphne and Peregrine came to Chatham, which was hardly the best environment for a tiny baby, as air raids offered unattractive music most nights, even if the balloon barrage overhead seemed to stop any bombs falling immediately around us. However I was expecting to be off to sea in *Triumph* as soon as the refit was finished, so Daphne and I wanted to have some time together.

Again came a rude shock at the medical check back in hospital, when the doctor spent ages with his stethoscope testing my lungs. The terrible word tuberculosis was mentioned and once more the verdict was "Unfit for sea service." I was still hoping to stay in submarines, and the submarine service seemed willing to wait for my fitness, so I was sent to the submarine base at Gosport to teach newcomers to submarines. It was the same job my friend Mervyn Wingfield had been doing when I first joined submarines. He had gone on to win the Victoria Cross for brilliant achievements in his submarine, so I was encouraged to feel that in time I would be back under the sea. Meantime it was satisfying to be teaching students about a subject which meant so much to me.

The Portsmouth area was a major target for enemy aircraft, so I felt it best for Daphne and the baby if we lived a few miles out in the country. We soon found a delightful farmer and his wife willing to lodge us. It turned out to be not so safe from the air. One night we were woken by many shells bursting overhead, and then saw a blazing plane dive very close past our window, followed by an explosion in the nearest field. Then the anxious cries from Mr Lucas "My ricks, my ricks", as the flames appeared to engulf them.

I rushed out with him, wearing a dressing gown, and we found the ricks were not alight, but there was no chance of anyone in the plane surviving. The Home Guard arrived very soon afterwards, so I turned to assist them in case any of the crew had parachuted and might be hiding in the farm buildings. We found none, but soon noticed a liberal crop of letters spread over the field around the burning plane. My torch showed some addressed to British warships, and when a R.A.F. party arrived they disclosed that it was a British plane that had been shot down in error; it carried no bombs but a full load of mail for Malta

My work with submarine training had been interesting, satisfying and was generally considered as a rest from the responsibilities of a job at sea. So I was confident that all would be well with the medical board. It came as a bombshell when a doctor explained gently that I was not fit, my lungs were still doubtful. I did not realise that for the present this meant shore service under the eye of a doctor, but assumed that the verdict was merely unfit for submarines at sea. So I went straight off to the Admiralty appointment department saying I wanted a job at sea. My papers had not arrived from the medical board, but my enthusiasm was obvious and there was an urgent need for a First Lieutenant of a destroyer due to go off on convoy duty. "Go straight to Liverpool and join *HMS Beverley*, which is due to sail tomorrow." *Beverley* was one of the 50 elderly four funnel destroyers loaned by the U.S.A. to support our war effort. Her Captain was a regular navy anti-submarine specialist who would be senior officer of the escort to an Atlantic convoy of merchant ships. He was pleased to see me, as his former First Lieutenant had just been found unfit for sea service. It was February, so he warned me to check everything was secured for severe North Atlantic weather. He went on to say that my experience in submarines would be a help to him because U-boats had become a major menace to convoys; indeed 27 merchant ships had been sunk in one week, and soon after that 20 were lost from an Atlantic convoy of 34.

Once clear of Ireland the weather lived up to expectations. I had to get used to seasickness with a destroyer's motion so different from a submarine. Keeping watch on the bridge was not too bad, but trying to deal with the domestic problems of the ship's company was as trying for me as it was for young sailors who had just joined the ship after shore training.

Fortunately the weather had moderated by the time the first U-boats attacked the convoy, so I had a splendid chance to admire John Grant's handling of the escort group. No wonder that before the end of the war he had won the D.S.O., and by the end of his career had become an Admiral.

There came a time in my trip with him when he was keeping off what appeared to be three U-boats, but the convoy's speed was so slow that they could overtake and have a go from ahead, which is where John wanted to take the ship; but just when needed so urgently her engines gave up, leaving us a sitting target. "I'd like to drop an occasional depth charge just to keep them away" John told me, "but with no throwers, we can only drop them over the stern and that would blow it off." Then after a moments thought he added, "I know you like boats No 1, so if we get a depth charge into the sea boat, set to maximum depth, you could take it clear, then heave it over with the crew rowing like hell." The sea boat was always kept ready for any emergency, so it was manned in a few seconds, and before I had time to explain to the crew our unconventional and rather risky task, there came a shout from the bridge. "Hold on. The engines are going again."

It turned out to be a good convoy without loss when our escort was relieved and we went to protect an incoming convoy. So as we went back to Liverpool I was feeling delighted at the prospect of a splendid job with a first rate Captain. I'd even got over seasickness.

Life ashore in Liverpool proved more hazardous than broken down in mid-Atlantic surrounded by U-boats. On the way into harbour I had sent a message to Daphne asking her to join me. I had a reply that her train would arrive at about 9.00pm, so I booked a room in a hotel near the ships mooring. Around supper time a heavy German bomber raid began with bombs falling in plenty. Taxis were unobtainable, so I set off on foot for the station, getting a vivid picture of searchlights, lighting up a pattern of bombers, while the whole area was lit up by burning buildings. The noise was a mixture of anti-aircraft fire mingled with bursting bombs, which my imagination suggested were concentrated on my route to the station.

I almost stumbled over a badly injured man, and did what little I could to help him until an ambulance arrived. Then right on my route was a tall building blazing vigorously, so I stopped to help the fire fighters - perhaps it was more than helping as with bombs bursting all round some had taken shelter and were not too happy to have a naval officer in uniform driving them back to their pumps and hoses.

Time was flying, so the thought of Daphne arriving at a strange city in the middle of a major air attack made me run to meet her train. Fortunately we met, and even found a taxi prepared to venture on the roads. At the hotel everyone had taken to the basement shelters, but we found our way in, and both of us were much too exhausted to stand around in the cellars. With the help of my torch, we found the number of our room and collapsed on the beds. By next morning at least our building was still standing, but we soon found that terrible damage had been done all around.

The ship had not been hit, but there was bad news when I got aboard her. An official letter stated that my appointment was a mistake because I was only fit for shore service. Thus I was to report to the Admiralty forthwith. Down in London the same officer that I'd seen before in the Admiralty did not welcome me this time; indeed he blamed me for misinforming him and added that he was taking me to his Director. The Naval Captain overlooked my offence and congratulated me on my enthusiasm to get to sea. He said that while striving to get totally fit, I would still be valuable ashore, training National Service men selected for commissions. Even that had to be postponed as another visit to hospital disclosed a duodenal ulcer, which meant the visit was prolonged, and submarine service seemed further away than ever.

It was well over two months from the day I left *Beverley* at Liverpool before I joined *HMS King Alfred* on the front at Brighton. In peacetime it was a municipal swimming bath and public lavatory, but its wartime task was training men to be Royal Naval Volunteer Officers. I was to be a divisional officer, joining up with several others who had commanded ships and were considered to need a few months rest before going back to sea. So I already knew and admired several of them.

Each of us would in turn take some 75 candidates through the course, with a team of three other officers to help with various aspects of training. My chief assistant, Douglas Collins, was an experienced R.N.V.R. Lieutenant, who I knew as a yachtsman, so he mainly taught seamanship. My first group gathered in the buildings of an evacuated preparatory school in Hove, then moved down to the former indoor bathing pools on the seafront, where the candidates slept in vast improvised dormitories, and the main part of the course was conducted. Then those who were keeping up to the standard moved to Lancing College, whose normal students had been evacuated. Much of the instruction in handling craft was carried out in Shoreham Basins, although I preferred to look out into the English Channel. The officer in charge of the boats was reluctant to let us out of the Basins because across the English Channel was a German training establishment, where potential Luftwaffe pilots would benefit from us as targets.

Boats were always a joy to me, so I particularly enjoyed taking a part in teaching others how to handle them. I even found classroom teaching could be interesting when enough questions were asked. A special treat cropped up one weekend when my cousin Peter Scott called in while his ship was in Newhaven nearby.

He had commanded a Motor Torpedo Boat with conspicuous success, and then moved to command a new type of craft - the Steam Gun Boat, which was very fast indeed, and could creep along almost noiselessly when required. He asked me to come out with him that night, but could not tell me his task until we were out at sea. Even out in the English Channel he still could not tell me where he was to creep in and 'take off' someone. Obviously the place used, and who it was, would have to remain secret in case someone gave a hint in such security affairs. For all I knew, it might on that occasion have been a practice on some part of the English coast, but later we heard how he crept into the French coast to land or take off an agent. Certainly I was impressed with his skill and complete control under difficult conditions in pitch dark. Later Peter's half brother, Wayland Young, was a candidate at *King Alfred*, so my aunt Kathleen, widow of Captain Scott of the Antarctic, came to stay with us to see how her younger son was progressing.

Another of my candidates happened to be Daphne's eldest brother. By profession a University don, with wide experience of leadership in various roles, he would obviously have no difficulty with the course. The divisional team kept careful records of our trainees who were known as cadet ratings, making continuous assessments of their work and progress, besides the examinations at the end. The decision whether to make each one an officer was made by a special Board, presided over by an Admiral, and included the Captain of *King Alfred*, besides an experienced academic and a psychologist. In practice the Board was mainly concerned with those the team considered doubtful, and it interviewed each of these. It did not normally see the rest personally, except that the Admiral liked to meet the top cadet rating, partly to congratulate him and perhaps also to check our judgement. When I was called in to give my report, the Admiral pointed out that I had given my top candidate unusually high marks. The academic said that this could be expected of a university don; the psychologist mentioned that an experienced Boy Scout leader was bound to be good. Yet the Admiral asked me whether I really knew the candidate well enough to award him the highest mark he had ever seen. "Yes, Sir", I felt bound to answer, "By chance he is my brother-in-law." "Well of course you know him, and that's quite all right" rejoined the Admiral, "Thanks for telling me."

Yet another session in hospital led to the familiar sentence of unfit for sea service; once again there was a hint of tuberculosis, that unconfirmed threat that had followed me since early Dartmouth days. The next appointment was to *HMS St George*, which had been evacuated to the Isle of Man. Lads entered there to train for a permanent career in the Navy, in the first place for 12 years, with the option of a further 10 years to earn a pension. By that time many would be Chief Petty Officers or Petty Officers, others would have gained Warrant rank, and a special few would have been promoted to General List Officers, with the possibility even of becoming an Admiral. Ashore in *St George* they had over a year of general schooling and naval training, before continuing the process at sea, until qualified as Ordinary Seamen, Signalmen or Telegraphists.

I considered my duties as a divisional officer much the same as a house master, to advise and help. But I quickly fell foul of my Captain, a rigid disciplinarian who had come ashore from an extremely demanding job in command of a cruiser, which had battled against a far more powerful German pocket battleship. One of my boys had been brought before him charged with lack of discipline, for which the

Captain regularly awarded six cuts of the cane. However I knew the boy to be timid and most unlikely to be undisciplined; while the instructor charging him was something of a bully who I had sometimes heard shouting muddled orders. Thus in defence of the boy I cross-examined the instructor briskly and made him almost admit that his order could have been misunderstood. The Captain had to let the boy off with a caution, but reserved a much more severe caution for me in the privacy of his office. "Don't you know that you main job is to enforce discipline. Yet you were failing to support a Chief Petty Officer doing just this."

By then Daphne and I had three children, Peregrine, Peter and Rosamund, living in a house we rented in Douglas. So we were delighted when an old friend, Hughie Hodgkinson, wrote that he was coming from his naval duties in the south. The reason for his visit was to consult a certain Dr Canon, from whom he previously had excellent medical attention. Dr Canon had moved to the Isle of Man from London as it was thought that some of his electronic gear might interfere with the radar defences. On his arrival Hughie strongly advised me to try this doctor as several years of other treatments had failed in my hopes of getting back to sea. Daphne supported this, so I made an appointment with Dr Canon, who introduced his secretary, and then put her into a hypnotic trance and questioned her. In answer to his detailed questions she gave an account of my medical history, even telling him that my left wrist had been set by someone not a doctor. Then came many

By then Daphne and I had had three children Peregrine, Rosamund and Peter living in a house in Douglas, Isle of Man.

questions about my recent series of troubles. Dr Canon brought the girl out of the trance with "You get more beautiful every day and you are never tired." As she stood up he told her to get on with her normal work elsewhere.

He then carried out a very careful physical examination, particularly of my spine. At the end of that he summed up saying that the whole problem had been a disjointed spine, suffered some years ago, which had upset the whole rhythm of my body when it came under physical or mental strain. He could cure me completely, he insisted, but it would take some three months and cost a large proportion of my salary. He suggested that I think about it and let him know in a week.

Naturally I went straight to the ship's doctor, who sent me for an X-ray. When that came back it disclosed nothing, so I returned with it to Dr Canon, who told me it had been taken from the wrong angle, and gave me a note for my doctor, which led to another X-ray. This time the report was that I should be admitted to hospital at once; but I had been through so many hospital admissions without cure, so I went back to Dr Canon. He told me that the private treatment would mean a couple of hours out of my normal working time each week, which would mean getting special leave from my Captain; this time my interview in his office was even more critical. He severely condemned my judgement for suggesting that oriental mysticism should come before sound naval practice, which cost me nothing. However he accepted that, if I persisted in such foolishness, he would allow me the time off, if I made up for it on other occasions.

Three months went by and although just about penniless by then, I felt very much better. I took on coaching the ship's rugger team, which involved a certain amount of fairly rough demonstration. In one critical match, the boy's 1st XV won, and as the Captain was watching he made a point of congratulating me as coach, adding that perhaps I would have got better in any case. With the summer term, boats took the place of rugger as my main recreational task. Besides the normal naval cutters and whalers, a fine old cruising yacht was available to me, and it could take many boys, while acting as escort to a couple of cutters cruising along the coast.

Before long two boys had passed my strict test as boat skipper, so could take charge of a cutter under sails or oars; this was a new departure as previously there had always been an instructor steering each boat. Sometimes we went into a small bay up the coast for picnic tea, and one day I was surprised to find that the Captain had come round by land to see what we were doing. He was first indignant that

I allowed two boys to take charge on their own, but after discussion and hearing what tests they had taken, he accepted this. Following a mug of tea I mentioned that it would be valuable training, especially for those boys who might in time blossom to substantial advancement, if on special occasions we had an overnight exercise with the boats, camping on the beach for a Saturday night. To my surprise he agreed, but added that he would not give any marks to a Divisional Officer who failed to be in charge of the division when he inspected it at Sunday divisions. I felt it best not to comment that my assistant Divisional Officer was very competent at parade work, and might benefit if the good marks went to him.

The overnight camps were very popular, and once or twice, after the tents had been rigged and supper finished, we all went out in the boats for a night exercise in the dark. Generally I could only guess the value of such training, but I chanced much later to come across the boy who was the first to qualify for charge of a boat; by then he was qualified as an officer, and mentioned what great confidence this boat experience had given him.

Six months went by without any sign of illness, so I reckoned it was time to ask for a medical survey; great was the joy when the answer was that at last I was fit for sea.

With the prospect of my absence in the Pacific war, Daphne and the children settled in our Dorset cottage, and prayed for peace...

CHAPTER SEVEN

East Again 1945

The appointment came to the cruiser *HMS Glasgow*, then nearing completion of a refit to prepare her for a special task. In the Far East naval aircraft sent out to attack Japanese ships were often used as guides by Japanese dive bombers back to their aircraft carriers. The American navy started a system of having a picket ship, effectively acting as a decoy, to which their returning aircraft could first return, allowing them to be, what they called de-loused, before continuing to their home aircraft carrier. The snag was that the destroyer acting as picket ship was often sunk, so the plan was to equip a large cruiser with additional anti-aircraft weapons, besides elaborate radar and fighter control equipment, replacing some of the main armament.

As First Lieutenant, I was number three in the command order, after the Commander, who was second in command, executive officer and president of the wardroom mess. In wardroom mess ranking I was much further down as there were commanders heading the departments of engineering, electronics, pay and supply, besides medical. At my level in the executive branch came the gunnery officer, the navigator and the torpedo officer; the four of us taking it in turns to be the duty commanding officer.

Once the refit was completed the ship set off for Scapa Flow to test every item of equipment and train the ship's company in its use. At action stations most of the senior executive officers were stationed on the bridges, in close touch with the Captain. But that was just where any dive bomber would aim, so a second command team was stationed well away towards the other end of the ship. I headed that second team, in touch only by telephone.

In spite of the excellent work done by the refitters in Newcastle, a mass of technical matters still needed attention, which took longer than the original plans. But at last we set off through the Mediterranean, and while on watch one dawn, steaming quite fast, I happened to sight a tiny object some distance from our track, so I turned the ship, and when Captain Clarke reached the bridge from his sea cabin, it was disclosed as a very small open boat with a body in it. We lowered a sea boat, the body stirred and was brought on board unable to do anything himself. When he could speak next day he proved to be a Spaniard who claimed to have been adrift 8 days, without water, food or shelter. He said that he had been out fishing when carried away by a storm. There was no fishing gear in the boat, but a good deal of Spanish money, besides barber's tools. We could only guess that he was trying to escape from somewhere, and he seemed very relieved to be put ashore, with the boat, in Malta. He even thanked me in person, using quite good English, as the person who had sighted his boat in the dawn light.

Just about then news came through that we would not have to perform our special fighting task in real life, as Japan had surrendered. However *Glasgow* was ordered to continue eastwards, but with less urgency. Indeed there was even time in Malta for me to conduct a sailing and camping exercise for some of the Boy Seaman on board, a couple of whom had done this with me in the Isle of Man. This time it was more realistic as Donald Peyton Jones, in charge of the Royal Marines on board, added much to it, while the senior sub-lieutenant also proved a splendid leader. The Admiral commanding naval affairs in Malta, went further than giving formal approval to such unconventional exercises and suggested that a pair of Wrens on his staff would benefit from taking part. So that time, instead of taking off pretended escaped prisoners-of-war past a patrol of the other boat, it was a matter of rescuing a pair of princesses who had been seized by a wicked king. Thus there could be a Wren on each side, and when the exercise was over, we camped on the rocks, with the two girls together in an improvised shelter.

Then on through the Suez Canal, the pace of life on board was much more leisurely and it felt crowded, with no need for the guns and equipment to be manned at wartime standards. Many of the ship's company were National Service men, called up for the war; as that was over, it worried them to be sailing away from home. For regulars it was different and the Captain gave priority to personal training; as I was the ship's training officer this gave me ample scope for organising classes aimed at helping those who wanted advancement to a higher grade. Not all officers sympathised with this, and some complained that it would mean the best leading rates being sent to another ship on becoming Petty Officers. However Captain Clarke gave real help and even lectured himself sometimes; then Tom Best, the Gunnery Officer, gave very strong support. We were joined by another cruiser *HMS Jamaica*, also making for the East. That meant we could exercise together in many ways. One which pleased me especially was man overboard drill, as each ship could compete to be fastest in lowering a sea boat and picking up the life buoy representing the man overboard. One day I asked if the regular lifeboat's crew could be replaced by Seaman Boys. The Captain agreed, but as it was rather rough he required that I should go as instructor. I was to watch the boy acting as coxswain in particular because he was a potential officer. *Jamaica* beat us by a few seconds and a senior officer commented loudly that I could learn some lessons from the leading seaman in charge of the other boat. That might have been so, but the satisfaction for me was that within a year Seaman Boy Sykes passed the selection board for promotion to officer.

Unfortunately there was already friction between that particular officer and me over another matter. I had been persuaded to take on the voluntary task of wardroom wine catering after some trouble over the accounts. It was clear to me that this officer was putting down some of his drinks to an officer I knew to be teetotal, no doubt paying him in cash, but giving a false impression when I submitted the wine books to the Captain for inspection. As my senior he was furious when I told him that it was my duty to present the Captain with the correct facts.

At Colombo we were all eagerly looking forward to letters from home; indeed the prospect of mail was one of the main subjects of conversation throughout the ship. I had been anxiously awaiting the latest news from Daphne because the last letter received in Malta told that Peregrine, our eldest boy and then aged 5, was unwell. It was a joy to hear that Daphne and all three children were in good health.

We soon heard that the ship was to take on board a large load of fleet mail and several hundred passengers for Singapore. Passengers, although nearly all naval officers and men, presented quite a problem because the ship already felt crowded with her full wartime complement still on board. Three hundred ratings had to be spread among the men's open messes, slinging their hammocks in scarcely suitable airless places. Then 30 officers had to sleep on the deck of the ship's officers' cabins. Captain Clarke gave up his entire harbour quarters to the few civilian passengers, keeping to his small sea cabin near the bridge.

It rained every day in the Indian Ocean on that voyage, making the upper deck seldom of use for passengers to relax. So we worked out a series of diversions with concerts, brains trusts and similar entertainments. Our greatest asset was the Royal Marine band, which scarcely rested all day. It played hymns at morning prayers, musical physical training, sing-song concerts and then popular extracts during supper.

Arriving at Singapore the passengers were quickly disembarked, but no one came to claim the mail, and enquiry received the answer that the Fleet Mail Office was already quite full with mail waiting to be sorted.

Next day the ship was ordered to sail back to Colombo with another load of passengers. Fortunately Tom Best volunteered to be assistant 'hotel manager' as his normal gunnery exercises were impossible with such a crowd on board. This proved a great success as among other things he thought out various new schemes to occupy the passengers. One of these proved particularly popular. It was an obstacle race with each member of the team doing something different, such as climbing a ladder wearing diver's boots, crossing a slippery pole suspended over a canvas bath full of water, or sliding down a slippery rope.

Next day an entirely different task cropped up when we heard that the large liner *Takliva*, loaded with returning prisoners-of-war, had gone ashore in a cyclone and caught fire. Several warships had managed to rescue everyone, but no one had boarded her since. So Captain Clarke decided to steam up to the Nicobar Islands to investigate.

I had at some time completed a course on salvage, so was told to hand over my other duties to Tom Best and prepare a salvage expedition. Almost every one else wanted to be included, but I cut it down to a few good swimmers and agile rope climbers. When we got there the sea was fairly rough, and the charts were not very precise; so the ship stopped a couple of miles out, where she lowered a motor boat and a whaler for the first investigation.

Close inshore it was still fairly rough and I saw that the wreck was well up among the rocks but heeling over, so that the ropes left by her boats, lowered for escaping, hung well out from the ship's side. Thus we could row the whaler among the rocks and reach the ropes without being smashed against the wreck. It was quite a climb, but having no gear to carry I went first, just carrying a pistol in case others had made a claim on her. But no one challenged me and from the height of the liner's boat deck I could look down and guide the motor boat in through the rocks.

Soon all eight of the salvage party were on board, leaving the boat's crews to tend their boats. Then looking round it was clear that there was no salvage to be done, as she had been gutted by fire. It was a terrible sight, still smouldering. Most of the ammunition had exploded, but some was still lying on the hot deck, so we threw that overboard.

The natives of that island were believed to be very hostile, so I was half expecting a shower of arrows from the shore, or even firing from machine guns, which could have been taken from the wreck. However there was no sign of life ashore, and clearly no one else had boarded the wreck. From outside she looked like a ship, but once aboard it was a derelict mass of molten metal, collapsed decks, gaping holes and desolation. Standing there I remembered that her sister ship had been wrecked in a typhoon some eight years earlier, and by extraordinary chance I was the first person to board that wreck too. There was a third great liner of that class, so I offered a prayer that she would not share the fate of her two sisters.

In a sombre mood I returned to our ship and made my report to the Captain, who had kept guns manned in case the natives attacked our small salvage party. Then on to Colombo where we disembarked our passengers before sailing back to Trincomalee, where we were promised ten days in harbour to get the ship sorted out and clean. We were practically on the equator so to avoid the highest temperatures, we would start work at 5.30am. and finish at noon. Then the afternoons would be free for games, sailing and bathing, or even sleep for those who preferred an extra tot or two of gin. There was always a run on football grounds from the Fleet, so it was easier at short notice to arrange hockey at which our ship's team soon earned a reputation. We had a really good centre forward in Captain Clarke and a splendid Sub-Lieutenant as centre half; somehow there was a shortage of left backs, so I was usually in the team. Trincomalee could have done with more games facilities to keep so many men fit. The tendency was for the same individuals to be good at several sports, so perhaps the best way to get exercise for the less skilled was by non-competitive boating and camping.

At the end of the comparative rest for cleaning I had arranged examinations for the various training classes, which meant getting suitable officers, sometimes from other ships. When I made my report to Captain Clarke he said that I had been through a very intensive time with all the passengers and special duties, so he felt that I should have a week in the rest camp up country, where it was cooler. However when it came out that no-one else was to go, I persuaded him to let me have instead a few days camping in the jungle locally with the sailors who had done best in the exams; this was agreed and better still, Donald Peyton-Jones could accompany me.

While we were camping, one of the favourite subjects between Donald and I was how best we would like to make the journey home, if our turns came before the ship was to return. My dream for us was to buy or build a suitable boat, then sail through the Suez Canal and perhaps on to Athens, picking up our wives for some Mediterranean cruising to the Gulf of Lyons, then on by canal to the Bay of Biscay and home. Donald was slightly more inclined to a scheme of travelling by foot, bus and train through Persia and Turkey; then to meet our wives in Constantinople, and the four of us continue across Europe. But our dreams in the tropical jungle did not cope with the problem of looking after the children, or many other practicalities. Nor did reality have much to do with such dreams, as within a month Donald was ordered to fly home for a special new job, while I was to complete nearly three years in the ship, returning home in her.

After visits to Indian ports the ship returned to Trincomalee, dropping one of my classes in a whaler 30 miles off, which would give us the satisfaction of 'discovering' the land. It also had another asset in that when the ship entered harbour Tom Best could have a turn at my normal job in charge of the forecastle, whether anchoring, picking up a buoy or taking a tow from a tug. Traditionally this was the First Lieutenant's job, but Tom was always keen to have a go at anything.

Tom took charge of another task after our arrival, which knocked spots off my improvised camping in the jungle. He took 150 men to a real camp, with concrete floored huts, kitchens and washing facilities, where they could have a week of rifle and machine gun practice. Each evening he sent a radio report of their doings - always interesting and amusing, but finishing off with "No incidents", as he had been warned to expect pilfering by the jungle folk. We knew how carefully he had organised sentries and guards to prevent this.

It had proved a laborious journey in lorries and a very primitive ferry to get there, so I made a survey in my *Dumbo* to see whether a landing craft could reach the camp, and decided that it was possible. Next day Robert MacNab and I set out in a borrowed landing craft to test the theory; half a mile short of the camp Robert and a midshipman, both disguised by grease paint and suitable clothing, landed in the jungle. I was duly met by sentries and escorted to Tom's tent, and while he and I were planning his return, a Petty Officer came in and reported that there were two strange people about, which he suspected could be sailors trying to be funny, yet closer examination showed them to be natives, although they did not belong to the camp staff. Tom rushed out shouting "Stop. Come here." No answer. "What are you doing here." They turned and began to run, saying in a high-pitched voice "A bing a bong a tring-a coo.""Call out the guards.

16 foot Dumbo often proved useful for H.M.S. Glasgow.

Man the defences" ordered Tom, but at that moment the loin clothes fell off the 'intruders', disclosing quite clearly a white body. "Excellent joke, thanks Erroll" Tom said, but I had to admit that he had won hands down, with "No incidents."

After one of the ships visits to an Indian harbour, again I was dropped in a whaler 30 miles out with a crew of Boy Seamen. This time the adventure was added to as we picked up two native fishermen whose boat had been damaged and was sinking. Naturally the Captain congratulated the crew, and following this, one of the officers heard two midshipmen complaining that their life was so dull compared with the boys. Certainly the midshipmen had a full programme with general education taught by an instructor officer with a University degree, semaphore exercises in the early morning and morse flashing in the evenings; outside of such working hours each had his ship's duties, such as keeping watch on the quarterdeck or running motor boats. Tom Best, as snotties nurse, kept these young officers firmly up to their jobs. However, discussing with me the feeling expressed by one of them about a dull life, he decided to take them off all duties for one evening and have a boat picnic in the jungle, approaching it in the dark through a maze of rocks. Captain Clarke volunteered to come as head cook, while the Chaplain offered his services as spud peeler.

Soon after that we set off with another load of passengers for Singapore. But I had learnt quite a few points from the previous run, so this time there was less acute discomfort. We were to remain in Singapore for our first Christmas since the ship left home.

On Christmas Eve 1945, Robert and I went to inspect a Japanese cruiser lying in the naval base 25 miles away, with part of her crew still on board. One of her Japanese officers had been to a British University, which made it very interesting as we discussed the treatment they were getting compared with that suffered by British prisoners-of-war in Japanese hands. No doubt he was being tactful, but he insisted that he never expected the Japanese to win.

That evening a ship's concert was held with officers and men combining to make it a thoroughly enjoyable affair. Then we gathered on the quarterdeck for carol singing, with several coming over from other ships to join in. The warships present were all decorated with coloured lights, their funnels flood lit, searchlights circling the sky and rockets fired from time to time. The Padre started Christmas communion at midnight in his small chapel, and such was the queue outside that he could have had little rest before Christmas matins, which were very well attended on the upper deck. Then followed the tradition of Christmas rounds of the mess decks, headed by the youngest sailor boy dressed as the Master-at-Arms and the youngest midshipman dressed as the Captain. Everyone cheered the real Captain Clarke, while another sailor boy dressed as Father Christmas presented him with a teddy bear. Then all the Chief Petty Officers and Petty Officers trooped to the quarterdeck dressed as monkeys, gypsies and who knows what, followed by the pipe band, the concert party and the brass band, where all took a drink with the officers.

On Boxing day *Glasgow's* officers gave a cocktail party, which was fun to prepare. Robert rigged even more coloured lights, Tom tied paper frills round his guns, while I went off in *Dumbo* with a pair of midshipmen to cut down a tall bamboo tree which we planted right down the hatches in the ship to offer a spread of leaves on the quarterdeck. All the Admirals and Generals present in Singapore were invited; the chief guest was the Supreme Commander of South East Asia, Lord Louis Mountbatten, who made a deep impression on everyone, as he seemed to remember any officer or man who had served in a ship under him. He even remembered that 15 years earlier I had helped to exercise his polo ponies. Some of these very senior officers had their families in Singapore, so I found a couple of midshipmen to introduce to a pair of girls, and asked who their fathers were. One seemed surprised that I did not recognise the initials defining his important military post; but the other girl answered modestly that her father had the peculiar title of supremo. So I could introduce her as Pamela Mountbatten.

CHAPTER EIGHT

Back to Peacetime Conditions 1946

By this time the Admiralty had sorted out the problems of turning the Fleet back to peacetime conditions. *Glasgow* and our fellow cruiser *Jamaica* were to remain in the East Indies Fleet. This meant a thoroughly interesting station, including the Indian Ocean, the Persian Gulf, the Bay of Bengal and the Arabian Sea. Yet it also meant another two years before we would see home, and there was very little chance of our wives coming out because the ship would spend so much time cruising throughout the station.

Early in 1946 Captain Clarke was appointed to an important task in the Admiralty, so the ship gave him an impressive farewell. That evening it was getting dark when he left in a whaler rowed by some of his senior officers in full uniform, while three canoes paddled by ratings formed his escort. On the ship's forecastle gathered every man not on duty below to give him resounding cheers as his boat drew abreast. Then it went clear, all were silent as the bagpipes played a farewell over the water.

Captain Hubback took over command with a thoroughly testing first voyage. When weighing anchor in the normal way, it hooked under the keel and stuck. He blamed himself, but it seemed to me to be sheer bad luck. Then a couple of days later, when nearly everyone was asleep in the tropical mid-afternoon, a man rolled over in his sleep into the sea. Another officer and I were reading on the quarterdeck and happened to see him go. While the officer ran to phone the bridge, I ran forward on deck shouting "Away Lifeboat's crew", the emergency call to man the sea boat. Although a special seaboat's crew was always detailed and would normally be the first to arrive, in this case they had been sent to secure something on the forecastle.

Several men sleeping on deck nearby woke to the call and jumped into the boat. So seeing a full boat I started to lower it, but then noticed that there was no-one in it with any knowledge as coxswain. So I climbed down a rope into the boat, thinking that all would be all ready when the bridge gave the order to slip. Before that moment came the ship heeled heavily as she turned, so the boat was in the water going too fast for safety. So I pulled the lever to slip her, and as we steered clear the order came over the ship's broadcast system "Away lifeboat's crew", showing that the bridge did not know we were already away.

The crew had never rowed together before, but because we were struggling for someone's life they put great effort into it. The life buoy sentry on duty right aft had let go his life buoy on my first shout, so I had a mark to steer by, and after rowing about half a mile at a cracking pace, we sighted the man still afloat, but only just; he went under when we stopped close to him. I jumped in and got a rope round him, but he was unconscious and we had a heavy job to get him aboard the boat.

The ship was steaming back fast, so he was in the sick bay under artificial respiration quite soon after falling in. A very fortunate young man, as he turned out to be a non-swimmer who had just joined the ship. Unfortunately I needed treatment too, as I was in great pain from my back, strained when getting the unconscious man into the boat. The Captain was thoroughly puzzled by the whole affair, with everything on board new to him. This particular event followed no normal routine, so the navigator could not enlighten him. Thus he had to come down to the sick bay to find out what had happened, both from the man rescued and myself as one of his rescuers. I do not know what we said to him, for neither of us were feeling too clear in our heads just at that time.

We were bound for Surabaya as the Potsdam Conference had widened the South East Asia Command to include Java, where there were many problems to solve. The course took us across the equator and it had been planned that Tom Best and I would organise the ceremony for crossing the line. But I was still confined to my bunk after the man overboard incident, so Tom did everything in what turned out to be a delightful occasion.

Many of the ship's company played a part in dressing Amphritite's full court of some 100 people. Wigs were made of teased out white hemp, bear skins of tarred rope, and robes of signal bunting. Queen Amphritite looked realistically regal, while her daughters Euphemia and Penelope were as beautiful and forward as any girl. Then there came the Lord Chamberlain, Lord Chief Justice, Herald, Clerk of the Rolls, High Sheriff, Chief of Police, Apothecary Extraordinary, Barbers, Physicians and Bears, with many more elaborately dressed up.

The ship's carpenters had previously been building stages and thrones, so soon all was set. Onlookers had a good view from the guns, the bridges and all around, as the entire Court formed up on the forecastle and was welcomed by the Captain with all traditional and elaborate ritual. Then King Neptune presented medals made of sealing wax and bits of bunting, hung on lavatory chain. To Captain Hubback was the Order of the Crusted Barnacle, to Commander Temple the Order of the Empty Paint Pot, and to me the Order of the Lifeboat's

Crew. Then came the special criminals, who were senior officers and notable characters in the ship. Each was charged with some appropriate verse and duly sentenced. There followed those who had not previously crossed the Line.

In each case the sentence came to the same thing. The criminal or novice sat on a little seat and was lathered with a mixture of mud, chalk and flour, then shaved with a 2 foot long wooden razor and given a pill of soap with a nasty flavour. At that moment the seat was tipped and he fell backwards into a canvas bath, where a row of bears caught and ducked him 9 times, before he was heaved out, when former novices were declared full blown Shell Backs. Eventually some 700 people had been dealt with after the "Police" had searched the ship for any hiding from justice. Finally the new Shell Backs rallied under the midshipmen, attacked the Court and ducked Neptune, the bears and all. It was all great fun and taken in the best of spirits by everyone, without anyone getting an extra ducking out of spite or malice.

Thus on to Java where, when the war ended, there were some 100,000 well equipped Indonesian troops, trained and officered by the Japanese; there were also many semi-organised troops. The Japanese had fostered some puppet leaders who actually had no power, and therefore no experience of administration under the Japanese or previous Dutch rule. The war over, their leader had no control over the army, and still less over the semi-organised groups, which were said to have shot or tortured Dutchmen who had been held in internment camps. Accordingly the Command decided to order the Japanese officers not to lay down their arms until its troops took over. It happened that British troops were most readily available and were having quite a stiff time from the Indonesian irregulars when we reached Surabaya. A bridgehead had been established, but fighting was still active, yet our presence was to give moral support more than armed assistance, and there was considerable recreational and social life going on besides fighting.

On the first day Tom and I were invited to go snipe shooting with the naval captain of the port and a brigadier, who had come straight from a tank battle not far away in which 80 Indonesian irregulars had been killed. The snipe were there, but in spite of our armed guards with machine guns, I tended to eye each bush and ditch for hostile soldiers.

That evening Captain Hubback and some of us were invited to dine with the General commanding East Java, who had recently moved from a dugout to a sumptuous palace;but a battle was clearly audible as we sat down to a splendid dinner. The ladies present came from the

Woman's Auxiliary Service, Burma, a select body who had really been through tough times, living in open jungle right in the front line. However that evening they looked as though they had scarcely been outside a drawing room. As the most junior of the guests I was seated beside the General's personal assistant, an attractive young woman whose husband had been killed on the Western Front soon after their marriage, so she had volunteered for the most dangerous duty in Burma. The whole party was delightful and around midnight armoured cars escorted us back to the ship.

Next day some of us went shopping using Japanese guilders, a hundred of which were available for anyone going ashore. The General had arranged for a group of the ladies to guide us and give us lunch, so I was delighted that Betty was again my partner. It turned out that she was a Dorset girl, so was intrigued to hear that Daphne and the children lived there. That evening the Captain and officers held a cocktail party on board and I was able to show her photos of Daphne, the children and our thatched cottage.

The following morning when officers as usual gathered in the wardroom for stand-easy coffee, a commander commented in a loud voice "So you took your bird to your cabin during the party Number One. No doubt you taught her a thing or two." He was far from my favourite fellow officer, so I was too infuriated to answer what he had meant as a joke. But Tom Best saw this and at once turned to support me with "Number One and I would not dream of letting our wives down, Sir, whatever your habits may be." Robert MacNab, a bachelor, also supported me saying that I had introduced the lady to him, and suggested that he escort her that evening. What Tom said was entirely true; our little group of married officers certainly enjoyed the company of ladies we met, but even with the prospect of some 3 years separated from our wives, kept firmly together in eschewing any improper association.

Back at sea two of the midshipmen could hardly feel their lives were dull after they were put in charge of whalers with boy crews and slipped in the middle of the night. The sea was rough enough for a wave or two to break over the ship's forecastle, but I assured the Captain that their training had reached the stage that was equal to the risk involved yet he insisted that I must go too. Perhaps lowering the boats was the most dangerous part, so I lowered one then rushed across to jump into the other one which was lowered by another officer, who made a good job of it, except for slipping in the dark a fraction of a second too late, so we landed awkwardly and smashed the rudder. However the boys had been exercised at that, so we were quickly under control with an oar as a jury rudder. Soon both boats had their masts up and a storm sail set, as we sailed off keeping fairly close together. Just about everyone in either boat was seasick, and there was still some 40 miles to go.

Before dawn came really heavy tropical rain, which began to quieten the seas, and continued when the strong wind eased, so it was no longer rough. Evening was approaching when the rain cleared and there was the ship at anchor a couple of miles ahead. Out came the oars and the boys rowed hard for their suppers. We were welcomed generously as small groups took over the boats, with hot baths and supper waiting for the boys. The midshipmen could truly record in their journals how they had grappled with the weather and navigation, a commendable feat. Even more so because once clear of the ship with storm sail set, I had reverted to being a mere observer, just occasionally helping to bail water from the bottom of the boat.

Ashore in Singapore things seemed rougher than the brisk wind at sea as some serious illness had broken out among the troops and others had mutinied. Tom Best's brother in the army was dangerously ill, so Tom was given leave to stay behind when we left for Colombo.

At Colombo I was very fortunate to be put in charge of a party of 20 officers and 300 men going up country to a rest camp. With Robert MacNab playing his bagpipes in the train's cab and myself driving the engine beside him, everyone went off in a very happy mood. Up country Robert and I met a retired forestry officer who knew every inch of the country and most of the native inhabitants as well. They welcomed him everywhere with a laughing call which was interpreted as Forest King.

Back on board again and round to Trincomalee for gunnery practices with ample sport and recreation. Tom was back preparing the gunnery part, but it was not to be as planned as we received the surprising signal "Proceed to Bombay with utmost dispatch." The Commander was ill, so I was temporarily second-in-command and the Captain told me that he still had no knowledge of the reason for our orders. However soon afterwards the world press news on the radio told us that there was a mutiny in Bombay in which the Indian navy ships present had joined. The news also told how Mr. Attlee, the Prime Minister, had informed Parliament that a cruiser was on her way at full speed.

It was exciting to be hurtling through the Arabian Sea, feeling we had an important task ahead. Tom Best and I worked through the detailed problems of any of the possible tasks mentioned by the Captain. We considered which officers and men were best suited for every situation, what equipment was needed and how to handle it effectively. In some cases we could rehearse the situation. Certainly nearly everyone seemed excited and keen to co-operate.

With the ship at Action Stations, guns at the ready and damage control parties at their posts, *Glasgow* led a group of Royal Navy warships into Bombay harbour. On the bridge the Chief Yeoman of Signals had his eye glued to his telescope. "Ship right ahead is hoisting a black flag", he reported, and that was the signal for surrender. Then all around the Indian warships hoisted the black flag and it was clear that the mutiny was at an end. Certainly, in our opinion, the prompt arrival of a powerful naval force was the reason.

Next day our mail from England arrived and we could land for shopping. A retired Admiral came on board to tell us about the mutiny, staying to lunch with the Captain, so I was honoured to be invited too. The Admiral insisted that Congress had given no support to their mutiny, which he said was not political at all, but had been inspired by similar troubles in Singapore, which he felt had been handled too timidly. "The prompt arrival of a strong naval force did the trick here" he said. The following day the ship was open to visitors and a great number of Indians came on board. Many talked to me of Indian problems, and all seemed convinced that if Britain moved out, all racial, economic and labour problems would cease. Indeed many told me that there were really no problems so long as the Hindus, or Mohammedans, or whatever each happened to be, had complete control. There seemed to me a certain amount of room for uncertainty over who it was that should have absolute control.

Perhaps my primary function on board was accommodation and I was becoming particularly concerned with living conditions of junior ratings, - that is all those not in Petty Officer or other enclosed messes. They seemed to me much the same as in Nelson's days, except that complex modern equipment needed much more space and also more men to operate it. Besides that, a steel box with no direct air or light is much less healthy than the old wooden ships with big gun ports. Certainly the food had become much better, but was often cold by the time it had come from the galley to each broadside mess, often having to wait, getting colder, until a man finished his job or came off watch. Then washing up had to be done in a bucket on the mess table, as in Nelson's day, but with less space. We had a hangar no longer needed for an aircraft, so I was keen to turn it into a dining hall, allowing the messes to become more comfortable and healthy. After careful consideration Captain Hubback accepted that it could be a useful experiment, so with the voluntary help of two carpenters, two officers and four sailors I created an Ideal Home Exhibition to demonstrate the idea of a future sailors' home on board. The Padre, Doctor and one or two others added a few homely touches before it was formally opened by the Captain for general inspection and comment. A senior officer insisted that the elder ratings would resent such changes to the system they had become used to; yet we found that it was these experienced men who were strongest in favour.

To my joy, an opportunity arrived sooner than expected to put the trial into effect, as news came from the Admiralty that *Glasgow* was to go for a refit in South Africa; what is more, approval was given for the proposed messing scheme. With the refit confirmed to start at Simonstown only a month ahead, we loaded up with passengers for Capetown. They included an Admiral and a Commodore, so Captain Hubback offered his accommodation aft to the Admiral, and my quite comfortable cabin went to the Commodore, putting me into what I called my kennel lower down.

Some of us sincerely hoped that the visit to Capetown would offer an opportunity for our wives to visit us, so I made enquiries about a ship in which they could come out together. Publication of articles I had written meant that I had the money to pay for Daphne's passage, if somehow she could arrange for our three children to be cared for while she was away. At that time I considered it unsuitable for a serving naval officer to write under his own name, so everything was published under the pseudonym Peregrine, which had become the actual name of our eldest son. Later another pseudonym, Eric Lorre, appeared when one editor wanted to use a separate name for a series of articles. However this time the fruits of the labour of Peregrine and Eric Lorre could not help Daphne to join me in South Africa because the illness of one of the children prevented her leaving.

The voyage of *Glasgow* to Capetown was broken by four days of showing the flag in Mauritius, once home of the extinct Dodo bird. The inhabitants then spoke French, although it had been a British colony for well over a century. The island threw everything open for our entertainment, and in reply we did the best we could on board. In advance we were asked to produce teams in many different sports, and there were ample volunteers. Yet when the time came several of our players had gone off with attractive girls, so as a result Tom Best and I found ourselves filling gaps in soccer, rugger and hockey. However the young officers were happy enough to fill their places at dances and cocktail parties. The young sailors also considered Mauritian girls particularly pretty, but some of the elder men suggested that time lends enchantment and if we had just come from England the local girls would merely seem normal.

Onboard showing the flag included visits each morning by school children, girl guides and boy scouts, with important people for lunch and the general public in the afternoons. A problem was that, as a sugar island, spirits were very cheap and a few people got completely out of control through drink. My analysis of the effect of practically free spirits in abundance was that generally sailors behaved well, several of the Petty Officers not so well, and a few of the officers scarcely well at all.

Some of our passengers could have behaved better too. Among them was a girl of two whose parents put her to bed and went ashore dancing, leaving the baby soon screaming its head off; fortunately there was no difficulty in finding a sailor to cope.

The Southern Ocean could still offer a severe storm in mid-March.

Off South Africa mid-March was summer time, but the Southern Ocean still sent us a severe storm which hit with enormous waves curling over beside us and spindrift driving over the bridge. A busy time ensued caring for passengers, with a few needing medical attention.

We berthed in the naval base at Simonstown, about an hour by train from Capetown, and made ready for refit in the dockyard. Mostly that was a matter of attention to engines and machinery, but for me the exciting part was the ideal home, which involved a certain amount of dockyard work. Yet South African volunteer organisations gave most generous help, so Captain Hubback and I went shopping in Capetown to buy suitable tables, chairs and other furniture. Then the ladies of Capetown sewed curtains, while pictures and darts boards were presented by ladies from various parts of the Union.

Onboard there were the usual housekeeping problems rather similar to continuing to live in a house while pulling it down and rebuilding. Half the ship's company were housed temporarily ashore in the naval base, but the other half had to live on board. Thus a dockyard craftsman drilled through a bulkhead as intended, but also into a 50 gallon tureen of hot soup; then an electrician left 200 volts loosely slung over lavatory door, so a sailor went in safely, but got a heavy shock on coming out.

One family who had been on board for some occasion very kindly invited Robert MacNab and I to their home some miles inland for two or three weekends. They farmed apples on a large scale, and on one occasion the daughters took Robert and I for a walk. It was a beautiful place and we were enjoying the peaceful surroundings when suddenly a bull came charging up furiously. We all got up trees pretty smartly with little time to think about decorum. The girls knew the temperament of their bull and said we had to stay there. We did, for what seemed ages, but luckily we were within talking distance of each other.

In time their Father arrived to rescue us in a Land Rover. "A bit of variety from being hove-to in the whaler through a gale," suggested Robert. The delightful daughters especially wanted to hear all about Daphne and our children, and the family made a point of celebrating our seventh wedding anniversary. I could tell them that as each year went by I loved Daphne more deeply, and how fortunate we were to have three growing children and a lovely thatched cottage in Dorset.

At last the new living arrangements was ready; the official Admiralty name was the Central Messing Scheme, but it got ample Press coverage under our title of the Sailor's Ideal Home. When the ship moved round to Capetown for a day or two she was open to the public, so that those who had so generously assisted in various ways could see what their efforts had achieved. By then it had started work and I found myself restaurant manager for the first few meals served, after which a duty lieutenant took on the job, and then it became a special Chief Petty Officer. The system worked well, and the men's messes were well appreciated by the sailors.

Ready to rejoin our fleet base at Trincomalee we were ordered to call in again at Mauritius to land some civilian passengers, as there was no regular shipping route there. This was my department, but had something new for me when a woman became seasick before we even left harbour and then turned hysterical, becoming even worse at the sight of the doctor. Her husband would not leave her for a moment, and in the opinion of fellow passengers who knew her, both he and the doctor were giving her excessive kindness. So they both left, and the doctor advised me to order her very firmly to get up and go on deck. This went against the grain, as she was young and pretty, but it worked until the husband came back oozing anxiety and she became hysterical again. The doctor ordered her to be taken to her cabin in a stretcher, and told me he would deal with her really firmly so I could get on with helping those who were not neurotic.

On reaching Trincomalee nearly 200 men were due to be demobilised, and it was my task to decide which of the wartime National Service men should go, under some rather complicated Admiralty rules. Some who were not included that time asked to see me about it, and oddly enough a young sailor who was on the list asked if he could stay until the next exodus, as he enjoyed the life on board and was not due to start his university course for several months. A similar number of regulars had come out from home and were waiting ashore to join us; these included several Seamen Boys replacing some of those who were Boys when we left England but had moved on to Ordinary Seamen - though many let me know they were still volunteers for any boat ventures.

There was much to be done settling the newcomers into their jobs. The greater part of this was Tom Best's concern to keep up the gunnery efficiency, which he had always maintained at a high level. A major exercise was a full calibre practice shoot with our main armament, and Tom's control of this in all previous shoots had been first rate. Yet the Captain told me that in discussion with Tom he had decided that the ship must not depend so heavily for such an important task on one man, who might be disabled in action or even knocked out by illness. So he wanted Tom to teach me how to do the job and actually control the guns for the next shoot. It was years since I had been taught gunnery control as a sub-lieutenant, and since then radar and complex electronics had altered things greatly.

Laughing, I said to Tom that I was reasonably good with my shot gun at snipe, but perhaps hitting an enemy cruiser with the main armament would be different. Certainly Tom was a first rate teacher, as well as a good friend; but it meant a great deal of work for us both before the actual shoot, which went off reasonably well. It was beside the point that he would have done better in actual control.

An unsettling affair for the ship was the court-martial of one of the commanders on board, who was found guilty of matters concerned with money. He was dismissed from the ship. My group of officers had no sympathy for him, but there was another senior officer who I felt certain was doing more harm to the ship; but I had sympathy with him as I felt that a very fine war record had left him something of a psychological casualty, who should have had a rest before being given important responsibility.

CHAPTER NINE

Flagship of the East Indies Station 1946-1947

A new task for *Glasgow* on that visit to Trincomalee in 1946 was to hoist the flag of Sir Arthur Palliser, Commander-in-Chief East Indies Station. He needed a large staff to be accommodated on board for a cruise around the southern part of his command.

Once at sea the Admiral expressed interest in our newly completed living arrangements for junior ratings, so was given a formal tour, and discussed it informally with several of the men. It was clear that he was favourably impressed, and gave generous praise to me. This embarrassed me as all my efforts had been under the control of my Captain, who had personally taken a big part in it. Captain Hubback sensed my feelings and afterwards was good enough to tell me how much he agreed with the Admiral over my part of it.

That evening I had further embarrassment as the Admiral expressed interest in the clay pigeon shooting which I often organised on the quarterdeck when at sea. Captain Hubback told me to start, and as a very regular performer with my own gun, I hit 9 out of 10, then commented "So it's quite easy" before handing my gun to the Captain, who had not tried it before and missed the lot. The Admiral took up his own gun and hit 4 out of 10; then invited me to lunch in his quarters next day. Captain Hubback, as Flag Captain, had his meals with the Admiral and on my arrival pulled my leg pleasantly saying, "Number One, you get better marks for shooting than for tact."

The first stop on our cruise was Mauritius, but the Commander-in-Chief's formal visit was quite different from our private ship calls. Formal visits included a great deal of ceremony with the leading figures ashore and afloat as the main actors, the Royal Marine band as the orchestra, with the Royal Marine and Military guards as the chorus. Then there was even more social activity, involving a great number of people from ashore and, all in all, some 700 from the ship.

The social side set off with a massive cocktail party at Government House at which it was clear that, for some at least, our private visit had been remembered; the Governor's lady asked after my children by their names. Her daughter was a very attractive girl, who certainly led the younger members of the community, and had arranged for me to sail with her in the regatta, as she was a keen sailor. However Captain

Hubback had planned that I sail with the Admiral, whose hobby was not sailing. Robert MacNab pulled my leg saying that my favourite sport was about to ruin my naval career. If I sailed with the Admiral, he suggested, the boat would capsize before I could stop him; yet if I sailed with the girl, she might capsize the boat while I was distracting her.

However when the regatta came I was saved from these hazards by a potentially bigger one. The Governor decided to sail, taking with him the Colonel of the Garrison, while I had the honour of representing the Admiral in His Excellency's crew. Our start was not impressive, as far as racing under sail goes, but soon after the wind increased enough to capsize three other yachts. My advice, as a simple sailor, was to reef the mainsail and stand out to sea, clear of the rocks. The Colonel's advice, as a master of tact, was that with many people in the water and others likely to follow, perhaps His Excellency would feel it advisable to give support to rescue operations from ashore.

The cruise continued, in similar style, to the Seychelles Islands, then to Dar Es Salaam, which perhaps was the most hectic of all. I got into trouble there when refereeing the main rugger match. At the last minute I awarded the Dar Es Salaam team a penalty which enabled them to finish the match as a draw. The Governor had not seen the foul, although it was clear to the players in the scrum, so he sent for me and insisted that I had given a 'political' penalty to ensure a draw. Later during a dance at Government House, His Excellency was good enough to say that the captain of the ship's rugger team had admitted that the penalty I had awarded was correct. In a speech he stated that this formal visit was a powerful symbol of the fact that the war was over and the British Empire was as strong as ever. Certainly that dance was powerful too, as it continued through the night, with bathing parties at dawn. Personally I returned on board fairly early, but was awoken by the officer of the watch asking for help. A Commander had returned at 6.00 a.m. apparently well, but had sent for a batch of junior officers, who had not been ashore the night before, and abused them violently. Then he did the same with a group of men, some of whom were not prepared to take it, so made formal complaints. Getting the Commander to bed was just another exercise in diplomacy, but soothing hurt feelings from the other side of the picture took me much of the morning.

But not all of it, as the local yacht club had organised a sailing race. Twenty-four yachts competed, each with some of our people on board; so no less than 50 of the ship's officers and men took part in the race and hospitality afterwards. I really enjoyed the race, but had to miss out on the hospitality, because Robert and I were responsible for the children's party on board which was followed by a very formal dinner ashore.

These many activities had their casualties, specially among those less accustomed to sport. One senior officer broke an ankle playing hockey, another came back on board one night needing stitches, while a third went to the doctor exhausted after a game and had to be flown home at once with tuberculosis. Even Tom Best, as active in sport as anyone, broke his knee. "The casualties of peace can be as heavy as those of war" suggested the doctor while bandaging yet another sports injury.

For me an even more enthralling part of the cruise was to come. When the Resident of Pemba Island requested a naval visit, the Admiral fell in with my idea of an independent boat cruise off the coast of East Africa. A visit to Pemba was impracticable for the flag ship, but could be done by boat. The plan was to leave Zanzibar in a 27 foot open whaler, and sail 80 miles to Pemba for an official visit, then to sail some 40 miles to rejoin the ship at Tanga on the coast of Tanganyika. However the staff suggested extending the cruise to start with a formal visit to Bagamoya. The town is rich in history and the town from which slaves were once shipped to the slave market at Zanzibar, where they were sold to Arabs, Persians and others. It was through Bagamoya that Dr. Livingstone entered 'darkest Africa' for his exploration, which eventually led to the end of the slave trade.

News of our intended cruise caused great interest in Dar Es Salaam, and I was told fierce stories of reefs, rocks and tides which discouraged local yachtsmen from sailing there. "You have no engine, so what happens if you get becalmed near the reefs?" asked one. "We have oars and strong men to pull them" was the answer.

My crew had been selected from many volunteers. There was Timothy Butler, an experienced midshipman but still to be introduced to the joys of night sailing. Then three sailors who were old hands at it - Bill Sykes, a bargee's son and a promising candidate for a commission, next Colin Guest, an East Anglian farmer's son also with good prospects in the navy. Finally Bill Butlin, a Boy Seaman who had been new to sailing until he became my messenger on board and had shown sterling qualities.

We set sail in the dusk, and as the boat drew clear of the ship, she turned a searchlight on us for a romantic departure as the moonlight showed palm trees waving gently in the breeze, behind the white sandy beaches. To seawards the waves could be seen breaking on the coral reefs, with a buoyed channel dimly visible towards them. We were flying a large white ensign from the masthead, with full sail set. We picked up a good wind outside the shoals and pounded along at a fine pace, with some water coming in and a certain amount of seasickness. By 2.00am, we were up to a lighthouse and had to turn in towards the shoals and hazards, while tropical rain fell to make pilotage more difficult. So sails were lowered and we anchored until dawn, when the rain stopped and the shoals were shown up by breaking waves. After a sandwich or two with a hot drink from the thermos flask, we sailed gently on. Soon afterwards an extraordinary object appeared in the sky ahead. It seemed like a mirage of the palace at Bagamyo, our destination. We found our way through the line of angry breakers to a sheltered sandy beach. On landing we were greeted by the District Commissioner and a trio of policemen who helped us unload our gear.

The officer's belongings were taken to the palace that we had thought was a mirage, while I went to see the lads settled in a delightful little rest house. Mr Webb, the District Commissioner, had practised as a barrister in Ireland before joining the Colonial Service with his wife. The British community also consisted of an agricultural officer and his wife, besides the game warden and his wife. These three households took turns to entertain us for each meal.

On the next day the five of us put on our best uniforms, which had come packed in waterproof bags for the voyage, and paraded through the town. There was the market place, then the magistrates court, with the Arab magistrate to salute, the Customs House with an Indian Customs Office, and the hospital under its Indian doctor. Thus everyone saw a section of the British Navy. Where ever we went people stood up and smiled.

On our return to the palace we found fellow guests, as Colonel and Mrs Murray with two children had arrived. It was an odd coincidence as they had been friends of mine many years before in China. The children immediately went to play in the boat, so we could add "children's party" to the programme. Then at sundown the District Commissioner kindly lent us the use of a reception room in the residency, so the group of us from the boat could entertain the community.

The plan was to sail at 5.30a.m., so just before that, with the tide up, I swam out to the boat and climbing aboard I heard giggles. I soon found two girls of 11 and 12 hoping to become stowaways. After escorting then back to their parents we set sail in a quiet breeze, finding it fairly easy to pilot our way through the reefs. My young sailors told me how at the rest house they had their own cook and a boy policeman as messenger; they were provided with two clubs each to play golf. Their clothes were washed as they took them off, and even bathing trunks came back ironed.

On reaching Zanzibar that evening I had expected to pick up a second whaler with her special crew, and sail off in company to Pemba. However the Captain told me with some annoyance that the voyage to Pemba had been cancelled due to some diplomatic muddle, although the people of Pemba wanted it very much.

It was obvious that the feeling on board in Zanzibar was different from the enthusiasm at Dar Es Salaam, and the official dance had been cancelled. It seemed that the local newspaper had printed a comment about the wildness of the dance at Dar Es Salaam, no doubt meant as a joke. 'Public Relations' was one of my ship's duties, as Captain Hubback knew that I sometimes wrote articles for the press under a pseudonym. So I called on the editor and almost forcibly got him to come on board and be introduced to the Captain. It was hardly an introduction as it turned out that he had served in the naval reserve as Captain Hubback's assistant secretary but had not proved entirely suited to the job. Perhaps there was a hint of revenge, but from then on the newspapers comments on the ship's visit were very reasonable. They even included reports on matches which the ship had won, when previously it seemed that only those won by the local teams were news worthy. I was not to see much of this, as instead of the boat trip to Pemba, I was fortunate enough to be included in the Admiral's party visiting Nairobi, thus staying in great comfort at Government House instead of camping in an open boat.

Next came Aden, where it was polo instead of sailing. Not having ridden for a long time, the game left my back so stiff that I needed a couple of sticks when going to lunch with the Attorney General. Some of the conversation at lunch was about a foul given against me. The onlookers shouted that it was the Colonel who came off when crossing in front of me, so was in the wrong. The Colonel was at the lunch party and decreed that of course he was in the wrong, but added amusingly that this was due to hospitality given to him by the Navy before the game, so the umpire had to consider protocol as well as polo rules.

On returning to Ceylon at the end of that cruise, I was to enjoy more of the Army, and polo too, when I was sent for a visit to the Army staff college at Quetta. It was to accompany the Fleet Royal Marine Officer as the college students had a few days studying combined operations, so needed some lectures from the other services. Up in the hills it was a delightful change from the damp and heat. The staff college students mostly seemed to be colonels, but actually had been promoted to acting rank due to war service, and most would go back to their substantive rank - probably major - when the course finished, except for those who passed out particularly well. Thus they worked really hard and found such academic work more difficult after some years of active service. About half were British and half Indian; for either of them the problems of the great country of India were a major subject of discussion. Knowing so little about it I found this intriguing. Part of my work consisted of joining a syndicate of five students working on a set problem. Yet for me there was ample time for recreation, and that was mainly riding. Indeed the Admiral's staff had probably selected me for this temporary task because they knew I played polo.

Back in Trincomalee after a month away *Glasgow* was at sea on exercises, so I joined the fellow cruiser *Jamaica* which was going out to meet her. It was very interesting to find how different the organisation and feelings were in these two ships, doing much the same work and at the same stage of their commissions. Both ships enjoyed excellent Captains, but with also a very good commander *Jamaica's* officers were happier. It was no wonder that those who worked with Commander Casement felt that he was to go further in his career.

When the ships met it was too rough for a boat to take me across, so the ships steamed side by side, perhaps fifty yards apart. Then a rocket was fired over *Glasgow* with a light rope attached, and with this a strong rope was hauled across, with slung from it a Breeches buoy, of the kind used for rescuing people from wrecks. The ships were rolling sometimes towards and sometimes away from each other, so one end of the rope was firmly secured in *Glasgow* and the other on board *Jamaica* went through a pulley to 15 men. As the ships rolled apart they walked back, then as the rolled together they ran away with it.

Every man in each ship not actually on watch came on deck to see this dangerous manoeuvre. First my suitcase went across, only just touching the sea momentarily. I was much heavier, so Commander Casement had some doubts and asked me if I would prefer to wait for better weather; a Chief Petty Officer came up and said "The rope is brand new, and the men well controlled, but the sea keeps to no rules and with the slightest slip the rope will break. Then you will certainly be killed." I felt that it would seem cowardly to back out in front of all those spectators. Out on the rope, the wind and the noise of waves were more evident, but I could clearly hear the general chorus of "Oohh" from both sides as a bigger wave missed my feet only by the amount I lifted them. Certainly no one on board *Glasgow* could fail to know that I had returned.

On reporting to the Captain on the bridge, he told me that the Admiralty had signalled that the ship could not expect to return home for nearly another year, due to changes in plans. Tom Best had already been relieved, and reliefs for many other officers who joined about my time were on their way out. A relief was also on the way for the commander, who joined a long time after me. Certainly I had been the longest in the ship among the officers, but the only hint for me was a personal letter from Captain Clarke, my first Captain in *Glasgow*, then serving in a personnel department in the Admiralty, saying "I think a training battleship at Portland will be just your mark, because I hear she needs a really good First Lieutenant"

Christmas on board was good fun as usual, and after church all officers followed the Captain round the messes to wish everyone a happy Christmas. Then the Chief Petty Officers came to have a drink with the officers. This time I poured out the whisky myself for everyone, so all would be able to walk away on their own legs; but one or two senior officers were not very pleased at this rationing.

Christmas dinner for the wardroom was a formal affair, with senior officers round the chairman; at the other end of the table I was put as vice-chairman, with around me junior lieutenants who played a good part in the ship's sports. During the stupendous meal I had a feeling that they had planned some prank. Sure enough, when the Chaplain had said grace and the chairman had proposed the royal toast, they jumped up shouting "Chairman overboard." The chairman was not amused and said firmly "If anyone puts his hands on me he will be arrested." The young officers were not very impressed, knowing that he was about to be relieved, but we elders knew that he meant it. We gathered round him, but were heavily outnumbered. I remembered a similar situation from my midshipman's days, when our well liked gunnery officer relieved the situation by suggesting that he be thrown in. So I said "Come on chaps, man overboard perhaps, but the vice-chairman's your man." "But would you arrest us?" asked a fairly moderate member of the gang. "This is sports time, and I can't object to being tackled." So they bundled me on deck, allowing me to remove my uniform shoes and badges of rank, before fairly gently throwing me in. Perhaps to show no ill feeling, two of the leaders jumped in too. Roast turkey and plum pudding float well, while the Chaplain lowered a rope ladder over the side to make it easy to get out.

After their enormous Christmas dinner our sailors had a water battle with those of *Jamaica*, who paddled over packed in boats and were met with hoses. Ours paid a return visit, and eventually the boats were swamped, with men swimming around and hoses playing in every direction. So all were having a good time until two men swam over to an aircraft carrier, which had not been part of the game, boarded her fast motor boat lying at her stern, and drove off at speed through the packed swimmers. As stokers they knew how to make the boat go fast, but had little experience of steering, yet it got all the swimmers out of the water faster than any order could have done. Fortunately that motor boat ran out of fuel before the next item for Christmas, which was a children's party on board.

As the children came up the gangway, the Commander came up to a Chief Petty Officer, who having half a dozen of his own back home, was one of the organisers, and pointing to a native child rather older than the others, said "That girl must have a sentry over her with so many ratings involved." That time he very nearly was thrown overboard, but the Chief Petty Officer first contented himself with "Our sailors are not rapists" but calmed down to "I'll put my cap on, Sir, and be the sentry." The children's party was a great success.

After a day or two we were off for another formal cruise, this time across the Bay of Bengal to Burma, steaming 40 miles up the Irrawaddy River to Rangoon, whose port was open although the town still showed much damage from bombing.

There was the usual orgy of official visits, and by that time I could watch them in a slightly detached way and with some sense of humour. Often it was quite an ordeal for the official visitor - be he Air Marshal, General or Governor. As his boat reached the gangway bugles sounded and the poor man would have to struggle with dignity up some 20 steps of the gangway. He usually tripped over the last one, as at that moment the band struck up the salute of 'Garb of Old Gaul' or 'Rule Britannia' if he was an Admiral. Recovering from his stumble he saw to his right an array of quartermasters with pipes, besides buglers and others; ahead was a line of officers, swords at their sides, telescopes under their arms; to the left was a guard of marines, bayonets fixed, arms at the present. Behind them a band of 20 with the loudest of instruments. As the band stopped its martial tune, he staggered forward forcing a smile. But there was not a move; the officers remained immobile, grim and at the salute. Once at that stage I saw the Very Important Person drop his hat and turn to look at his line of retreat; but that was cut off, as the boat had left the gangway. I felt that he was just about to jump for it, when the guard completed their contortions with arms. Then he relaxed slightly as he noticed that the line of officers was no longer saluting. But it was still a row of statues, who all refused to catch his eye. Again he seemed about to reach despair when the furthest statue melted to disclose itself as the Admiral.

Next came Calcutta, with the normal formalities and social programme. I was hospitably invited to stay with the Commander of the Governor's Bodyguard, who was a delightful host and could tell me about all that went on, besides being an authority on the numerous parties and the people I would meet. Perhaps the most ostentatious party was in the Governor's box at the Calcutta races. My host was also very well informed about the horses, so I won on the tote almost every race, after venturing no more than the minimum stake on the first. The Admiral was staying at the Governor's luxurious palace, but his host did not study the form of race horses. However, he was a unique character by all accounts, appointed by a Socialist Government after a valuable career with the railway Trades Union. One story I remembered in particular was that on arrival in Calcutta, an Indian Prince invited the Governor out shooting; it was said that he answered amusingly "My predecessors have been great men for huntin', and shootin', but I'm more familiar with shuntin' and hootin'." Whoever had been appointed Governor of Bengal would have had a truly different task as, with independence round the corner, there were several riots with many people killed, besides famine and other troubles. Yet all was peaceful during our visit.

About this time news came that my brother Merlin, four years older than me, had been promoted to commander. Promotion to lieutenant-commander was automatic after 8 years as a lieutenant, but the next step up to commander was by selection and, at that time, about one in three of the executive branch was chosen. "No doubt you will follow him when your time comes" commented a fellow officer. I had to admit that this was unlikely; although my Captains had been generous enough in their reports, the Navy is a fighting sea service, and I had spent most of the war medically unfit for sea, and then I was still judged to be suitable only for serving in a ship with a doctor.

The next formal cruise took us across the Arabian Sea and into the Persian Gulf. We first visited Bahrein and then up the Euphrates River to Basra. It was interesting to drive out over the desert with the curator of the King of Iraq's local shooting. In a strong wind there was a curious phenomenon in which the mirages galloped along the horizon in a rough sea effect. We disgorged into the king's tent then, after shaking hands with the inhabitants of some 20 thatched huts, we set off in two shallow boats, pushed by a bamboo pole at each end. They cut through the bullrush beds until we came to a patch of clear water with hundreds of duck on it, but were told not shoot until all was ready. Then the boats were loaded with rushes and from them hides - each with a shooting stick - were constructed on shallow patches, from which one got a good view although partly screened. When all of us were ready in this way, a signal came from our host and at once there were hundreds of duck consisting of many varieties flying in every direction. One I shot fell straight at me, actually knocking my hat off, but it soon became clear that those falling in the bull rushes were difficult to find for the Arab boys detailed as retrievers; so the trick was to bring them down into open water. Between the four of us the bag was 80 birds; about half teal, the rest shovellers, pigeon and mallard. Royal shooting indeed, and a thoroughly romantic adventure, with the long drive back across the desert interrupted when we came to a railway line and waited a few minutes for the Bagdad express to go by. We also saw in the distance two trees, and were told that they were all that was left of the Garden of Eden.

The next visit was to Kuwait, then ruled by a Sheik under British protection, and at that time reasonably prosperous from pearl fisheries. But oil had been located and tapping had just begun by combined British and American effort. Driving out over the desert to see the oil well, we swept through a cloud of locusts. For half a mile they were as thick as flakes in a heavy snow storm, then, for the next three miles, they came in batches.

During this cruise Lady Palliser, the Admiral's wife, was on board the flagship, which was a great help with the busy social programme. At each party on board she would take various officers to be introduced to the Governor's lady, or whoever was her hostess ashore. When it was my turn, the lady quickly came to a frequent question "Do you happen to have met ..... in the Navy?" mentioning some name, to which so frequently my reply had to be "There are so many people in the Navy......." In Kuwait I was ready to give this answer when I realised that the name she enquired about was mine. She turned out to be the mother of three children who for years has spent their school holidays with us at Herstmonceux and had become almost part of our family while she was abroad with her husband in the East. The youngest of those children had married the Sheik's political adviser and was actually my Admiral's hostess. She had given birth to her first baby only recently, so her Mother had come out to help her. It was a moment when I felt perhaps the world is not so big after all.

Then followed a visit to Karachi, but by then I was feeling exhausted with a slight chill, so I neither asked to be slipped in the whaler for training, nor accepted an invitation to go shooting at dawn. Captain Hubback was quite annoyed with the doctor, saying there must be something seriously wrong with me to drop out of such activities. The doctor agreed to have me examined when we reached Bombay. Of course I regretted missing a shoot after sand grouse and partridges. It was a good shoot, the bag was 70 birds - a help to the ship's catering, which since leaving South Africa had seldom enjoyed any fresh meat except that which came from the shooting parties.

At the Bombay hospital, X-ray examination disclosed nothing much wrong, but I was advised to do less work in that hot and humid climate; indeed rather more alcohol was recommended. This did not impress me. My own diagnosis was that some of my trouble was due to indignation at the amount of alcohol drunk by an officer with whom I had to be in close contact. However his relief was already on the way to the ship, and on his arrival, and the other officer's departure, all my symptoms disappeared. However, I had one good piece of advice from the Bombay consultant. This was that the Persian carpets available in the Bombay shops were of higher quality and cheaper than any likely to be offered for sale in the Persian Gulf. So I managed to afford a couple of nice ones, which seem as good as ever after 40 years of hard use.

When we put into Colombo that was really the end of the cruise for the Admiral, as he turned from formal visits to his annual inspection of the ships, including detailed examination of the living accommodation of his flag ship. In preparation for this my regular 30 'housemaids' and 20 'kitchen maids', with another 40 part-time ones, had been painting, scrubbing and tidying for this great day. All went well, and the Admiral was pleased. Another great joy came a day or so later, with the arrival on board of Commander Hodgkinson as executive officer. Fresh from England he brought new enthusiasm to a ship which had worked hard, much of the time in a really difficult climate. The next major affair was the fleet rowing regatta, which involved a high proportion of the men of the fleet. The programme allowed about a month for practising, which was nearly always in the early morning or the evening because of the sticky heat.

As I was the ship's regatta officer, my duties included making the arrangements for practising - allocating times and boats to the different crews and coaching one or two of them. Yet now much of the drive came from Commander Hodgkinson, who even took his part in coaching one of the crews, as did Captain Hubback. One evening many of us were on deck as several of the rowing crews returned exhausted, when there came a strident call of "Away Lifeboat's crew", and we saw a small plane was crashing into the sea. Robert MacNab and I both rushed for a motorboat lying alongside the gangway, with its coxswain probably in the ship getting orders for a routine trip ashore. We went straight off at speed, while arranging life saving and salvage functions for those who happened to be in the boat. Unexpectedly our padre appeared from the cabin and said sleepily, "Surely there's some mistake, I'm playing tennis with the Captain of the Fleet, so must be punctual." We all burst out laughing, but a Stoker Petty Officer said in an awed whisper "A plane's just crashed, Sir", so the padre said a prayer for the life of anyone in the plane. Fortunately it was only one, and he had suffered no more than bruises. The plane was less fortunate, yet we got it to the beach before it sank.

Commander Hodgkinson continued to build up enthusiasm in the ship, while Captain Hubback presided over the fleet organisation of the regatta, which included a totaliser so that everybody could back his favourite from on board his own ship, and this went by radio to the central organisation. The moment the judges decided upon the winner, a flag indicated which it was and the tote in each ship could at once pay out the fleet odds. His committee also had to create the rules with as many as 23 boats competing in one race.

The fleet organisation proved a great success, and *Glasgow's* rowing certainly pleased us, as we won the overall fleet trophy. In one race Captain Hubback could not be among the judges, as our officer's crew included him besides Commander Hodgkinson; with the rest of the crew also veterans, backers in other ships considered us much too old and this put the odds up, so when we did win it was very popular with those in *Glasgow* who had backed us.

When Captain Hubback convened the final Fleet Regatta meeting a few days afterwards, it was the only one I had not attended since it was formed several weeks earlier. However my small share of general congratulations reached me in hospital, where I had been taken after an almost complete collapse. Also that day came Lady Palliser, wife of the Commander-in-Chief, with welcome encouragement. The doctor had just announced that there was nothing wrong with my lungs or heart, but it was a matter of extreme overwork for some two years, mainly in a very trying climate.

The treatment was three weeks in an up country rest camp, high above sea level, and the instructions were that I must not mention the word *Glasgow* during that time. Instead I could count down the days, then some 70, before I would be re-united with my family when the ship reached Portsmouth. I was helped by the chance that an old friend from submarine days, but then a senior staff officer ashore, came to ask if he could borrow my cabin on board for the ship's next cruise about to start.

H.M.S. Glasgow's officers rowing crew duly won a regatta trophy.

He mentioned that his wife Yvonne, who I knew fairly well, was going to the rest camp with her very small children, and would welcome any help I could give. Taking a very small boy to spring a leek in the jungle, as the lorry stopped on that long drive, might not seem conventional treatment, but it was just right for me and certainly helped me to think of Rosamund, then 4, Peter 6 and Peregrine 7. Actually the short walk was not literally in the jungle, as the lorry driver was anxious about leopards so asked me to bring the baby back to the verge of the track.

My return to *Glasgow* three weeks later was back to form. This time it was not by Breeches buoy, but as the ship steamed in with a very strong wind, I watched her lowering a boat to take the rope to her mooring buoy. Suddenly the foremost fall broke with the bows falling into the sea, and the boat capsized, strewing out its crew. Those on the bridge would not be able to see this, so I rushed to a motor boat lying at the jetty and seeing no coxswain jumped aboard and shot out to pick up the capsized boat's crew, hearing from the ship the call "Away Lifeboat's Crew." Then, with the one Petty Officer who happened to be in my boat, backed up by the soaked crew of the capsized boat, we took the ship's rope out to the buoy. Back on board again Captain Hubback laughed at me saying "I suspect that you pray for people to fall in, so that you can rescue them." He added the very welcome news that we would arrive at Portsmouth on 27th August - just 54 days ahead.

A hospital check had further welcome news that I was much better. However it was accompanied with a note to the ship's doctor that I should do as little work as possible until we got home. My doctor added that I had already done the equivalent of several years work for the ship, and we would be setting off for home in just a few days.

That very evening things changed, as word came through that there was trouble ashore in Rangoon. We raised steam and clearly I had to do my job in preparing for sea, but that was made better when the Admiral, who was no longer aboard, signalled that our departure for home would not be affected, as another ship would soon be ready to take our place. Better still came the signal that we were not needed in Rangoon after all. Captain Hubback had even further good news, which was that his next appointment meant promotion to Commodore in a shore job with an official house for his wife and himself.

At last came the day to leave Trincomalee, with all the traditional farewells. Arrival at Portsmouth was even more thrilling as Daphne and I were reunited after nearly 3 years apart.

CHAPTER TEN

Admiralty and Atlantic 1948-1950

After having been away from home for so long I was given a good
period of foreign service leave, but when in London I visited the
Admiralty to enquire about my next appointment. The Naval
Assistant to the Second Sea Lord told me that my work over improved
living conditions on board was known, so I would be appointed to the
Admiralty to work on similar matters. Unfortunately he was also aware
that my health had not been perfect, but I could pull his leg by saying
that anyone left to serve in a ship on the equator as long as he had left
me there, might have the same problem.

Certainly leave with my family in Dorset was very important, and
soon brought my energy levels back to normal. The prospect of work
in London involved deciding where to live, so we sold the lovely
thatched cottage in Dorset to provide the money for another house. My
eldest sister Rhalou, with her family of many boys, lived in the Surrey
countryside near Dorking, where her husband Kirkby Peace had a
veterinary practice; so she helped us by suggesting a bungalow a mile
or so from her and much less than that from the railway station of South
Holmwood, which had frequent suburban trains to London. There was
a day school nearby, and friendship with their cousins, the Peace boys,
made life interesting for our children. Then I shared a rough shoot with
Kirkby, who was always known as K. The shoot helped our family
needs for meat, rationing still being in force.

By the beginning of 1948, I joined the Admiralty in the Welfare and
Service Conditions Department. This came under the Second Sea Lord,
whose responsibility on the Board of Admiralty was for personnel. The
departments were housed in Queen Anne's Mansions, a short walk
from the main Admiralty buildings, and a pleasant stroll across Green
Park to the Royal Ocean Racing Club, of which I was an active member.
On arrival my Director was Captain Ralph Heathcote, but my work
came under his deputy Captain John Whitfield, who soon afterwards
became the Director. Much of the work was writing comments on
Admiralty dockets, passed round to get many points of view before
decision by a member of the Admiralty Board. Sometimes it meant
researching and then writing a paper on some new subject. My Director
soon remarked that he noticed my comments were often very different

from those of officers more senior than me, and he welcomed this as originality, even if it was often wrong.

Captain Whitfield, while deputy, was far from stuck to his desk and frequently went out to naval establishments and ships to keep in touch with a navy accustoming itself to post-war conditions. Soon after I joined, he took me with him to the Staff College where his lecture gave me a valuable conception of the whole range of the department's concerns. The next time it was a lecture in Scotland, and on the way he suggested that the name Bruce would be well known in Scotland, so he wanted me to take over a section of the lecture.

John was an inspiring lecturer himself, so his advice was of special value to me. He stressed that no lecture should ever go even a minute beyond the arranged time - often one hour - but even that was too long for one voice without a break. "Often as much value comes from the questions as from the, lecture itself" he said, "So you should plan on a good proportion of the time going to questions, and tune your talk to inviting them. If the talk is stimulating enough there will be no lack of questions." Thanks to his coaching and further instruction, I soon began to enjoy lecturing, especially dealing with interesting questions. Thus I was used more and more for lecturing, both to officers and men.

The department's range included sport and recreation, although I was not in the section dealing particularly with this. However I was concerned with certain aspects of sport in other ways. For instance, I had been a very modest polo player, my tuition aided greatly by Dickie Mountbatten, when he was a lieutenant. Thus I could hardly say no when he suggested that as I was serving in London, I was well placed to take on the position of Honorary Secretary of the Royal Naval Polo Association. The chairman at that time was Admiral Charles Lambe, who taught me much about administration of a small organisation. The post also involved being editor of the Association's magazine.

Following his appointment as Supreme Commander South-East Asia in the war, Mountbatten eagerly returned to the navy as a Rear-Admiral serving afloat in the Mediterranean. He asked me to help with correcting the proofs and dealing with the publisher for a new edition of his well known book 'An Introduction to Polo'. This led to a quite unexpected incident.

Lord Mountbatten commanded a squadron of cruisers, which he told me was only half a day's work; so his Commander-in-Chief gave him further responsibility for the important combined exercises in the Atlantic, with the Mediterranean Fleet taking on the Home Fleet. While passing through the Straits of Gibraltar before the exercises started, with the Home Fleet still in harbour at Gibraltar, he sent ashore his postman to pick up mail. Among his letters was one from me sending corrected proofs of the book, and he had time to deal with this before the first exercise started, so sent a signal to me at the Admiralty correcting a mistake.

The Operations Division was taking a very close interest in the coming exercises, and knew that the postman sent ashore at Gibraltar was not the normal corporal, so suspected that he might have some intelligence task, which could help to assess the Home Fleet plans. Thus the Division kept a close watch on any signal coming from Mountbatten and stopped the one to me, as it was known that twice recently I had lunched with a friend serving in that Department, so might also be collecting intelligence. Anyhow my friend suggested we lunch together again, and then said that his Director would like to speak to me; this did not surprise me as I had known him in submarines - a strict disciplinarian with a brilliant brain.

In his office he handed me a signal, addressed to me from Rear-Admiral Mountbatten. It read "No No Keep your right arm straight." "What does it mean?" asked the Director, so I turned in my chair to demonstrate playing a ball under the pony's neck. "Rubbish", said the Director very firmly, "It's a coded message and you will tell me precisely what it means". I protested innocently that it was purely a polo shot, but he would not accept this. "You will not leave this department until you tell me the truth. It's all right, I will inform your Director." Later my friend in Operations agreed to telephone my secretary to bring over my file on polo. When it arrived his Director sent for me again. "I am satisfied that your explanation was correct, Erroll, so I will thank your Director for your help. But I insist that you do not mention this to anyone until the combined exercises are over." "But surely, Sir, I should not keep any secrets from my own Director?" I said. "This does not concern his department" he replied. It was the only time he had addressed me by my christian name, perhaps to rub it in that it was a private subject.

Another interesting matter came my way as Hon. Sec. of the polo association. Admiral Mountbatten wrote to me mentioning that his nephew Philip was coming out to Malta as a lieutenant and would probably want to play polo. So he invited me to contact him to tell him what might be needed. I had not met Prince Philip, but like everyone else in Britain, knew that he had just married Princess Elizabeth, the heir to the throne. I phoned him and was invited to lunch, when the conversation was mainly about sailing, as Prince Philip suggested that his ship's duties and interest in sailing made it unlikely that he would take to polo. As a committee member of the Royal Naval Sailing Association, I could comment on sailing in Malta. But, a month or so later, Lord Mountbatten wrote that Prince Philip found his wife was so keen on polo that he had joined in. Indeed, he became a good player, but this certainly did not reduce his interest in sailing.

A further polo communication with Lord Mountbatten got me a reprimand from His Lordship. The naval polo committee decided to invite Princess Elizabeth to become Vice-Patron of the Association; so I was instructed to find out whether this was acceptable. When Admiral Mountbatten got his copy of the minutes he was annoyed to find that I had asked Buckingham Palace. The Princess had her own staff at Clarence House, so might not want her matters to be handled through Buckingham Palace. Such was His Lordship's displeasure that his letter was not only typed in contrast to his usual informal handwritten letters, but also his handwritten signature just read 'Yours sincerely', instead of the usual 'Yours very sincerely'. He was good enough to add 'I appreciate that you did all of this in good faith, not realising the situation'.

My Department was responsible for recreational sailing, including allocation of ex-German Windfall yachts, which had been used pre-war by the German Navy for racing inshore. Windfalls as sailed by the British Navy were often raced offshore, although they must have been the wettest and most lively of competitors. It was well within the Department's responsibilities to see how they were getting on, and the best way of doing that was to race in them. Sometimes I was invited to skipper, which I did when I had established there was no-one else experienced enough to do so without further guidance.

Much of my own experience of offshore racing came from crewing for other skippers. Among these were John Illingworth, Adlard Coles, who became a life long friend, Colonel Dick Scholfield, later a flag officer of the Royal Ocean Racing Club, and Group Captain Teddy Haylock, editor of a major yachting magazine. Fortunately my Directors all considered this valuable, and were satisfied that I would make up for the time away from the office when weekend races sometimes stretched out beyond Friday evening to Monday morning.

It also meant that I was away from home many weekends in the summer; but it was still much less than if serving in some naval shore station with the need for frequent night duties. At Holmwood it was a pleasure to play with the children - Peregrine about 8, Peter a year younger and Rosamund 5. In summer we could listen to the nightingale's song in the small wood beside us, and there were frequent family visits to my sister Rhalou and husband K, with their six sons and many ponies. We also went further from time to time, visiting Daphne's family in Dorset and mine in Sussex.

Daphne became pregnant again, and at the same time we were faced by the need for boarding schools for our children. It was part of naval life to move every two or so years and we decided that boarding school was better than the unsettling effect of such frequent changes of schools and home. My naval salary in a relatively junior rank was inadequate for this, there being no marriage allowance for naval officers at that time. Thus came the need, more than ever, to follow the example of my Father by writing. I had always done some, but now I had to write much more. I kept the pseudonym of Peregrine, especially suitable perhaps, because the first income of these articles all went to my son of that name's schooling. Naturally I got agreement from my Director with the assurance that I would not write about naval matters. Honorary editorship of the polo magazine also proved valuable experience at this time as well as in later life.

Some slight anxiety on appointment to the Admiralty that such a desk job would prove dull and unattractive to a simple sailor like me, proved quite unjustified. My fellow officers tended to be of a high grade, and nearly all were senior to me in rank and thus naval experience. Inspite of this they seemed quite willing to consider any ideas I had. I met and worked with people from many walks of life. There was the home life, which I had missed so deeply in my three years on *Glasgow*. I also enjoyed a reasonable amount of time afloat in yachts. In a ship at sea I seldom met admirals except on ceremonial and formal occasions, yet serving in the Admiralty I was often dealing with people holding highly responsible jobs; thus in my files today are personal letters from no less than five First Sea Lords - the highest job of all for a serving naval officer. So my life was far from dull.

It seemed that my Directors were satisfied with my work and my reports were favourable. When the time came to leave, I was eagerly hoping to go back to sea in command. Once again my health let me down; the medical recommendation considered me fit for sea, with the stipulation that it be with a doctor aboard. However, an opportunity to command at sea came before any formal appointment, although it was a yacht of only some 5 tons.

John Illingworth had inspired the conception of an economical all purpose yacht, of the minimum size for ocean racing, also capable of racing effectively round the buoys inshore, yet equally suitable for cruising. This was known as the RNSA 24, with her waterline length of 24 feet. Designed by Laurent Giles, a first batch of six boats was built

*Royal Naval Sailing Association's 24 foot yacht
Samuel Pepys.*

by Camper and Nicholsons, and one of these was for the club members. She was named *Samuel Pepys* after the distinguished Secretary of the Admiralty. I was fortunate enough to skipper her several times, with reasonable success in races, although always beaten by her sister yacht *Minx of Malham*, sailed by John Illingworth.

Apart from the actual sailing, I found voluntary work for the RNSA very interesting. It also gave me practice in administration and management. John Illingworth had done very well sailing his bigger yacht in the famous Bermuda race, so suggested to the Cruising Club of America, which organised this race, that the RNSA 24 boats should be eligible as a special exception to the rule limiting entry to much larger yachts. This was agreed, and it followed that the RNSA decided to enter its own *Samuel Pepys*, crewed by members of the club. Other British yachts seemed likely to enter, so the Royal Ocean Racing Club announced a Trans-Atlantic race back from Bermuda.

Adlard Coles, an outstanding ocean racing skipper of small yachts and a RNSA member, asked the Cruising Club of America if his *Cohoe II* was eligible for the Bermuda race. Thinking it was another of the RNSA 24 class, this was accepted. Later the mistake was realised, so Adlard had an extension built on to her stem bringing her within the lower limit allowed. The RNSA formed a small committee to plan the venture when the Admiralty agreed that those selected could be given special leave for 3 months in the same way as those competing for Britain in the Olympic games. Three months was not enough to sail out to America, and compete in the race back to England. We had to find a quicker way of getting to Bermuda.

So, after we had done a good deal of spreading the gospel, the Royal Mail Line, whose ships sailed to Bermuda, agreed that the crew could sign on as deck hands, taking the yacht as their luggage. By then it had become an RNSA team, with both *Cohoe II* and another small yacht *Mokoia*, offered the same facilities by the Royal Mail Line.

It was soon clear that John Illingworth's duties in the command of a naval air station would prevent him skippering the club yacht. I was selected as skipper, and also given the responsibility of Captain of the RNSA team.

Mokoia's owner, Major James Murray, an Army officer, and his mate Wing Commander Marwood Elton R.A.F., had been made honorary members of the RNSA. In return for that, James' daughter Jean, who was to be part of his race crew, acted as team secretary. In *Samuel Pepys* I had a splendid crew with Lieutenant Commander Stephen Sampson as mate, Lieutenant Pat Ovens, Royal Marines, and Chief Petty Officer Flux, who had joined the Royal Navy as a shipwright after helping to build and sail racing dinghies under Uffa Fox.

As team Captain there were scores of letters to be written, assisted by Jean as secretary, and numerous meetings to attend. When it seemed that every detail had been planned, I found how wrong I was. After the three yachts had reached London by road, a dock strike started which meant that no cargo could be accepted in the dock area. However, people were not part of the embargo, so the yacht crew all went on board the Royal Mail Vessel *Araby* of some 5,000 tons. We were introduced to Captain Bolland, the Master. He was a powerful big man with a bluff manner who made clear that no action could be taken which would cause conflict with the strikers, but everything that was allowed would be done to get the yachts to Bermuda. Working for the Port of London Authority was Mr. Dowden, an RNSA member, who got his Authority to waive all charges for wharfage and porterage. He also knew

Samuel Pepys being hoisted aboard a Royal Mail freighter for crossing the Atlantic before the 1950 Bermuda and Trans-Atlantic races.

who was who in the world of London docks, and introduced me to Trade Union officials who had sporting instincts. When I told them that we represented Britain in America, in a non-commercial race, with no money involved either with the Port of London Authority or the shipping company, it was agreed that the yachts could be embarked if the work was done by the ship's crew, of which we yachtsmen were a part.

Ship's bosun of S.S. Araby telling off temporary deck hands working on the masts of their yachts.

All this took a day or two, but the time came when the ship's cranes, operated by the ship's officers, hoisted the three yachts on board. Once there, the ship's bo'sun and carpenter arranged special equipment to secure the yachts whatever the weather might do. What a relief it was to be at sea, even if a few days behind programme, but still scheduled to reach Bermuda in time. Aboard, the three yacht crews acted as one group, helping each other whenever needed. Adlard was renowned as a good dead reckoning navigator, but this was before the days of electronic navigating equipment in yachts and he was not familiar with sextant navigation. Although he was expecting to have an experienced sextant navigator on board for the Atlantic race, he felt it important that he should be instructed so he could act as a second string. So I started each day with a navigation course. Stephen Sampson saw to it that the yachts' bottoms were brought to a fine polish.

On arrival in Bermuda we found that my old ship *HMS Glasgow* was the fleet flagship. A note from the Second Sea Lord in Admiralty had invited the Commander-in-Chief to give us any support possible. So while preparing the three yachts for the 650 mile sail to America, we all lived as guests in *Glasgow* and were certainly given every possible support.

After five days alongside *Glasgow*, all three yachts were ready, so we set out for Newport in company. It was still May, so weather in the Bermuda triangle could be stormy. With my full crew on board I hoped we might have some rough weather to practise in, but the other two yachts had only three on board, so would be happy with more moderate conditions. Oddly enough, all three were satisfied. The other two were within a mile or so of each other when, on the second day, the barometer began to fall and the wind reached gale force, so both lowered all sail and lay to, noticing 38 knots of wind on their anemometers. *Samuel Pepys* was by then 30 miles ahead and by chance fairly close to Humphrey Barton sailing his *Vertue XXXV* across the Atlantic. Both of us recorded much the same weather, with a full Horse Latitude Storm, reaching force 10 around midnight, while with the dawn the anemomenters showed gusts of 60 knots with seas building up to 30 feet high. It was a wind which 'no canvas could withstand', but we had the sails down in time so suffered no damage. *Vertue XXXV* was less fortunate; a huge wave burst over her, smashing her doghouse window, splitting her coachroof and half filling her, besides breaking some of Humphrey's ribs.

Later the met office told us that it was a two-eyed storm with winds of hurricane force. At its height, *Vertue XXXV* and *Samuel Pepys* were where the winds was strongest, while the other two yachts were fortunate to be between the eyes where conditions were more tolerable. Certainly after hearing this full report, I felt confident that we could cope with anything that the North Atlantic could hurl at us in the two races ahead of us.

In Newport we joined up with *Galway Blazer*, another RNSA 24, which had been in America for some time. Her skipper, Bill King, had previously sailed the Bermuda race with John Illingworth and was a very experienced ocean racer. Moreover his yacht was ketch rigged, which many felt was an advantage for the Bermuda race. So we looked upon her as likely to do best of British boats in the small class. Yet no one expected these yachts, so much smaller than any others in the race, would be anywhere near the big class. *Gulvain* was the only British entry in the big class, and Humphrey Barton was her sailing master. He was a very experienced ocean racer but was still recovering from the ribs broken in the storm we had shared with him.

In *Samuel Pepys*, boat and crew were quickly ready again, so we sailed various passage races in Long Island Sound, helping to tune our race technique. We also greatly enjoying the chance to meet many famous American yachtsmen who welcomed us warmly. For the

Bermuda race itself, at that time the world's most famous ocean race, there were 50 really fine yachts, arranged in three handicap classes, with four British among the 17 in the smallest class. Conditions were quiet throughout the four or five days of the race, with a good deal of light winds, but with the usual disturbed sea when crossing the Gulf Stream. In each class, first on corrected time was a twin-masted yacht, with the ketch *Galway Blazer*, fourth in our class as the best British entry overall. In *Samuel Pepys* we were content to place half way up our class. The race had done much towards preparing us for the Trans-Atlantic.

Actually in the Bermuda race we were chiefly competing with our team mate *Cohoe*, and particularly exciting that proved to be as we approached the finishing line side by side, eventually getting there a tiny 24 seconds ahead, after nearly five days of concentrated racing. Under the American handicap rules that put *Samuel Pepys* three hours ahead of *Cohoe*, but for the Trans-Atlantic we would compete under British handicap rules, and although *Cohoe* would be more than a foot longer even after removing her false bow, *Samuel Pepys* would need to reach Plymouth some seven hours before her to beat her, mainly due to a greater sail area.

Removing the false bow quickly was quite a task, as the yacht yard was already busy, so our Fluxey offered to help Adlard and his crew. Even then *Cohoe* might be a late starter, so I cabled the R.O.R.C. in London and asked that the start be postponed for 24 hours. This was accepted.

For us the main task was to provide attractive food for perhaps five weeks, as we had no refrigeration. We also had to take ample fresh water, which meant cans as well as an extra water tank. Both of these matters were Sammy Sampson's department, and much of my time was spent writing, as that would provide part of the costs of the venture. I had expected the yachting press to be interested in the Bermuda race, which proved to be so; but I had not reckoned on the general press interest in the small pair for the Trans-Atlantic race, so was most grateful to Jean for typing much of this. Thus the crews of the three yachts of our team were helping each other.

Five yachts lined up for the start off Bermuda's Farewell Buoy. It seemed that all Bermuda had come out to watch, and nearly all had put their money on the fine new 55ft length *Gulvain* with a powerful crew including Humphrey Barton as Sailing Master and Bill King as Navigator. There was also a worthy contender, *Karin II* which, although elderly, was very much larger than the small trio, and considered well suited to a race of nearly 3,000 miles across the Atlantic. The three small yachts had the good wishes of everyone, but I doubt if any of the spectators had put a penny on any of them winning.

At the start, in the lightest of breeze and a glassy calm sea, *Samuel Pepys* was a matter of inches in front of *Gulvain*, but would never head her again. The small pair, laden with the greatest weight of stores and water in proportion to the displacement, plodded sluggishly along and by next morning no yacht was in sight of another, and none was to see another in the race before the finish.

The Great Circle or, shortest route, led up to the Gulf Stream, then for some 500 miles ran north of a thick red line on the American weather chart for July, which showed the limit of drifting ice and also 10% chance of fog coming from the Grand Banks. We knew that there had been seven previous Trans-Atlantic yacht races since 1866 when the American schooner *Henrietta* of 107 feet reached the Needles in 13 days. The most recent race was in 1936 when a German yawl of 59 feet won in 21 days. But in none of these races had there been a yacht anywhere near as small as our trio, so we could expect to take at least 4 weeks.

It was hard work trying to squeeze every inch out of the lazy breeze. Sammy, Pat and Fluxey took 4 hours watches in turn, while as skipper and navigator I was available any time at a moment's notice; in the area where icebergs might be, I also remained on deck as a look out throughout the hours of darkness. There was precious little comfort below, until some of the provisions were eaten to allow more room; we also carried a large number of sails to meet all conditions and allow for storm damage as this was before the days of terylene sails.

Those first few days were the toughest on morale, with the prospect of a very slow passage. Yet when a stronger wind came, our spirits livened up too. On the eighth day we sighted a ship, which turned close enough for us to signal "Please report me to Lloyds of London" and when she answered, it really cheered us up. Next dawn, sextant sights showed that we were clear of possible ice area, which added to the general cheer. I noted in my diary, 'Now we are ready for a gale'.

Amazingly it came, giving us a splendid lift, but *Cohoe* was less fortunate, as we learnt afterwards. She was making slow speed under a bare pole when an Italian liner came very close at high speed, perhaps not seeing her in the high seas. There was a roar of breaking water and the yacht was thrown on her side; she had been pooped and the cockpit was half filled. Then a second even bigger wave broke over her, causing her to broach, completely filling the cockpit and throwing the yacht on her beam ends. By then the liner must have sighted the yacht, so slowed down and circled round, with a crowd of passengers watching from the upper deck. Adlard checked that all was within the ability of he and his crew to put right, so signalled "Please report me to Lloyds of London."

Gulvain also had her share of trouble. In the middle of the night, she lost her spreaders so could carry no sail until Charles Gardner and Bill King had spent long periods working aloft in the gale.

Two weeks out we were in the maximum gale area for the time of year with 4% of observations Force 8 and above. I was annoyingly apprehensive, and my mind turned to the possibility of hitting heavy flotsam, which at high speed would surely sink *Samuel Pepys*. We had no radio so it would mean taking to the rubber dinghy, towing half filled cans of fresh water, with the nearest shipping lane 115 miles away. So with the night I ordered a trisail instead of the reefed mainsail, and a genoa instead of the spinnaker. An amazing co-incidence came to light after the race was over. About the time when my mind was on hitting flotsam, Adlard recorded in his log, 'Passed some heavy wreckage, big enough to have sunk the yacht if we had struck it'.

Sure enough, it blew up to around gale force before midnight, then at 2.00am the wind veered after a squall and the sky cleared to show some stars. Although the barometer was still falling, those stars had a magic effect on morale. So I called all hands and we struggled to set a reefed mainsail and larger genoa. By the time we had finished that, the sky had clouded over again and wind freshened once more taking the yacht creaming through the breaking waves. But that half hour of stars had done the trick, sweeping ideas of rubber dinghy from my mind, stressing instead that Plymouth was only some 1,000 miles away.

Come midday, a glimpse of the sun and the moon confirmed that we had 997 miles to go. My pre-arranged plan for the last 1,000 miles was to race flat out, as though turning round the buoys off Cowes. So this was the time - barometer low and dropping, sea rough, wind Force 6 - hoist spinnaker. Perhaps it would not last long, but the needles were sharp and sewing cotton ready. Actually that spinnaker held for 32 hours before it split to keep the watch below sewing with the second spinnaker hoisted.

Another gale threatened, but moved across south of us, so although tired helmsmen led to a few broken ropes, that time we really had no more than half a gale. *Cohoe*, 50 miles to the south of us was right in the path of the gale so got its full strength. Like us, she had also declared the final thousand miles a sprint.

With some 200 miles to go, when sailing some 170 miles a day, both Adlard and I recorded in our journals 'Prayed for one more gale'. His prayer was slightly more effective than mine, as I recorded 'Modest seas suggest a young gale'. However cloud was heavy, so there was no chance of taking sextant sights, and navigational worry added to my exhaustion. It was a massive relief when Stephen shouted down the hatch "Wolf Rock lighthouse in sight, right ahead." The sky was clear and sun shining as we passed the Lizard, where the coastguards signalled that *Gulvain* had finished three days ago. There was no answer to my question whether any other competitors had been sighted.

The land looked quite delightful, after 21 days from the start - a very fast race indeed. But a ragged gybe round Rame Head failed to show me that we were really far too tired to keep on under spinnaker in the dark with a fresh breeze blowing. We finished at midnight, and in the calm of Plymouth Sound the simple tasks of lowering the mainsail and spinnaker was like a school girls outing, showing that my judgement had been wrong in keeping up the sprint when all were so exhausted. I was even too befuzzled to know which way to steer within the harbour.

The hazy blink of what I thought was an unknown light buoy turned into a boat's light with the hail "Well done *Samuel Pepys*. Am coming alongside to take over your yacht. Daphne is with me and will board with the Customs Officer also on board." It was Dick Hewitt, so I could relax utterly at last. By breakfast time *Samuel Pepys*, *Cohoe* and *Mokoia* had secured alongside each other, while I was asleep ashore. "Well done" said Adlard as I joined them, "my navigator has worked out that you win by 10 minutes." "Rubbish", answered Pat Ovens, "You've forgotten to wind your watch. I reckon you've won by at least two minutes." It was evening before the formal results came through, when *Cohoe* was confirmed as the winner, with *Samuel Pepys* second.

That day we had many visitors on board, headed by the Commander-in-Chief, Plymouth and the RNSA Branch Captain, followed by the Press, BBC and many others. A representative of the Met. office interested me; "Surely", I asked him "there were more than normal gales for mid-summer in the Atlantic; or was my anemometer over-reading?", "Our records show a very unsettled three weeks" he answered. Pat was listening intently and added, "What do you expect when the skipper kept praying for gales?."

It was three days later when *Karin III* finished her race, after a well-sailed crossing suited to a cruising yacht over 30 years old. By then we had handed *Samuel Pepys* back for her normal club tasks, while each of us had returned to our naval duties.

Cohoe with her false bow showing, which was removed when she won the 1950 Trans-Atlantic race sailed by Adlard Coles.

CHAPTER ELEVEN

Fleet Aircraft Carrier 1950-1951

Back with the family in Dorset a vital matter for me was getting to know our second daughter, Errollyn, who had been born when preparations for the Atlantic race were in full swing. But there was still a good deal of work from the venture to finish up, including a full report to the Royal Naval Sailing Association, and dealing with the financial side of the endeavour.

The expedition was very much a club matter, with *Samuel Pepys* in the races as a club entry. The costs worked out very reasonably, the greatest expense being for additional sails and bosunry, besides an extra water tank for the Trans-Atlantic passage. Transport was minimal, thanks to the generosity of the Royal Mail Line and the Port of London Authority; but we still had to build a cradle and pay road freight from Plymouth to London. There was special insurance for the races, and a few administrative costs. The whole lot came to just over £600.

The conditions for the crew were that each should contribute the equivalent of a month's pay, which between us came to some £200; the receipts from Press and Radio were much the same. The Royal Naval Sports Control Board contributed £150, so all this meant that the club entering its yacht for the races only had to find some £50 and had the asset of some new sails and gear. The Commodore and the committee, considered it a very good bargain indeed, while each of the crew felt he had excellent value from being a partner in the expedition as well as the satisfaction of sailing.

The Admiralty showed it was pleased that its contribution - allowing the crew special leave on full pay - had brought credit to the Royal Navy, besides encouraging recruitment among adventurous young people. Its interest was shown by both First and Second Sea Lords sending for me to hear my personal report on the venture. Admiral of the Fleet Lord Fraser of North Cape said that courage, enterprise and seamanship brought the adventure to a successful conclusion. The Department of Admiralty in which I had served before the race came under the Second Sea Lord, so I had met him previously. He was very complimentary about the whole thing, and as the Board Member for Personnel went on to say that he intended to suggest that I should skipper the royal yacht *Bluebottle*, an International Dragon Class yacht of about the same length as *Samuel Pepys*, but designed for racing inshore. He saw that I looked worried and managed to draw my anxieties out of me. Although I was aware that this would be a great honour, I hoped that coping with all the strains of the trans-atlantic race would allow me to escape from the medical limitation that I was fit only for a ship with a doctor, and then I might be sent to a destroyer or similar warship. He rang up the Medical Director General at once to arrange that I see him personally, when it was explained to me that a few weeks of stress in the Atlantic was very different from commanding a ship for two years, perhaps in difficult climates. Naturally I was given a very full examination, besides research into my not very satisfactory health record. So no change in recommendation could be made.

Soon my appointment came as First Lieutenant of the Fleet Aircraft Carrier *Illustrious*. The ship's normal function was housing, operating and maintaining aircraft. Thus even in my job, dealing mainly with living conditions and discipline, there was a great deal to be learnt. Fortunately the Commander Flying was particularly helpful and all those in his department were excellent shipmates and found time from their flying duties to take their ship's duties seriously.

Traditionally the First Lieutenant was in charge on deck forward when anchoring, picking up mooring buoys or securing to a wharf. In most warships the Captain, on the bridge, could see all that was going on forward, and give orders accordingly. Yet in an aircraft carrier the

Fleet Aircraft Carrier H.M.S. Illustrious.

flight deck completely blinded the bridge from the forecastle. In one way this was an asset, as my Captain, with the Navigating Officer, always gave me detailed briefing of exactly what was intended because after that any changes would need to be passed by telephone. Thus I quickly got to know my Captain really well, and realised that with Shorty Carlill I was once more very fortunate in my captain.

Operating in home waters, sometimes going as far as Gibraltar, life was interesting. It was so different from foreign service, and there was a fortnight's seasonal leave three times a year.

At one stage all aircraft and their personnel went to a naval air station ashore while the ship refitted in Devonport dockyard. Again fortune came my way, when a sailing friend, Captain Brown, was appointed with little notice to take command of a warship off Korea and invited me to take over his converted sailing trawler *Dayspring*. Built in Rye during 1906 with an overall length of 56 feet, she was described as a Ramsgate 5-day sailing trawler. On converting her to a yacht, the original trawler rig and spars were kept; thus with a powerful great bowsprit sticking out forward and an overhanging mizzen boom aft, she felt twice her length when manoeuvring in confined waters. Her fish hold had been converted into a comfortable living quarters, and she was to be our family home during the time *Illustrious* was refitting. By then the family included four children, the youngest, Errollyn, only a few weeks old.

Dayspring was lying in Gosport, so with the elder children still at school, volunteers from the ship helped me to sail her down to Plymouth, where we put her in a mud berth at St. Germans. The school holidays then began which was perfect for the two boys, Peregrine and Peter, aged 11 and 9, as *Dayspring* had a 11 foot sailing dinghy, actually built by Captain Brown himself. The boys had the whole Lynher River to sail in perfect safety. Perhaps things were not so perfect for Daphne, as although the boat lay alongside a disused wharf, the boys were as often in mud as in the water. This problem became acute when the Commander-in-Chief, Plymouth, kindly invited the whole family to lunch. I had my work on board *Illustrious* that morning, so Daphne had to get the whole bunch to Plymouth by land, and hosed down in a public bath. On reaching Admiralty House, her Ladyship, who turned out to have children of a similar age, greeted them with "Hot baths all ready. I assume the boys will have been in the mud." So it was a splendid party for all.

With the completion of the ship's refit in sight it became necessary for *Dayspring* to get back to Gosport. It was still school holidays for the

Peregrine climbing out on the bowsprit, and Peter in the dinghy, when the converted sailing trawler Dayspring was our family home during a school holiday.

boys, so they were very keen to take part in the 120 mile cruise. It would be the first open sea passage both for them and for Daphne. Rosamund would at first stay with her grandmother and help look after the baby, but she was to join us at Weymouth. There were two honorary members of the family for the cruise and their strength was really valuable for a vessel with such heavy equipment. John Clutterbuck not only taught the boys throughout the school terms, but accepted their invitation to cruise with them for part of the holidays as well. Then there was George Moyes, a naval leading seaman on leave before joining a ship off Korea. While serving in *Illustrious* he had been an important part of my crew for the voyage west from Gosport. On that trip, in really nasty weather he had developed acute appendicitis so, short-handed, the rest of us struggled through Portland race in an urgent effort to get the pain-wracked George to hospital. He recovered from the operation quickly and came back to *Dayspring* for sick leave spent helping with splicing and sail sewing.

Out at sea, a 7 foot high swell excited the boys with the boat's motion and an occasional swirl of water on deck as she dipped her nose under a wave. I felt sorry for Daphne struggling below to secure the crockery, picked out of its rack by the steeper waves off the harbour entrance. With such a heavy boom and gaff it was hard work to get the mainsail up, and even destroyer-hardened George was feeling not too well after mistakenly taking a sniff at a petrol can. With a head wind it was not really the right conditions for novices, so to the disappointment of the boys, I turned back for the harbour to wait for better weather.

At dawn the next day the conditions were just right, the wind round to a moderate westerly. So off we went and the boys in turn had no difficulty in steering a good compass course. As the wind increased on the quarter, with plentiful white crests to the waves, steering needed close concentration, but the boys took their half hour tricks of steering with the adults, until with land out of sight and supper finished they willingly went to their bunks.

During darkness a hand bell was placed on the deck beside the helmsman, so that a tinkle could call for help from below. Usually it called me to adjust the sails with wind shifts, but once there was urgent ringing, followed by the crash of the main boom gybing as John's concentration had lapsed during his middle watch. Back at school next term when Mr. Clutterbuck, as he became in term time, sternly corrected Peter for some lapse in the class room, the boy mischievously mimicked the ringing of a handbell.

However, back at sea, we were off Portland Bill with the dawn, this time keeping well out beyond the tidal race as there was no urgency, then turned in for Weymouth. The auxiliary engine had failed leaving Plymouth harbour, so we planned the arrival carefully. John and I would lower the mailsail. George would handle the jib, while Daphne and Peregrine would deal with the mizzen. That left Peter at the wheel making for the only berth visible, which was alongside a fine white yacht. By then those of us handling sails were invisible beneath them, so the yacht's owner, from down below, saw approaching him a big black tarred hull, with a long bowsprit sticking far out ahead, and a child at the wheel apparently the only person on board. He rushed on deck, still in his pyjamas, waving a mop and shouting "Not here, away!"

However those on board a motor yacht, within heaving line range, invited us alongside hospitably. Safely secured in harbour we later picked up Rosamund to make it three children on board, ready for the sail to the Solent. Nothing we could do would persuade the engine to work so our kindly motor yacht neighbour, which was also about to set off, offered us a tow out of the harbour, where a gentle breeze and evening sunshine offered conditions that would encourage any child to come again.

Approaching the Needles soon after dawn, Daphne complained "But they're not like needles at all. They look like razors." "They would feel like them too," suggested George, "if you let the tide take you onto them." Indeed the spring tide was running fast against us, but with a fresh wind astern we got some of the excitement of a rough sea, with none of the discomfort. So we came into Yarmouth, Isle of Wight, with the dinghy first a vital aid to picking up a mooring, and then to provide endless joy for the children. They were even able to enter the town's regatta, finishing about last in each race. Then we were off again in *Dayspring* to find ourselves amongst the racing fleet off Cowes. "Can't we join in the race?" asked Peter. In later years he did, winning in his own yachts many a fine trophy.

Next we came into Portsmouth harbour, still without help from an engine, but with George standing by the kedge anchor as we crept up Blockhouse Creek. Sentries aboard the submarines and motor torpedo boats watched us with interest, combined with suspicion for the safety of their paint work. When the direction of the creek turned ahead into the wind, it was down all sails and the boys to the dinghy, Peregrine rowing 50 yards to a mooring buoy and Peter letting out a light line over its stern. George and I hauled away on this, as Rosamund steered to the buoy. Finally it was warping from pile to pile until *Dayspring* was in her own berth. "Need we ever live in a house again, Mummy?" asked Rosamund, leaning sleepily back on the saloon berth, replete with food and adventure.

Back on board the *Illustrious* the re-fit was nearly over, so we made preparations for the aircraft and their teams to come back to the ship. It was a pleasant feeling when the first of the planes landed safely, to be quickly handled back to the lift, and lowered to the hangar, so that the next one could land on. Then normal fleet exercises became the routine again.

Of course there were no newspapers at sea, but radio news was regularly received and sometimes read. Those who did so knew that there was some crisis in the Middle East, but off the Scottish coast that seemed a long way from us. So it was a surprise when the Admiralty ordered *Illustrious* to disembark aircraft and proceed to Portsmouth at speed.

By the time we reached Portsmouth, where most of those concerned with flying went ashore, we knew that *Illustrious* and the Light Fleet

Carrier *Triumph*, of approximately half our size, were to be converted at the rush to troop carriers, taking much of the Third Infantry Division to the Middle East. "You will be Trooping Officer, Number One" ordered Captain Jellicoe, who had taken over command from Shorty Carlill. "We are to embark as many troops as possible under austerity conditions, for passage to the Middle East; but we don't know exactly where. I gather you have experience of this sort of thing in a cruiser."

I formed a ship's trooping staff, including representatives of all departments, but of course heads of Departments and the Executive Officer were to be consulted as necessary, although each had ample to deal with of his own. Very quickly we measured up the hangar and decided that with jackstays rigged we could sleep 1,500 men there in hammocks, while mess tables could be fitted below them for cafeteria messing. Some 400 more soldiers, mostly sergeants, could be fitted into ship's messes. 100 officers could be crowded into cabins vacated by the air department, and fed in the wardroom mess. Some 170 Army vehicles could be parked on the flight deck, leaving about 100 feet forward for men to exercise in open air. Latrines would be rigged on the boat deck each side, so that one side would always be leeward.

Very quickly a meeting was held on board with Portsmouth dockyard officers, and the work was assessed as needing 4 days with

With some crisis in the Middle East, all aircraft were put ashore and the hangar became a mammoth dormitory.

full overtime. Dockyard workers started that very evening welding ring bolts to the flight deck, so that the loading of some Army vehicles could start the next morning, using the ship's cranes with nets.

By then the trooping office had its own separate G.P.O. telephone, and also direct phones to military headquarters. The trooping office had to be manned day and night, so between us we had very little time to eat. This was ironic when arranging that extra naval cooks should join the ship, along with many more electric hot lockers and a thousand other items. Nor was there much time to sleep when 2,000 soldiers were on their way to add to the 1,050 people of the ship's company.

With the grave risk of fire and the possibility of other accidents, strict orders had to be prepared for the soldiers embarking and living on board. There came the problem of language, as military understanding would not always fit with naval usage. This was helped when two majors arrived with the first of the vehicles, and were at once co-opted into the trooping office. But before then some slips had been made. For instance, my instructions to a group of 400 soldiers coming from the other side of the country included the information 'sandwiches will be provided on arrival'. The unfortunate men arrived in mid-afternoon still carrying the sandwiches they understood that they had to provide on arrival. Making enough fresh water was going to be a heavy task for our engineers, so my orders to officers included 'No long baths', meaning that they would have to be content with showers. Thus I was annoyed to find an officer luxuriating after his journey in 10 inches of hot water. "But I've only just got in, and won't be in here for long" he answered.

Somehow all was ready when the various special trains arrived, and each soldier changed into gym shoes as military boots would be too slippery on iron decks. The sudden rush of troops was front page news, with many graphic details described. This was before the days of computers for everyday use, so somehow headlines were given to the simple fact that I had planned it all on my slide rule, which gave no credit to all the effort made by the Captain and everyone else on board. However, on return I was presented by the ship with a new slide rule.

The Commander-in-Chief was more realistic in congratulating all on board, adding his hopes that we would be rewarded by good weather in the Bay of Biscay. Perhaps this was expecting rather too much for November but the severe storm which hit us next day was scarcely reasonable. The wind blew up to 80 knots, and as the eye of the storm passed over it shifted 120 degrees in a few minutes. So the ship had to slow right down from the high speed planned for the voyage. We were grateful that the special stores embarked included a vast number of seasick pills. At all times the Field Officer of the Day and Orderly Officer of the Watch were on the bridge, and able to broadcast in military language any instruction needed by the ship's officers. Finally there was a Transport Officer of the Watch, also continuously on duty to ensure safety of the vehicles and any soldier on the flight deck. It said much for the dockyard welding that throughout that severe storm nothing came adrift. Perhaps it was all those instructions that helped us to weather the storm without even a broken arm or ankle.

Life for the soldiers became almost reasonable speeding through the Mediterranean, with a few hundred at a time brought up to the patch of flight deck clear of vehicles for physical training. Certainly the doctors were not overwhelmed. By then signals had come through saying that our destination was Cyprus, so plans for disembarking could start. The ship anchored about a mile offshore, and Z lighters were used to land men, taking 600 per lighter as the sea was calm. Planning assessed that if rough it would take 10 more hours compared with the 17 hours it actually took. Vehicles had to be off-loaded of stores down to the 5 ton maximum that the ship's cranes could handle, then hoisted out each side into three Z lighters, each of which could take ten vehicles. Army stores weighing some 100 tons, besides 2,000 kit bags, were slid down chutes into dumb lighters. The weather remained fine, and amazingly the whole operation proceeded to time without accident or loss. Then up came the anchor and ship set off at speed for another

The flight deck was mainly Army vehicles with only a limited space for men to exercise.

helping at Portsmouth. That time more Army officers were carried, the same number of troops, but only 167 vehicles. The weather was much kinder and lessons from the first trip certainly were a help to me. The whole lot was safely disembarked in Cyprus before the end of November, and we returned home at economical speed, preparing to be an aircraft carrier again.

During 1951, a small committee of the RNSA had been considering an entry for the Bermuda and Trans-Atlantic races the following year, and when not at sea, I had attended these meetings. For the Bermuda race itself researches suggested that a two-masted yacht of around 50 foot length had the best chance, but I personally stressed that there would be many American yachts in this range. So the vital thing was the best skipper and that for the Trans-Atlantic race it would be best to consider it in terms of adventure training, perhaps using one of the 100 square metre windfall yachts. Much had gone on during the summer when I had been unable to attend, and with the intensity of trooping tasks I had not even noticed the full committee decision that *Samuel Pepys* would go again as the club entry, while support would be given to the venture planned by my good friend Sam Brooks in the 100 square metres windfall *Marabu*, which had done well racing in British waters that year. Volunteers were called for to race *Samuel Pepys*, but it did not occur to me to forward my name. I felt I was doing a useful job in *Illustrious*, and that John Illingworth should be skipper. However a letter arrived from a very high authority saying that the first *Samuel Pepys* venture had achieved far more for naval prestige than anyone had anticipated, so it was important to repeat the series with a chance of doing even better. John Illingworth could not be made available, so my experience as team leader and skipper was important.

Faced with this it seemed best to ask my Captain's advice. He was firm, and rather annoyed that I should even consider a step which would mean leaving his ship. He was kindly about my service under him, mentioning the trooping, but insisted that if I took my naval career seriously I would not dream of asking to leave so good a job as First Lieutenant of an operational Fleet Carrier for the sake of what was merely amateur sport. I could not help remembering also that this job had been arranged for me by the Second Sea Lord when I felt it important to have a professional appointment instead of one with the sport of sailing.

I replied to the letter in those terms, stressing my loyalty to the Royal Navy, and was then firmly instructed to attend an interview at the Admiralty. At this meeting I was told that I was putting my personal career before genuine loyalty. It was stressed that there were many officers of the rank well suited to take over my job in *Illustrious*, but none had the experience of skippering *Samuel Pepys* in a Trans Atlantic race. This was a task which could bring further credit to the Navy, but could become a calamity in a boat so small, if the skipper lacked the special experience.

So my appointment to *Illustrious* came to an end after 14 months, instead of the expected two years. My Captain was very generous in his report, in spite of the fact that formally I had left at my own request.

CHAPTER TWELVE

Atlantic Again 1952

A s a temporary expedient I was appointed First Lieutenant of the reserve fleet battleship *H.M.S.Howe* laid up at Plymouth. This was not a demanding task, and moored alongside her was *Samuel Pepys*. Once the Admiralty had accepted the request of the Royal Naval Sailing Association that I be her skipper for the 1952 Bermuda and Trans-Atlantic races, I was given a postion that meant I was strongly placed to prepare her for this.

The Cruising Club of America had confirmed that the yacht would be welcome again, although shorter than the minimum length still normally acceptable; her handicap would be similar to the previous visit. So my next major task was to select a crew in conjunction with the Admiralty. Chief Petty Officer Flux had been sailing regularly in *Marabu*, which therefore had first right to him for this series, and the Admiralty could not release the other pair of my former crew. However some 60 names had been sent as volunteers, nearly all with good ocean racing experience.

A further example of the strong support at a high level came when the Admiral Commanding Reserves wrote that it would be valuable to Reserve prestige and recruiting if a member of the Reserves was included in the crew. This was most fortunate, as while still serving in *Illustrious,* I had met an R.N.V.R. officer who had come for a short period of routine training under my direction. He had shown himself an outstanding leader with excellent experience of small fighting craft, and I soon found that he could volunteer, as he could get special leave from the Bank of England, where he worked. Thus Ian Quarrie was quickly nominated as a crew member. The RNSA Commodore, General Thomas Royal Marines, strongly supported Lieutenant Commander Larney Wise and Lieutenant David Coaker, and the Admiralty agreed that they would be released on three months special leave, while representing their country.

The Admiralty also agreed to release the 9 members of *Marabu's* crew for three months on full pay. She was a much bigger yacht, so Sam Brooks planned to sail her out to America, and she was entered in the two races in the name of *H.M.S. Hornet* Yacht Club, so she would not be part of an RNSA team, but as Sam Brooks was a highly regarded member of the RNSA, we would give her any support we could. *Marabu* was 17 years old and hardly expected to win the Bermuda race, yet she might do very well in the Trans Atlantic and her entry was splendid adventure training for the Navy.

A professional yacht surveyor checked *Samuel Pepys'* hull and rigging. The excellent condition showed how well Dick Hewitt had cared for her since her last big race, and very little extra equipment was needed this time. Once more the Royal Mail Line generously agreed that the crew could sign on as deck hands, taking the yacht without charge. To save the cost of road freight I sailed the boat round to London with two of the new crew backed up by my sons Peregrine and Peter, then 11 and 10. This route also had the asset that on reaching London we sailed alongside Tower Pier for a visit by His Royal Highness Prince Philip, the Lord Mayor of London, and several members of the Admiralty Board. This got excellent Press coverage, which the Admiralty was keen to support, perhaps to encourage naval recruiting. Indeed this time much of the venture brought *Samuel Pepys* onto the front pages of the main London dailies, besides provincial papers far and wide.

Fortunately there were no strikes or problems on this occasion, so off we went in *M.V.Brittany* for an excellent crossing to Bermuda. There we were put up as guests of the Royal Bermuda Yacht Club for the couple of days needed to get the yacht ready. Then there were two more days of sail drill and provisioning before we set off for Newport as planned.

As usual I hoped for some rough weather to practice in. It came, and might almost have been scheduled for training purposes; in mid-ocean, far from any land hazards, and in broad daylight, the wind steadily increased to a Force 8 gale. After an hour came a shift in direction to give confused seas before it steadily decreased to a pleasant fresh breeze, so skipper and crew could eat their supper in comfort.

We sailed on to America and, with 25 miles to go, thick fog came down. Again we turned this to our advantage, practising a landfall in low visibility. Larney Wise, an electrical specialist, had brought an experimental radio direction finder, which were rare in yachts at that time. Getting no sensible answer from the machine, I impatiently told Larney to stop playing with toys and come up to strengthen the lookouts. Just at that time he got a bearing which seemed right, but by then I had lost confidence in the device and hove to. This gave a splendid opportunity to try the machine out and all get used to it. Soon the fog cleared to show that the instrument was no toy at all but an accurate aid to navigation.

As we came to City Island we sighted our fellow British competitors, one after the other. First there was *Bloodhound*, a beautiful 63 foot yawl, flying the flag of Myles Wyatt, Vice Commodore of the Royal Ocean Racing Club, with an excellent crew to support him. We were backing her to get a place in the large class, and therefore likely to be placed overall. Next we sighted *Iolaire*, flying the flag of Bobby Somerset, Commodore of the R.O.R.C. She was a fine cruising cutter, nearly 50 years old, and not really expected in the prize list. Then came the 55 foot *Lutine* of Lloyds Yacht Club, a modern design of ocean racer first launched that year. *Joliette*, in our small class, had sailed from Bermuda at the same time as we did, but she had been hit harder by that gale and suffered some sail damage. *Marabu* was to arrive soon afterwards from her good Atlantic crossing. Thus there was a splendid half dozen British competitors, with some of our best skippers and crew. So that year there might be a British Bermuda race prize for the first time.

There were still a couple of weeks before the start of the race, which gave us valuable time to polish our techniques. We were made very welcome by American yachtsmen and Blunt White, Commodore of the Cruising Club of America took us all to his home for dinner. By then we were joined by Commander Robin Graham of the British Naval staff in Washington who was to be our fifth man in *Samuel Pepys*, just for the Bermuda race.

So we came to the race itself, starting on June 21st with 58 good competitors, for a course of 635 miles. It was just what we had been training for, and each of us on board put the very last ounce of effort into it. Easily the smallest yacht, it was most encouraging that even on the fourth day there were several other yachts astern of us at dawn At the finish off Bermuda, we were told that allowing for handicap *Samuel Pepys* was very well up. Then as we sailed in to anchor near the yacht club there were rousing cheers, from American as well as British yachts. Word came from ashore that *Samuel Pepys* had achieved the highest overall place ever won by a non-American yach. That was fifth overall, and third place in our class. Soon afterwards His Excellency the Governor and the British Naval Commander-in-Chief managed to cram into our cockpit, followed by the Commodore of the Cruising Club of America, who had beaten us by one place.

The American yacht *Caribee* with a crew of nine headed by the brilliant skipper Carleton Mitchell was the overall winner. It was the first time in the history of the race that a small class yacht had won the Bermuda trophy. *Bloodhound* with four of the Wyatt family among the nine people on board, had a popular success as second in the big class, but on handicap she was five hours behind *Samuel Pepys* .

It left six days to the Trans-Atlantic, and they were very busy ones for us. Perhaps past experience meant that I took these preparations more seriously than some, but everything was so much easier the second time around. Certainly some were still struggling with details when the club launch arrived to tow yachts to the start. As I had nothing more to do myself, I was asked to help carry water bags to a fellow competitor. Indeed the start was delayed by two hours for all five competitors to get there - three British, one French and one American. The American entry was *Caribee* which had just won the Bermuda trophy and was to be sailed by Carleton Mitchell again. Both *Bloodhound* and *Iolaire* decided to cruise back, not racing, while *Lutine* was still under repair.

Off we went, with the finish at Plymouth 2780 miles away. It was a big advantage to have raced the course before, as so much depends upon the crew keeping up their driving enthusiasm for perhaps 4 weeks. Strong winds can stimulate a competitive crew, but it is harder to keep up the pressure in near calms by night. I was confident that I had the best crew of all for gales, and it was encouraging to have a short brisk gale in the first week, but we did not know that 100 miles away or more the others were sailing flat out with only a strong breeze, while for an hour we were running under a bare pole, in 45 knots of wind.

But that was the only gale and we all had a good deal of light weather. Even that was not too bad for me as Ian Quarrie proved such an excellent mate that I could confidently have a ration of sleep knowing that he would keep up the pressure. Indeed the whole crew kept really alert, even when it needed full attention to make use of a mean wisp of wind coming from a new direction.

Again we were sailing much the smallest yacht and with less than half the crew of some of the others. Nearing England my assessment was that *Caribee* as our keenest rival would have to finish some 4 days ahead to beat us. As we came up to the Lizard the coastguards signalled that she had finished giving us a few hours in hand "Have you seen any other competitors?" I signalled. We waited nervously for the answering signal. Relief swept over us all when the signal came that they had not.

But there was still the chance that we could lie becalmed with a contrary tide in those last few miles. Fortunately a gentle breeze from the north kept us going. As in the first race, I was utterly exhausted at this stage but I knew that I could depend on Ian Quarrie.

We crossed the finishing line and once more there was Dick Hewitt waiting in a motorboat. It was 25 days out from Bermuda and on time corrected for handicap we beat *Caribee* by 6 hours and 45 minutes to win overall and the Commodore's Cup. *Marabu* had finished only 4 hours after *Caribee* having sailed a very good race. Then, 70 minutes after her came *Joliette*, with French *Janabel* half an hour after her, both on corrected time. Thus, after handicaps, all of the competitors came within 18 hours of one another.

It took only two or three days to get the yacht back for normal chartering to members. Then the four of us went to London where in the Mansion House, in the presence of Prince Philip and many others, the Lord Mayor of London formally paid off the crew. However he pointed out that this traditional expression might be misleading, as each had handed over a proportion of his naval pay towards the expenses of the venture. The Lord Mayor certainly made us feel that we had done our bit for the prestige of our country.

The Admiralty's interest in the project had been strong, although it was a Royal Naval Sailing Association entry more than a formal Naval one. I was sent for by the First Sea Lord, Admiral Sir Roderick McGrigor, and the Second Sea Lord, Admiral Sir Alec Madden, with warm praise for the contribution to naval prestige. Surprisingly I was also summoned by Sir John Lang, Secretary to the Admiralty who received me in quite a different way. "As a civil Servant" he said, "I have always understood that a naval officer's career depended mainly on his Captain. I understand that you actually asked to leave his command, which must have concerned him." "Sir," I protested indignantly, "You can't know all that went on; I have respect for my Captain" His mood changed and smiling he said "I do know what went on actually. Congratulations."

CHAPTER THIRTEEN

Orcadian Home 1952-1954

The Admiralty had been generous enough to grant us special leave for sport, but the Board members went much further by showing a lively interest and appreciating the value of our venture to the Navy. Thus for six weeks I was lent to the Director of Naval Training, who sent me to a succession of training establishments to lecture on the human aspects of the race.

One of the places I went to was in Scotland, and while there the Flag Officer Scotland told me that he wanted to discuss another subject as well. This was Scapa Flow, which I knew from past visits in different ships. He said that a new Resident Naval Officer Orkney would shortly be needed, with isolation and severe weather conditions making it a very demanding task.

"Your name had been suggested by the Admiralty, and I have little doubt that you could cope. However it is even more difficult for the wife, so I would like to be satisfied that your wife could manage it."

I explained my family affairs and stressed that Daphne loved the country and wild creatures. I reckoned that she would be happy and would not feel deprived of the social round of cocktail parties, so important to some naval wives. I quoted the name of a naval captain who knew her.

Soon afterwards I was officially informed of my appointment as Resident Naval Officer, Orkney: Queen's Harbour Master, Scapa Flow: Commander of the Dockyard, Lyness: and Admiralty Pilot for Royal Fleet Auxiliaries. This was a Commander's appointment, so I was made an Acting Commander just for that job.

It was October 1952 and so term time for our two boys at a boarding school in Devonshire. Our two girls, Rosamund then 9 and Errollyn just 2, travelled up to Orkney with Daphne and me.

My predecessor was clearly not very happy. It seemed unfortunate that he had been given the job, as early in the war he had been Officer of the Watch in the battleship *Royal Oak*, anchored in Scapa Flow when a brilliant submarine attack by Lieutenant Prien sank the battleship, with the loss of 786 officers and men. To be sent back ten years later for an isolated life nearby must have been traumatic. Sadly his wife disliked the life of Scapa Flow as much as he did. He was pleased to see me, but his description of life and the duties was far from cheerful. He told me that to make matters worse his First Lieutenant was also to leave, without relief. This meant that my only naval staff would be a Warrant Engineer as Base Engineer Officer. However there were 150 civilian staff with competent dockyard civilian officers. We all lived in wooden huts, and he assured me that the wire ropes holding the roofs on in storms had recently been tightened.

The naval base was at Lyness on the Island of Hoy. There were motor fishing vessels well suited for communication across Scapa Flow to the Mainland of Orkney, where there was a second naval office in Kirkwall, the capital. Lyness had a village school, with most of the children coming from the naval base families. Rosamund at once joined that and quickly made two or three friends.

The Orkneys are at a latitude nearly sixty degrees north, so in mid-winter the hours of daylight are very short. However a leg of the Gulf Stream current runs past, so average temperatures in December are much the same as those in the Solent. Yet the winds are very different, with many a storm each winter. The first one came the very day my predecessor left by air, when a sudden blast shattered a window pane in our sitting room, and the house jolted violently against its holding-down hawsers, bringing down pictures and saucepans. I quickly donned oilskins to visit the pier, where a dozen reserve vessels from a thousand tons downwards were lying alongside under a couple of watchmen. It was a snow blizzard, gusting up to 90 knots, and threw me into the ditch beside a coatless figure. "My children are missing," she screamed, "Husband's away at the boiler." Then she was out of sight in a moment, and I did not know who she was or where she lived. It was a Sunday morning, when the camp bar might be full, but raising a search party could have its problems, as probably no-one would recognise the newly arrived Commander.

How wrong I was. The men crowded there immediately appreciated the problem. They not only guessed who the missing children were, but quickly found them in a neighbour's house.

The only other serving naval officer kept close to his engineering, except that he was in charge of the cinema. Thus I was mainly dependent upon my secretary, a reliable civil servant, to know who was who. I mentioned to him that regular meetings of heads of department might be useful; he suggested that the Base Engineer might feel this was interfering with his responsibilities, but felt others would appreciate that this would give them a share in the total control of the base. So this began, and certainly helped me. Soon afterwards I brought Trades

Union representatives in as well: it was one of these who lent me manuals of industrial management, and also helped with technical words and expressions of the trade.

Christmas holidays were not far ahead, so we had to work out how our boys could get home from their school in North Devon. A school train would take them to London, where one of my sisters would meet them and take them across London to catch the night sleeper train to Aberdeen. There they would be met by Miss Duffie who we had not met, but knew about through love of dogs. After giving them lunch she would take them to the plane flying to Kirkwall, where I would meet them and take them back across the Scapa Flow. Quite an adventure in itself, as well as the interest of visiting Scotland for the first time. My Admiral, based at Rosyth near Edinburgh, had asked me by phone about these arrangements, as he was keen to help if required. He mentioned that should the plane be held up for any length of time, he could probably have the boys picked up by a warship going our way on fishery protection patrol. However that never happened, and throughout our time in Orkney the journeys to school and back were completed without fail, winter and summer.

It was soon after the boys had gone back to school from their first Orkney holidays that the biggest storm struck. Indeed the wind recorded at the nearby research station, 135 knots, was claimed to be the highest wind speed ever recorded in Britain. Much damage was done, although all the vessels attached to my base were safe. I wondered whether my Admiral thought we might have been blown away when a message came that his Chief-of-Staff was coming for a visit. Yet when I met him from his plane he told me light-heartedly that as there had been none of the former string of complaints from Orkney through the winter, they felt on the Admiral's staff that something must be wrong.

He was delighted to find no damage to any craft, and that the extensive oil depot was operational. Fortunately no major tanker was present when the storm hit, although there were regular visits of Royal Fleet Auxiliary tankers. Up to that time none had asked for my services as the pilot, and the Chief-of-Staff explained that they would only do so when the weather made the approach especially difficult. He gave me an idea of the year's programme, with a large fleet aircraft carrier visiting in July, followed by 16 submarines with attendant craft. I would be required to fly south for briefing before each came. Then in late August the Admiral would come for his official inspection. He mentioned that the isolation in Orkney might be a strain, and hinted that if I wanted to sail in the Fastnet race, special arrangements could be made to borrow an officer as I no longer had a First Lieutenant. For me it was a very pleasant visit, and the weather was quiet throughout the two days, but was not to last long. The following weekend the winds returned, and there were gusts to 90 knots when the Norwegian cargo ship *Basra* radioed that she was in trouble off Hoy.

The next marine casualty off Hoy was not due to gale but to fog. The Grimsby trawler *Leicester City* was returning home from Iceland fishing grounds when she hit a rock in Hoy Sound and, listing heavily, seemed in danger of rolling over. The Danish skipper gave orders to abandon ship, but the ship's lifeboat was hurled over by a wave, scattering the crew. Seven men drowned, but the RNLI lifeboat from nearby Stromness picked up some of the survivors, while others were swept to the shore, which was actually only 200 yards away in the fog. The alarm was raised by a woman returning to her croft after visiting a friend. It was her call that brought out the lifeboat, and although it was the middle of the night, all those living near, including five women, turned out to join the search and they found other survivors washed up. News came to me through the coastguards, so I roused two men with first aid training and we drove the seven miles as fast as we could in my car. The ship's mate died before our help arrived, but others had already been dealt with by Isaac Moar, volunteer in charge of the Hoy Lifesaving team. One of the joys of such islands was that so many were involved in giving voluntary help to others.

Soon after that came the first warship visit since I took command. Admiral Sir Henry McCall, flag officer of the reserve fleet, came in the destroyer *HMS Trafalgar* to inspect the group of reserve fleet ships laid up in Lyness dockyard. It was of special interest to me as when I first joined Dartmouth College as a cadet, he was an officer there. We had much to talk about as well as the ships in which we both had an interest.

With well over a hundred wives and children of people from outside Orkney working at the base, there seemed a strong need for a social club. It was really satisfying when a committee was formed and rapidly set to work redecorating some rooms which could be spared. Before long they invited me to open the club formally with time in hand to get settled before the dark days of the winter. But this was June when the sun scarcely set, so it was ideal for a regatta to celebrate the Coronation. During the dark winter nights I had built a sailing dinghy in one of our spare bedrooms, and its first race was in this regatta, where it sailed quite well; but as the trophy was presented by me, I had to disqualify the boat. We also had a rowing regatta with races for women, men and boys. Next day the newly formed Base Sports Club had an open air meeting, ending with a baby competition for which there were ample entries.

Soon after that came another event to celebrate, in that a big cargo ship, aground in the Pentland Firth, survived. With its very strong tides and numerous rocks, the Pentland was traditionally known as the Ship's Graveyard. Thus when the American *Rutgers Victory*, with 12,000 tons of cargo, hit a rock in thick fog, few felt she could get off. Two special salvage tugs stationed in the area rushed to the scene, but I can confirm that the Longhope lifeboat got there first, as I was by then a member of her crew. Coxswain Fred Johnston ordered me to board her and discover her state. On her bridge her Master protested to me

"See here, your Limey sailing directions say the tide goes at 13 knots. What could I do with only 11 knots in the box?" Actually he was short of the worst, as the Admiralty Pilot went on to write "but higher velocities undoubtedly occur locally in the Firth."

The Longhope lifeboat was one of the busiest voluntary life saving team in Britain, so I felt it a great honour to become a member of the crew, helping in the rescue of many wrecks in the Pentland Firth. Sadly the whole crew were drowned not long after I left.

With the help of the salvage tugs the ship was refloated, and after temporary repairs to the 30 foot rent in her bottom, she was able to go under her own steam to Belfast for docking.

My place in the crew of the RNLI lifeboat came about following another rescue call. During the previous winter a ship ran on the rocks in the Pentland Firth, during icy cold weather, and all on board were rescued by the lifeboat, whose crew were well aware that some of the survivors had helped themselves liberally to whisky before leaving their ship. They mentioned that there was more whisky lying around on deck. Past experience suggested to the lifeboat crew that the ship was bound to be a total loss, and in such cold conditions it seemed a waste for that whisky to be lost as well, so they went back and rescued a few bottles.

By amazing chance the ship was not a total loss and was towed to Aberdeen for repair. There rumour got around that things had been taken from the ship where she grounded, and the word reached RNLI headquarters in London, which took anything of that nature very seriously. An inspector was sent up north to investigate. The lifeboatmen at once admitted that they had salvaged some whisky.

"Well, what happened to it?" came the enquiry. "It was very cold, so we drank it on return to the slip."

The inspector paused to think, as the Pentland Firth is one of the main areas for wrecks in Britain. Then the Lifeboat Hon. Secretary suggested a solution which would preserve honour all round.

"You know", she said, "Brims folk may find it difficult to understand London talk. But the new Naval Commander is a proved boating man, so we could have him in the crew."

The inspector queried whether the commander would be able to volunteer with so many other responsibilities.

"I'll see to that" answered the Hon. Secretary, "You see I'm the only grocer around here."

The plan seemed to satisfy both sides, and certainly pleased me. Although my house was five miles from the lifeboat station, my car was always ready beside it, so in practice I got to a call as soon as several of the crew whose crofts were half a mile away on foot.

Ocean racing in the south seemed a very long way off, but Adlard Coles wrote inviting me to sail with him in the Fastnet race. For the first time the smaller yachts were able to enter since these had made out well in the much longer Trans-Atlantic races, and had also been allowed in the Bermuda race, which is the American equivalent of the Fastnet. This extension to Class III craft led to the largest international entry ever known, with yachts from eight different countries. In *Cohoe II* we had a good race, and our small class winners were far ahead of any in the large classes. It was my first sail in that yacht, which Adlard Coles had built to replace his famous *Cohoe*; it was also my first ocean race of the season, so I was not really up to the crew standard, but thoroughly enjoyed racing with Adlard.

The Longhope regatta had a score of boats, including one sailed by my wife Daphne, who took a major part in so many Orkney matters. This must have been one of the few Naval appointments where the Commanding Officer's wife could take as responsible a part as him. Indeed by the end she was more vital to all in the area as my wartime injuries were trying and there was no doctor on our island.

Thus all I saw of England in 1953 was a brief glimpse of Cowes at the start and Plymouth at the finish. Then I went back to Orkney, where our two boys had enjoyed sailing our home-built sailing dinghy.

Soon after my return, the Base Engineer Officer asked for urgent compassionate leave after the death of a parent. Naturally I granted this, but asked that temporarily he hand over the cinema accounts to my secretary. His accounts proved difficult to follow, and when the Royal Naval Film Corporation was called in, it showed that several bills had been unpaid. Then, on opening the cinema account safe, we found what looked at first sight like packets of bank notes but were actually blank paper. So I had to ask my Admiral to send up an Accountant Officer to sort things out. When the Engineer Officer was interviewed at his home near Chatham, it was found that the death of a parent was fiction. Sadly it was disclosed that he had got into financial problems. He admitted borrowing the cinema money, which he could not repay, so was ordered to Rosyth, where the Admiral had no option but to have him court-martialled. His defence was the difficulty of life in Lyness, leading to him and his wife smoking very heavily. He was found guilty and dismissed from the Navy. It was a blow to me that I should have failed to realise that my only naval officer was getting into this state, and we had never got to know him and his wife.

With the summer we walked a great deal, climbing the high hills of Hoy and exploring the coast. We got to know many of those living in Hoy, as well as those in the naval base. One great character was Isaac Moar, who had played such a valuable part in rescuing survivors of *Leicester City*. He ran a shop in the north of the island, and took his van around with many wares. He was also the undertaker, so some wit commented that his van brought kippers and coffins. Malcolm and Mary Stewart often came with us exploring small islets by boat. He owned the north part of Hoy, and rented sections to crofters; he had retired from his large family firm of London Brick to enjoy the life of Orkney, particularly studying birds. Others who frequently joined our expeditions were Jo Grimond and his family. He was Member of Parliament for Orkney and Shetland. Rosamund made friends with his daughter, Grizelda, a friendship that remains today. On Swona, surrounded by the violent tides of Pentland Firth, James Rosie told Jo Grimond that there were many more grey seals than people on his island, "But they don't have a vote."

Often walking with us in the summer was Sir Claremont Skrine. He had retired from a distinguished Foreign Service career, and alarmed me by skipping over precipitous high cliffs, until I learnt that he had been quite happy on the slopes of Mount Everest. Lady Skrine remained in Hoy through the winter, claiming that she preferred the company of wild creatures to human beings; but she got on very well with Daphne. Thus in summer months we had ample social life, but most of these people tended to go South through much of the winter. Our children also thoroughly enjoyed life in the Orkneys. Even Errollyn, at two, had her social life, as Laird, our boiler man, and Kenny, the dockyard sweeper for our corner, happily joined her for dolls' tea parties.

A big event for the naval base was the Admiral's annual inspection, and much work went into seeing that all was at its best by then. Rear-Admiral Robson had just taken over as Flag Officer Scotland, and one or two Orcadians remembered him from many years before when he was an officer of the then very large wartime base. He arrived flying his flag in *HMS Largs Bay*, and first paid formal calls on the Lord Lieutenant of the County and Provost of Kirkwall. Then he inspected every detail of naval interest, speaking personally to each person employed for the benefit of the Navy. This was splendid reward for good work done, but

*Rosamund at the local school became well used
to boats of many types.*

he went further by inviting all ninety children of the Lyness school for
a cruise round Scapa Flow in his flagship.

Rosamund, then aged ten, was a bright child, very well up with her
lessons, so Jo Grimond suggested that she might share a governess with
a daughter of his sister, Lady Rowallen. So she left at the end of term to
live during term time at Rowallen Castle in Kilmarnock.

Soon after that came the first of the winter storms, when gusts up
to 80 knots struck the Hull trawler *Hildina* off Orkney's Suleskerry
lighthouse. She foundered with the loss of six lives, including her
skipper, but the rest of the crew were rescued.

A few days later came a 5.00 am telephone call from Coxswain Fred
Johnston, and I made a full speed dash by car as the first of two maroons
exploded with a brilliant fireball that spread wide the news. Then oilskins
were pulled on, life-belts strapped, engines started - all in seconds,
smoothly and with scarcely a word. Next came the order "All hands
forward", still with no flurry, then "All together - Jump", and the boat's
nose tipped down. The coxswain rasied his hand, and as it dropped,
down the slip she went. It was black, not just that velvety darkness that
one feels is mere lack of light. This was a devil black darkness that struck
the mind as violently as the strong South-Easter bit into the cheeks.

Steering by compass, she plunged and soared out of Aith Hope. There was not a sign of land, although the cliffs were scarcely a hundred yards away. Then Dunnet Light peeped clear of the cliff, and the boat turned for it, with the strong ebb tide helping and the waves doing all they could to stop her. "Where will she be?", "How will she be lying?", and a hundred more questions flooded into my mind.

I ducked below the cockpit shelter for a heavy wave. A dim light gleamed from each of the thigh-high sea boots, firm footed as water swirled around them. Dimmer still, in the tiny light from the engine switch board, were the shapes of Engineer Bob and Soldier Bob, who sat rigid at their controls as though part of the hull itself. Soldier Bob had two sons aboard, Robbie up forward and Jimmy in the cockpit. Engineer Bob was brother to coxswain Fred. The radio spoke:

"Our Lassie has taken off all the crew." A minute or two later, "Longhope lifeboat no longer required."

Speed was eased and Fred took her gently back until there was light enough to see the way into Aith Hope.

There were other lifeboat calls, but it was that one off Dunnet Head which remained closest in my memory. Especially poignant, some years later, was news that the Longhope lifeboat had capsized in a storm with the loss of all members of the crew. Brave, brave men indeed.

To return to Orkney, it seems that in the winter the gales were more stimulating than depressing. In spite of the short hours of daylight, output in the yard actually increased as did my personal writing in the evenings. Many of these dark winter hours were devoted to my book "Deep Sea Sailing." Also largely written in Orkney evenings was "Challenge to Poseidon" which described adventures in small craft the world over. It included stories based on research in Orkney of special interest to me as some of my ancestors of a thousand years ago were Vikings based in Orkney, including Lotha the Earl of Orkney. Later Orcadian descendants from these Vikings visited America in small boats long before Columbus.

Winter was no season for walking, but I got around the whole county of Orkney giving evening lectures in the towns and villages, thereby meeting many more people.

Thus it was not the winter storms that proved a strain, but after them, at the time when in South there would be spring. The wind would persist without pause from the East, and with scarcely a tree on our island, whose buds would show promise of summer, everyone seemed depressed. We were told that in the Aberdeen hospital which took our longer-lasting cases, a special ward was usually opened at this time for what was named locally as Orcandensis Melancholia. That might be a layman's myth, but we had vivid proof of the effect. One night around 2.00am it was not a lifeboat call, but a bang on the front door and I got up to find a neighbour from five miles away in Hoy.

"I've bungled it" he said in a highly emotional state, and repeated it several times as I asked him to come in out of the cold wind.

"Bungled what?" I asked, and after a time he came out with the story that he had tried to commit suicide but missed. We took him in and, after I had searched him for weapons, we put him to bed. It was a day or two before we could arrange for him to fly south.

On another occasion it was the well respected parson who succumbed. He normally visited our island for a service about once a month and telephoned one day to ask if I would send a boat for the six mile trip across Scapa Flow. I was at the pier to greet him and it was a surprise when he insisted that all was finished as he no longer believed in God; the strain of that East wind had even been too much for him. Our doctor visited Hoy when the need arose, but had not been for some time, so I tried to phone him to suggest a visit. Getting no answer to several calls, I rang his neighbour who told me that the doctor was ill himself.

Among my men in the base and their families, depression was most apparent among 'foreigners', most of whom came from the Glasgow area. As a 'foreigner' myself, and in my third winter, I was feeling short of energy and somehow inadequate to deal with any emergency. So I rang my Admiral with a personal call, and wondered whether one of his staff could visit for a day or two.

"What is the problem", he asked, "Is it engineering, finance or what?",

"None of these, Sir. Its just that we would benefit from another face for a day or two."

"How long has the East wind been blowing?" he asked.

"Eleven days without a pause" I answered.

"Right" came the reply "Get the sheep off the airstrip and I'll fly up myself straight away."

What a man to have as my Admiral. He knew from experience in Orkney what the problem was, and acted promptly. Full of cheer he walked round the base speaking to everyone, man to man. The problem was solved, and soon after his plane took off, the weather gave up the struggle with a wind shift to the West. Daphne felt that perhaps the East wind was not the only cause, but also the bleakness of Lyness, with its grim oil tanks and treeless landscape. She managed to persuade the Forestry Commission to give us a thousand trees, mostly quick growing pines, hoping to give a splash of green to the desolate scene. There was no lack of volunteers to plant them around the base, but sadly, we heard a year or two later, the trees mostly found the climate too difficult. Did an East wind affect them too?

With summer came the first post-war visit of the whole Home Fleet to hold its regatta in Scapa Flow. Before that I was ordered to fly South for instructions from the Commander-in-Chief, Sir Michael Denny. Then back again, I had meetings with the Kirkwall Town Council, stressing that this would be an operational and not a courtesy visit. Obviously the town hoped that the sailors would be given leave to visit it, but the local police would need help.

So the Fleet came - the battleship "Vanguard", flying the flag of the Commander-in-Chief, then the cruiser "Jamaica" flying a Rear-Admiral's flag, two destroyer flotillas and five other ships. On board the fleet flagship were also the First Lord of the Admiralty and the Under Secretary of the Admiralty.

The weather proved perfect for both rowing and sailing regattas, the behaviour of the liberty men in Kirkwall was exemplary, while the base provided oil, fuel and anything else asked for. The Commander-in-Chief had previously inquired whether there was anything he could do for me, so I asked that the lifeboat could carry out an exercise with one of his ships at anchor, He answered that it would be his flagship and the Captain of "Vanguard" asked me what was required. Tactlessly I quoted the lifeboat name of the exercise which was "Rescue from unapproachable wreck". He laughed and asked if we could use another name for his very smart ship. However, when the time came, it was thoroughly realistic. As we approached her in the lifeboat there were figures at the forecastle waving clothes in distress; then closer to, we saw they had mock plaits of blonde hair and skirts - no doubt borrowed from the ship's concert party. We fired a rocket line over the ship and with the lifeboat lying well clear for the pretended gale seas, these four survivors were brought across in breeches buoys to the cheers of what seemed the rest of the ship's company, watching from further aft. A white flare signalled the exercise completed and then the lifeboat was invited to come alongside. Coxswain Fred Johnston was presented to the Admiral, while the rest of us crew were shown round the ship. After the Fleet had left, the formal report from the Commander-in-Chief mentioned how impressed he was with the good will towards his Fleet exhibited by the people of Orkney.

Following a lecture at a newly formed sailing club across the Pentland Firth at Scrabster, its Commodore challenged me, as Commodore of the Longhope Yacht Club, to a dinghy race across the

Firth. So many big ships had been sunk or wrecked in this Firth, with its exceptionally strong tidal stream, that this seemed absurd. However the challenger was a very lively young woman of twenty-four who was already well known in Scotland for show jumping, and apparently found her life as a farmer's wife needed further excitement. I felt that if I refused, as a prudent seaman should do, she would try to sail across the twenty-one miles on her own, at considerable risk. So I accepted the challenge under my conditions. These were that we should be single-handed, with no escort, and that both of us must agree on the day and time of the start. That would mean I could ensure we could only go in fine weather and neap tides.

Rosemary Vickers and her husband came across by ferry to stay with Daphne and I beforehand, so that she could get to know the coast our side. She also came out in my dinghy to practice rough weather and even capsize techniques. I reckoned that after all this she would appreciate the sense of keeping together. We sought advice from the ferry Captain and from Fred Johnston, while another authority's advice was simply "Make your will and say your prayers."

On getting to Scrabster I checked that Rosemary had fitted extra buoyancy tanks and a bigger rudder. Life-belts caused a problem as the one I recommended was a bright orange colour to show up well in the water; but this clashed with the red of her sails, and what young woman would wear clashing colours when there were many cameras around? Indeed next morning our start was on the front pages even of the national dailies.

The race was on, and the weather started excellent with ample wind to make good progress. Again, very favourably, it decreased as we approached the main tidal race off Brimms Ness. Even at neaps the tide was running at 5 knots so in the tidal race we both needed hard work with buckets to reduce the water that came in. Fog drifted across the Firth, but that cleared in time and we had only been racing some five hours. Once into the safe waters of Carrick Sound my bucket was needed again, but this time trailed over the stern to adjust speed so that the photos could show a dead heat. "Housewife Beats Killer Firth" read the Scottish Express front page, while the Daily Mail told of her courage. What fun for all, and for me it was about my finalé to life in Orkney.

During my time there one of the Admiralty's regular list of promotions to commander included my name, so I was confirmed in the rank for further jobs. Actually this surprised me as only one in three executive officers at this date gained promotion, and after injuries and illness I had very little experience of wartime service at sea, which the

Navy must surely expect of its officers. I wondered whether planning and leading the trans-Atlantic sailing ventures could have helped, but among letters of congratulations this was refuted by two very senior officers. One had been Second Sea Lord, mainly responsible for Personnel, and he wrote that when away from normal duties on special leave I could not be considered for promotion. Admiral Mountbatten mentioned the same point.

So my next job would also be as a Commander, and I was told it would be in Malta, so popular for families, to compensate for the deprivations (as most people considered them) of Scapa Flow.

The aircraft carrier Triumph was the largest ship to berth alongside Lyness Wharf during my time. But the Home Fleet, led by the battleship Vanguard, anchored in Scapa Flow.

CHAPTER FOURTEEN

Mediterranean Adventures 1954-1957

In contrast to wooden huts in the north of Scotland, our next home was a 17th. century stone fortress in the Mediterranean. Fort Ricasoli had been built to guard the entrance to Malta's Grand Harbour to the design of the Marquis of St Angelo. My appointment was as Commanding Officer *HMS Ricasoli*, then the Fleet training centre, besides a barracks for naval officers and sailors waiting to join their ships after flying out from Britain.

Entrance to Fort Ricasoli.

Of special interest to me was the Leadership School, where sailors were given training for higher responsibilities, and occasionally young officers were sent as well. Then came the Signal School, with advanced training for men already qualified in visual or radio signalling. The Cookery School dealt with men already qualified as cooks, but enabled them to improve their skills. Beside the fortress itself, on a stretch of the coast, were the small arms ranges for rifle, machine gun and pistol shooting. Then on the harbour side of the fort was the Fleet bathing centre, and also moorings for several boats.

Quite separate from my naval appointment was a warrant as Sea Scout Commissioner for Malta and Gozo. It was signed by General Laycock, Governor of Malta and Gozo, also by Lord Rowallen, who we knew personally as our elder daughter Rosamund lived with the Rowallan family in term time sharing a governess with their daughter during our last year in Orkney. Thus I had very high level backing for Maltese Sea Scout activities

It was November 1954 when we arrived in Malta with our two daughters, Rosamund and Errollyn. By then our two sons had moved on to public schools to suit each one; Peregrine was at Canford and Peter at Sherborne. Coming out to us for the holidays was easier and quicker than their previous journeys to Orkney, as planes flew regularly, direct from England. Even in the Christmas holidays the climate was milder than an Orkney summer and there were many friends of their age. In particular there was the Kennard family: John had been one of my closest friends since we first went to Dartmouth, and was also living in Malta with his daughters Joanna and Judith the same age as our boys, while his Caroline fitted well with our Errollyn, by then four years old. Indeed there were many children with interests similar to ours, with sailing and swimming coming high in the list.

On taking over command it was normal custom to drop a visiting card on the Commander-in-Chief, who was Admiral Mountbatten. A week or two later came an invitation to lunch at the Commander-in-Chief's house. Surpise was even greater when the Flag Lieutenant telephoned me with a brief on my fellow guests; they included a British Cabinet Minister, Mr Mintoff - the leader of the Maltese Labour party - and other distinguished names from Italy and France. There was certainly no one else of my less senior calibre.

On arrival, Mountbatten greeted me warmly and told me he had seated me next to his daughter Pamela, and added he hoped I would keep her amused. This was no chore as Pamela was a delightful young woman. Conforming with the Mountbatten custom, Pamela was well briefed and knew that I had two daughters and also of my interest in polo and sailing. Converstion was light-hearted and easy as she told me that her father was thoroughly naughty in diving far too deep in his new sport of underwater swimming, although he still enjoyed polo.

Thanking Lord Mountbatten for his hospitality, protocol put me at the end of the queue. He cut me short saying

"Thank you for coming. You know Pamela had a tough time with formal entertaining when her mother is away, so I felt she was due for some light relief, and you would be just right."

Sailing could be enjoyed all the year round, and I soon found myself Hon. Secretary of the local branch of the Royal Naval Sailing Association, which had many boats for the use of members. One of these was *Samuel Pepys*, the boat which I had twice raced across the Atlantic. So I introduced a programme of offshore races, starting the season in April with a course of some fifty miles, working up with races to Sicily, then in mid-season races of 250 miles, perhaps to Tunis. After the first season, some French, and occasional Italian, yachts entered.

The fort was fully exposed to strong easterly winds, known as gregale.

Of course there could be gales in the winter, especially those known in Spanish waters as 'levantes', or in Italian waters as 'gregales'. Around Malta these usually blew from the north-east, so in Fort Ricasoli we got a splendid view of the waves storming onto the breakwater leading out from the fort. They sometimes reflected back into the incoming waves to form a vertical face. One day in just such conditions

I was watching from the lookout position on the fort wall, when a destroyer came down the harbour with men still working on the forecastle; as she reached the entrance the wind and seas tended to push her off course, so she increased speed, but the men were still on deck.

A tall vertical-faced wave stood well above her stem, and as she went into it, the whole forecastle was under water. As it cleared I could see several men in the sea, and others still hanging over the side until the next wave took them in also. It was a desperate situation, so I rushed to order an emergency signal to all ships and then jumped aboard a boat lying at the fort pier to start picking up men in the water, followed by many other boats from the Fleet. Several were saved, but others lost.

This suggested to me the importance of dealing with emergencies in the Leadership course. Practice in taking charge was traditionally exercised by students giving set orders at squad drill. Within this framework we introduced emergency situations, which would teach students to act quickly to unexpected situations. For instance one of the squad would be briefed to slip as though he had broken his ankle; on another occasion smoke would come pouring out of a window nearby. These special situations were given the name 'Exercise Dynamite'.

The two senior leadership officers, Tom Cotton and Tom Baird, enthusiastically developed this exercise, with many ingenious tests. After each one, it was discussed in the classroom, with mistakes

Leadership exercise Dynamite.

analysed and learnt from. We also gradually developed night exercises to instil confidence, as well as exercising endurance, courage and initiative. Normally the groups embarked in small craft at sunset, then landed perhaps two hours later by dinghy on a rocky coastline unknown to them, assumed to be hostile-controlled in a state of cold war. They had to find an agent nearby who would direct them to other objectives. The officer directing the exercise could control the problems through radio to the agents. Then when the time came to withdraw, it had previously been arranged that a different member of each class should take charge of the boats returning to the one who had been in charge of embarking.

As the directing staff gained experience of the area, which included the Island of Gozo, they used great ingenuity to make these night exercises valuable and exciting. Once or twice, for instance, rescuing women came into it, and ample realism came when one of them was in real life an admiral's daughter. Each exercise would last all night, whatever the weather, and they certainly kept the training staff, as well as the candidates, alive to the practical realities of leadership in difficult conditions. Indeed as Commanding Officer I gained too, as I always took some part.

The Leadership Training in this imaginative form became popular with the ships which sent the men, and in time 220 men came from 30 different ships. Often we were told how much better certain Petty Officers had performed when back to their duties on board. Indeed one prize letter from a Divisional Officer wrote that one of his men, in spite of a good education, had tended to fade into the background with ship's work. However since the course he exuded enthusiasm and was well on the way to be recommended as an officer.

We had strong support from senior officers. The new Commander-in-Chief, Admiral Sir Guy Grantham, visited informally one day, and after watching an Exercise Dynamite, spoke to that class. Each of the other Admirals of the Mediterranean Fleet also visited and spoke informally.

Admiral Grantham suggested extending the leadership night exercises into recreational activities on similar lines. For this I formed a fleet committee, assisted by the Commander-in-Chief's deputy secretary Roger Fisher, besides certain officers with special experience, such as rock climbing, camping and under-water swimming. We called these activities Outward Bounding, and in time they spread throughout the whole Navy.

In a typical exercise a Fleet signal was sent in advance stating that it would start on Friday evening and was expected to finish at noon on

Monday. It would consist of a night landing from Motor Torpedo Boats, a night cross-country scramble, camping, rock climbing, under-water swimming, followed by sailing in cutters and whalers back to Grand Harbour. I was in charge of the exercise, with Roger Fisher as deputy, and we arranged six specialists on the directing staff. For that exercise we selected 14 teams from 25 which volunteered; team leaders ranged from Lieutenant-Commanders to Midshipmen. It was great fun, and all seemed to agree that the weekend promoted mutual understanding between officers and men, while every one of us learnt something new about leadership; but of course the purpose was mainly recreational.

One day while lecturing in the class room a real Dynamite situation arose when an emergency signal told of a major crash by a civil aircraft on Malta. I got there about as soon as any rescue party with part of my class rammed into my car and the rest in the cars of the two senior leadership officers.

For administrative purposes, especially when dealing with officers and men living in the fort while waiting for their ships, or from ships refitting, *Ricasoli* came under the Flag Officer Malta, Rear Admiral Brittain, who lived nearby. His daughter, Bunty was a contemporary of Rosamund's and they became friends. However the training aspects of my work came under the Flag Officer, Second-in-Command, while for a few days *Ricasoli* was flying the flag of Admiral Air, whose own flagstaff at the naval air base was being repaired.

Thus I saw a good deal of Admirals, and held them in high regard. Yet another one came our way, this time retired: Admiral Sir Lennox Goldsmith, whose repute as a yachtsman was well known to me. He lived aboard his small sailing yacht *Diotima* in the Mediterranean and spent two winters with us on a berth alongside Fort Ricasoli. Lady Goldsmith had retired from sailing and so arranged for young ladies to come out and help him on board. One winter he called at my office to ask for help because his regular medical check at the naval hospital advised that he might not live much longer. As a very fine seaman his reaction was to consider the consequences; among them was that, if he died in some isolated anchorage, it would be difficult for the accompanying girl to deal with the corpse. So while she was ashore shopping, he had rigged a simple tackle for hoisting the corpse out of the cabin, and invited me to come aboard the yacht to test it. Of course it was just right, but when I told Daphne she commented that the anxieties of a young woman in those circumstances would be eased if she had a cat. So the Admiral arranged that too. Indeed he did die on board in mid-summer with the yacht in a quiet Greek anchorage. The rig worked excellently, and the body was put in a taxi and driven to the British Embassy.

Many other cruising yachtsmen visited us, among them two adventurous girls, Penny Hughes and Sally Hinchcliffe, in their small open boat called *Crab*. Then there was Isobel and George Millar, the author, in their fine yacht *Amokura*.

Apart from sailing and swimming, riding was a popular family sport. Rosamund did quite well in her class for the Malta Horse Show, while before we left Errollyn had reached the younger class. My interest in riding led even to mounted duty for the combined services Queen's Birthday Parade. His Excellency the Governor, Sir Robert Laycock, represented the Queen, and he certainly would be mounted. This meant that the senior officer of each service must be mounted too, which was the reason that I was selected for the Navy as Second-in-Command of the Parade, with a Brigadier as Parade Commander.

Rosamund at the Malta Horse Show having reached the 12 year old class.

During the rehearsals it became clear that the Brigadier's horse disliked loud orders, and perhaps his rider too. Yet as the mounted officers had to be ahead of the parade, with a thousand and more men behind them, the orders had to be shouted really loud, so in one rehearsal he was thrown off. Thus he rearranged things and delightfully told the whole parade that for the real thing they should not take much notice of his orders. They all knew by then the formal sequence, and what mattered was the timing so all would act exactly together. Thus he had high up and well behind the Governor a sergeant with a flag on a pole. As the flag was slowly raised all should know what command was coming. Then as the flag was briskly swept down, all thousand and more would act as one.

All went well for the great occasion, watched by half the people of the Island. Then the Governor invited those mounted to have a drink with him, and knowing the Brigadier well, laughingly told him

"I was wondering if you fell off what sort of orders the Navy would give."

So I felt emboldened to say "Your daughter did very well at the Horse Show, Sir."

"Not bad" His Excellency answered, "But yours beat her."

It was the following year that international troubles began to rumble. So sport, and even parades, had to wait. The news told of trouble in the Middle East, but it was not clear to us how things stood until there came a clear directive that the Fleet must prepare for hostilities. Ships would need all their men and could not spare any for personal training, thus *Ricasoli* training had to cease, and the training staff was a reserve. The possibility of a landing operation gave special importance to the Amphibious Warfare Squadron, so at once Ken Alan-Williams, my senior leadership training officer, was sent to command *HMS Portcullis*, a Tank Landing Craft. Commanding this squadron was Commodore Robert Franks, a good friend of mine who had often given support to my fairly adventurous exercises. Thus I called on him and told him that there were no more training courses during the present situation, so I could probably be made available if there was anything I could do in his squadron. He commented that with so many newcomers what it needed was training, and straight away too. If this could be agreed by my immediate authority he would at once ask the Commander-in-Chief to have me appointed temporarily to his staff. It was a Sunday morning and I knew that Admiral Brittain would shortly be going to church, so rushed to intercept him to ask if I could hand over command of *Ricasoli*.

"I bet Robert Franks is after you. I knew he would be. Certainly I agree if you are satisfied that your First Lieutenant can cope temporarily." The Commander-in-Chief agreed the same day, so I started work straight away. Two days later came a formal Admiralty signal appointing me to *HMS Meon* temporarily for duty with the Amphibious Warfare Squadron, as Staff Officer Training.

The frigate *HMS Meon* was the Commodore's headquarters ship. Then there were eight large vessels classified as Landing Ships Tank,

Appointed Training Commander of Amphibious Warfare Squadron.

abbreviated to LST. Next nine rather smaller Landing Craft Tank, LCT. Then there was a Maintenance and Repair Craft, and finally a Motor Launch, whose asset was that it could get around fairly fast. All the landing vessels were designed to run aground and lower a ramp onto the beach so that tanks, vehicles and men could quickly get ashore.

"You will be training some very experienced officers commanding the ships, although others will not be used to them" the Commodore told me.

It was stimulating work ensuring that every ship had ample practice in loading and unloading tanks, besides so many other tasks. I was on board every one of them several times, keeping at it until each had overcome the many problems. One problem was manoeuvring the vessel into difficult positions, and just occasionally an officer seemed unable to master this; then the Commodore would come too, and that would probably lead to someone else being found to take command.

The vigorous enthusiasm of the Commodore, which stood out a mile at every one of the staff meetings, led to things going really well. So there came a time when he announced that his squadron would have a quiet weekend, and vessels which had passed the many training standards could come on a cruise with him to Sicily. He made good use of every hour at sea on the way there, exercising one thing after another. Yet once in the port of Syracuse there were restaurants for a quiet evening.

The sight of a smoking volcano in the distance seemed a challenge to the Commodore. He announced that after church next day he would like to climb Mount Etna and would welcome anyone to come too. A bus was arranged to take the volunteer officers and men some 20 miles to the mountain, where the climb began towards its 10,000 foot smoking summit. The Commodore was first to the top and as the next group staggered up beside him, we were truly concerned when he jumped down into the crater, bounding between pools of lava for the highest pile of sulphur. It was a relief when he returned to the crater's rim and we could begin our descent. Back at our bus a count showed one man missing. We searched for a time, but with no sign of him, and the Commodore committed to a meeting with local dignitaries, he put me in charge of a search party in conjunction with the local police. The Chief of Police politely expressed his regrets and handing me a form said

"Would you kindly fill in the details of the dead man."

I protested that I felt the man had merely lost his way - as a Royal Marine he would be quite able to sleep rough on a mountain side. But the Chief of Police explained gently that the mountain regularly claimed a life, and this must be another.

The search went on the next day. Perhaps Etna had won, I felt. Then came a radio message from the Commodore to Search Leader,

"Marine Page has returned. Squadron will sail as arranged. One ship will wait if search party is not back. Over."

Back in Malta the feeling of urgency seemed to have eased, and soon it became clear that the plans had been modified. While still with my task in the Squadron, my home when not at sea was still Fort Ricasoli and returning there I found that Daphne had a guest. He was Captain Ronald Brooke, who had been appointed to relieve Robert Franks when the situation allowed. Meantime he felt it best to make no contact with the Squadron until his time came.

Training continued, but at a less intensive pace. A couple of weeks later the operation seemed even less likely, so orders were given for reliefs waiting ashore to take over. Daphne was involved with the urgency for Ronald Brookes uniform to show a Commodore's gold stripes, so although we had breakfast together with Ronald as a Captain, I was surprised that for his formal arrival on board *Meon*, he was a Commodore and Robert formally introduced me to him as his senior staff officer.

At that stage none of us knew exactly where the landings were to take place, and certainly not when. We just knew that an operation might take place to free the Suez Canal, which until June that year had been the responsibility of the Anglo-French Suez Canal Company, with a garrison of British troops. Then Colonel Nasser was elected President of Egypt and promptly nationalised the Suez Canal Company. But in late October came the first of Israel's attacks on Egypt, and orders were given for Operation Musketeer to proceed, apparently with British and French assumption that Egypt's defence against Israel would leave our landings virtually unopposed.

When the order came for Operation Musketeer to go ahead, it came as a surprise. Several of the tanks were on the west coast of Malta in Military Bay so two Tank Landing Craft were sent to bring them back to Grand Harbour. I went in one to see half the tanks embarked in rather difficult weather conditions. Then we set off back, and the other vessel moved in. Over the radio I heard that she had lost two men overboard and was having difficulties. So I was put ashore in a boat on the east coast of Malta, and rushed over by taxi to Military Bay to find that the two men had been hauled out of the sea among some rocks; but *HMS Citadel* had lost her ramp in deep water and was quite unable to embark the group of tanks. An ex-Polish sergeant was in charge of them and he had been told that tanks must not use the roads. He could not disobey the order of his officer, who was in the other vessel, but he agreed that if I took charge of his tanks then he could obey me. This led to the unusual sight of a naval officer in oilskins and seaboots directing a group of tanks from the leading one, and it impressed a Maltese Policeman enough to hold up the traffic to let us by.

Thus there was no delay, and the squadron of 20 ships set out to sea led by Commodore Brooke in *HMS Meon*. Bringing up the rear was the Tank Landing Craft *Sallyport*, which was carrying no tanks, but had been converted into a headquarters ship with her tank deck full of radio vans, jeeps and ambulances, while her sides were decorated with whip aerials. At first she was my headquarters ship, but once established in Port Said, she would be the headquarters of another Commander on board, who would be deputy to the Port Naval Officer in Charge. The load included 14 passenger officers, so the Royal Engineer Colonel was the only one to have his own bunk; I had six feet of deck at the back of the bridge for sleep, so as to be immediately available.

Once clear of Malta I had been able to open the secret orders, so by then the 'Inner Cabinet' of the four naval and army officers on board with special responsibilities in the operation could work through a system of action to be taken for every situation we could think of on arrival in Port Said.

A few miles off the coast the armada split into three sections, advancing like the prongs of a trident, aimed at Port Said. To the right went the British assault ships led by *Meon* towards the beaches of Port Said; to the left went the French assault ships aiming for the beaches of Port Fouard. The centre prong was led by our *Sallyport* bound for the

H.M.S. Sallyport into the Suez Canal.

harbour of Port Said itself. We knew that British and French paratroops had already dropped and captured the vital bridge that gave an exit from Port Said along the west bank of the Suez Canal, and that they had captured the airfield to the west, besides the whole of Port Fouard, which meant that the French assault would be unopposed. Intelligence suggested that there were many block ships in Port Said, and the assault on its beaches would be opposed by an abundance of guns, plentiful mines and Russian built tanks, technically better than ours. However bombing by the Fleet Air Arm and the destroyers' guns drove off the defenders' gun crews.

I had been told to wait until mine sweepers cleared a passage into Port Said, but they were delayed elsewhere, and I assessed that the mines were on the beaches and not in the channel so when a signal came to me on the bridge "*Portcullis* sunk", and she was part of the assault on the beaches, I wondered if I should go ahead without waiting for the mine sweepers. A minute or so later a communicating officer clambered red-faced onto the bridge.

"There's no such signal as *Portcullis* sunk" he exploded, "some blinking idiot de-ciphered the signal wrong. It should be *Portcullis* retracted."

That was a relief, but rather illogically it encouraged me to go ahead. When the mine sweepers did arrive they soon lost their sweeps as there were more block ships than expected, mostly not visible below the surface. So I decided to land at once and open up some Tank Landing Ship berths by moving a bunch of fishing boats. This would also provide a good berth for the Deputy Port Officer, as the ship would then become his headquarters, while my task would be to represent my Commodore in the harbour.

Radio signals seemed a confusion of uncertainty. The first Landing Ship HMS *Ravager* had been called into the harbour to unload tanks, but was still waiting to be told where to berth. Ashore the Army told me that tanks were urgently needed, so finding more water than expected in the Fishing Harbour, I hailed her that this was free, but her Captain told me that he had two confusing radio signals, neither of which came through clearly. So I boarded her and piloted her to the berth, where she quickly started to unload tanks. The next Landing Ship HMS *Puncher* was circling round in the channel made very narrow by block ships; so I boarded her and, finding she also had confused signals, told her to ignore them and follow my verbal directions to a berth. Next I boarded the third Landing Ship and took her to a berth. By then some of the smaller Tank Landing Craft had come into the harbour from the beaches, so I directed them alongside their sister ship *Sallyport.*

The Port Captain arrived in his destroyer, so I called on him. He was rather annoyed with me and said

"Each ship is in a different berth from the one I ordered, so who is in charge of the harbour."

Not very tactfully I answered that as the representative of my Commodore, it seemed that I had been, as each ship had gone to the berth I ordered. He took it very well and ordered *Sallyport* to berth alongside him. He accepted that when inside the harbour, block ships made things look different, and also agreed that radio had not on this occasion been as effective as personal touch. He added that as from that moment he had borrowed me from my Commodore to work directly under him.

There was a good deal of shooting from ashore, but it was not clear where it was coming from, so Captain Briggs told me to take an assault craft up the harbour to investigate, as we felt there might be berths near Navy House. But I met with heavy machine gun fire, fortunately badly aimed. Later it was found that this was a major defence position, so it was as well that a boat manned by three Royal Marines and one Naval Officer had not attempted to capture it by personal touch.

After the Naval Landing Ships came War Office ones with civilian crews; piloting them made me realise how valuable had been the training of the Amphibious Warfare Squadron under Robert Franks. When I returned from piloting a Landing Ship into a brute of a berth amongst the wrecks, some totally submerged, Captain Briggs told me that this would be the last movement of the day, as it was getting dark. He was very complimentary and I gratefully accepted his offer of a drink, with the prospect of a good night's sleep, actually on a bunk.

The pleasant party in Captain Briggs' cabin was interrupted by an irate French officer, coming straight from the French General, who had noticed that every ship brought into the harbour was British. This was so, as the French landing had been entirely successful and there was no fighting on their side of the harbour. It was difficult, as all normal berths were full. Movement by night had been considered impractical and, added to that the two French Landing Ships had not answered any radio signals, and their positions outside were not known. Two ships would have to get out to leave berths, and after weeks of training I knew two Captains who would accept changes and difficulties, as it would be a real test to get out with no navigational lights and many submerged wrecks. So I boarded *HMS Reggio*, where Ian Stoop agreed to set off straight away. Aboard *HMS Suvla*, Robert Gilchrist would be able to move in an hour. Back to report to Captain Briggs to find there was still no radio answers from the French ships, and that probably hostilities would cease at midnight; so it was essential for the sake of honour that French ships would get in before then.

Then out to sea in the little assault craft, and wet it was too in the fresh wind which would have made the beach landings impracticable soon after they were completed. All ships were darkened, and it seemed that I hailed almost every ship at anchor before discovering where a French ship lay in the pitch darkness. I boarded her and made my way to the Captain's cabin with the hope that he would understand English better than I could speak French. He was naturally suspicious, but after a glass of wine eased up when I explained that he was required to enter the harbour for the honour of France. I mentioned that attempts had been made to call him by radio.

"Yes", he agreed, "But when we looked up the code letter of the sender, it was a spare group. Of course I will obey an order from a British Admiral, but I will not obey a spare group." Next came the point "How can I enter a strange harbour in the dark. I must have a pilot."

"I am the pilot" I answered, having been on the bridge when most of their vessels of the same type had entered harbour that day.

Several fires burning ashore showed me the way to the entrance. The best was the oil fuel depot at the head of the harbour, which had been fired before the attack began. There was also an ammunition dump which gave useful firework displays from time to time. In that flickering, eerie light the harbour looked even more cluttered than it had in daylight, and the wind was stronger. Our berth was immediately beyond a pair of black-painted Army Landing Ships and near to a wreck of which only a fragment broke surface. I could not see the light of the berthing party ashore, and the task was even more difficult as it seemed that the only choices were to touch the submerged wreck or to ram the wall ahead with the force that might jam the bow doors shut. It was then that Le Capitaine asked in faultless English

"Are we O.K., pilot?" I squirmed at the word pilot, which I had used so confidently out at sea.

"Splendid" seemed the essential answer, and perhaps it shocked that wreck to back away in astonishment. We must have missed it by only inches. We gave the black Army Landing Ship a glancing blow and cannoned into the berth without damage.

Back to Captain Briggs' congratulations, I said in despair that it was quite beyond me to get another ship safely into harbour in the dark. He pointed out that a thing once done should be easier in the repetition. The French staff officer, by then in a jocular mood, wrote out a hand message which he said would make things easier with Le Capitaine, who was asleep when I boarded his ship around 11 p.m. However, the hand message caused an outburst of orders and partly dressed officers arrived at the rush. This turned out to be because the French staff officer had put in a bit that there might be danger from E-boats in their present berth. When I pointed out the paragraph that said I was the harbour pilot, Le Capitaine led me straight to the bridge, still in his pyjamas.

Certainly it proved much easier to enter harbour the second time in the dark, and I had checked some leading marks by the fires' glow from my assault craft on the way out. Again Le Capitaine spoke excellent English, and with an easier berth this time, all went smoothly until the ship was pointing into her berth and scarcely half a length away. The wind was strong on the bow so I was content with a good speed of approach. But Le Capitaine was not and took over control with a stream of orders which overtook my understanding of French after I had taken in "Full astern", "Collision Stations." The ship lost way and drifted sideways towards a wall, then another staccato of orders resulted in three guns firing lines ashore and a searchlight lighting up the wall. In its light I saw the beachmaster's berthing party run for the shelter of a pile of rubbish and throw themselves flat. Our stern bumped hard against the wall and it was not a neat manoeuvre. Yet judged by the feelings of the moment it was an overwhelming success.

When my assault craft came alongside Le Capitaine himself climbed down the ladder to bid farewell.

"It is magnificent," he repeated several times, "We have arrived in Port Said two minutes before midnight. And our first salvo put to flight the British Army."

The bunk in Captain Brigg's ship was certainly comfortable that night, with the Cease Fire confirmed. After a leisurely breakfast I set off in the assault craft to report to my Commodore in *HMS Meon*. Ronald was in great form, as well he might be after the success of the assault.

"Your task is completed. Really well done" he said. "There's bound to be work waiting for you in *Ricasoli* so you can join *Puncher* which is leaving for Malta and England in half an hour's time. Love to Daphne."

All was well in *Ricasoli* but of course there were many matters awaiting my decision, although training class could not actually start until the Fleet returned. One letter was from the editor of Blackwood's Magazine asking for a personal story of the Suez campaign. I had often written articles under pseudonyms, but never about naval operations. Indeed I doubted whether, as a serving officer, it would be right to do so. However I happened to mention the subject to a knowledgeable friend on the Commander-in-Chief's staff and to my surprise he said that they were well aware of my pseudonyms and what I had written - mostly about sailing or natural history. He added that knowing my work he could see no objection to me writing personal experiences in the campaign.

"Should I let you see it before sending it off?" I asked.

"Certainly not. That would tend to make it official. There's no longer any censorship on the affair, so we'll wait until we read it in print. If you said anything you should not, we'll take you out on your own pistol range and shoot you."

In Parliament and the Press there was discussion about whether the British and French should have landed in Egypt, but that was the political side and far outside my knowledge.

In *Ricasoli* a significant event was the visit of the Archbishop of Malta, Mgr Gonzi, which meant a great deal to my Maltese personnel. Soon afterwards came Christmas when by tradition I stirred the sailors' Christmas pudding, while my First Lieutenant, Edwin Kite, poured in the rum. Christmas dinner was the ship's occasion when my family were invited to join in, as were any sailors' wives and children in Malta.

So all was peaceful compared with the intensity of the Suez campaign, but one day I was reminded of action when a storm of unusual intensity for Malta hit with winds up to 65 knots, wrecking a sizeable passenger ship on Gozo with loss of life. But that was very much the exception and our sons Peregrine and Peter managed ample dinghy sailing in their Christmas holidays, while Rosamund, also back from boarding school in England, enjoyed her riding.

In the New Year of 1957, training was back to full flow, as was Outward Bounding and other recreational activities. It was longer than the normal two and a half years before my relief arrived, but even that fitted in well with our family plans.

CHAPTER FIFTEEN

With a Donkey in Calabria 1957

On weekend sails to Syracuse from Malta, we met the British Vice-Consul, who had so intrigued Daphne with stories of Calabria in Southern Italy, that we planned to visit it when the time came to leave *Ricasoli*. As my successor was due in early June, this meant three of the children would be at boarding school for another two months while Errollyn, then seven, was a close friend of the Kennard family and could travel home with them, staying with them until we returned.

On one of our preliminary visits while I was still commanding *Ricasoli* we crossed from Sicily to Messina by ferry and then took a bus to a village high up in the Calabrian mountains, where there was a primitive inn. Daphne had taught herself some Italian, which was as well, as tourists were unknown in that village. We came across two men leading their mules back from the day's work, and astonished them by asking to hire the mules next day. The muleteers came too and taught us much, including great respect for the mules themselves. Mules live long and work throughout their lives, so are highly valued. Later we had confirmation that to buy a pair would cost more than the money we had to spare. Donkeys would be cheaper.

Thus plans went ahead. Captain Van Der Byl, a good friend who commanded the Mediterranean Submarine Squadron, kindly offered to take my car in his depot ship to Venice, where lived my cousin Nancy Guarniera, who had been born a Bruce. Some other friends had offered to sail us in their yacht to Syracuse, so when the time came to leave *Ricasoli*, what better way than to leave by sail, and it seemed that half Malta was there to wish us well.

At Syracuse we boarded a train which took us along the coast of Sicily and over the Strait of Messina to Calabria. This might seem the simplest section of our journey, but turned out to be far from that. Crossing the Strait we travelled on deck of the train ferry to enjoy the view, then approaching harbour we went below, but in the dark I got into the wrong train which, when the lights came on, proved to be the Rome Express. Realising my mistake I was just getting out, with my heavy walking shoes, when the bump of the ship as she hit her berth made me fall, not just to the deck, but through an inspection hatch leading down to the propeller shaft. It really was a bang and much later, on reaching England, I was to be told in hospital that the crash cracked two vertebrae in my neck.

So things were painful, especially in the bus leading up the mountains to the little village of San Eufemia d'Aspromonte, where we had tried our mule riding a couple of months earlier. This time we had our camping gear so had no need of the extremely simple inn. But I was quite unable to sleep and feeling feverish, lay in a cooling stream. By morning it was quite clear that I would not be able to ride a donkey, so we settled on buying just one to carry our camping gear. Our earlier mule riding visit meant that we had friends, who helped us to find a large brown stallion donkey, which we called Bruno. For the first time, loading was a lengthy process, as it was essential to dispose the load evenly on each side across the wooden pack saddle, stuffed with straw and secured by ancient leather straps and pieces of wire. Daphne felt that the bitless bridle was cruel, as a toothed metal bar behind his chin stuck its points in the flesh to control him. So she set to work to improve this, and we were delighted to find that he could still be controlled - that is until we met other donkeys. If the unknown donkey was a male, Bruno wanted to fight and, if female, to get closely acquainted. In either case, we would hang on either side of his braying, careering body and, in a cloud of dust, struggle to stop him. My damaged neck did not help.

Bruno carried all we owned for day after day along the woodland tracks of Calabria.

One day we had camped as usual near a farm and, while Daphne chatted with several local women, I was taken by the farmer to the hamlet's equivalent of a pub, where several men gathered. By then I was able to understand and speak a few simple words of Italian with a decidedly Calabrian brogue. Especially they spoke of the route to the north, as we were keeping off the roads and sticking to tracks more suited to a donkey.

They had just explained a way though the woods, which came to a sheer cliff with only one path zig-zagging down it to the plain below. Suddenly came silence as three more men came into the bar. My host signalled me not to speak. Soon afterwards he beckoned me to leave. "Banditi" he whispered, then when well away he told me that those three were part of a gang which normally worked on the road down by the coast, where tourists drove past in their cars.

We usually set off with the donkey soon after dawn, then rested in the heat of the day. The farmer was up early too and tried to persuade me not to leave until the bad men had gone away. I wanted him to explain this to Daphne, whose knowledge of Italian was so much better, but he was reluctant to mention bandits to women. I felt we had little to steal, except our donkey and he would easily be recognised. True I had a small number of lira hidden in my belt, but no more than would be a reasonable price for the experience of being held up by bandits. We certainly would not appear prosperous enough to be worth taking for ransom. Indeed many of the country folk we met assumed that we were on a religious pilgrimage.

So off we went to the woods, gently gaining height. The trees were well spread, so we had no need to keep on the track, but followed its direction. About an hour later I heard a lorry coming along that track and as it drew abreast, I saw quite clearly that it was manned by the three men I had been warned against. Our friends had told us that there was only one path down the cliff, with no way to avoid it. So there was nothing for it but to walk on. Then I saw the lorry stop. It seemed likely to be at the top of the cliff path, which I had been told no vehicle could use. Daphne had not seen the men at the inn, and had not been let into the warnings. So she thought I was pulling her leg when I said they were bandits. They got out of their lorry and stood spread, a few yards between each, commanding the path.

My mind went back to the leadership exercises in *Ricasoli* and surely this was as definite a Dynamite as any I had set for the students. It was Daphne who answered this one while I was still wondering what an unarmed pair like us should do.

"What a lovely day", she called out in Italian with a slight Calabrian lilt. Then called out again in a totally relaxed way, "You are out early for your work in the woods. We go slow with our old donkey."

Now it was the gang that faced a Dynamite situation. They knew exactly how to act if we tried to run away. They also had rifles ready should we be armed. Yet friendly talk in their own language was quite new to a hold-up and they did not know how to answer. We walked up to them quietly and Daphne paused to offer some compliment.

We continued on, down that almost vertical zig-zag path, and at first they could still stop us by rolling down a boulder, so it was a relief to me when we reached the level track. Yet when I saw a vehicle stopped on the track ahead, I thought it might have other members of the gang. But no - it was police who jumped out to greet us.

"There are bandits about, we have come to rescue you" one said in English. Brave of them perhaps, especially as one well knew that among Calabrian bandits at that time, a killed policeman counted for extra points in the scale of prestige.

I was in too much pain from my neck to write my diary, but Daphne's showed that each morning we got up when the sun rose, reloaded Bruno with the tent, sleeping bags, cooking pots, spaghetti, onions and a large bar of olive oil soap. We had no schedule as water and weariness governed our route and the distance we covered each day. We had to find water of two grades; clean spring water to drink from and river water to wash ourselves and our dusty clothes in. Sometimes we had to pant on in the fiery mid-day sun to find water in the next ravine, or the next again, hoping that there would also be shade, room to pitch our tent and some grass for Bruno. Excellent would be a farmyard, as they all proved hospitable, but very best of all was a valley where the wild water slid swiftly down, shattering on the rocks into roaring foam. There we stepped out of the dust into the trees and unloaded Bruno's sweating back. When he had quenched his thirst and was happy munching grass, we bathed and changed clothes, then brewed tea, before Daphne waded into the torrent with the bar of soap and our travel clothes, which dried in less than an hour in the brilliant sun.

Nightingales sang night and day, while golden orioles called to one another with notes of lucid purity. Along the river banks feathery rush flowers bowed up and down with the constant hosts of shimmering dragonflies of many varieties, like winged jewels, rubies, amethysts, ebony and translucent gold. Nor were they nervous, but allowed us to look into their magnificent rainbow eyes. When night fell, fireflies crept out and danced by the light of their own winking brightness.

Day after day we tramped northwards, taking turns to lead Bruno. We stopped in villages or hamlets to buy food and ask the way, usually surrounded by a crowd of questioning, friendly young Italians and all were eager to know who we were, and what on earth we were doing; then offering advice and help. Many of the villages had no water and no school, perhaps with just one shop. At the shop we bought spaghetti, rough heavy bread and a delicious cheese called provoloni. These, with olive oil, onions and an occasional egg, formed our diet for several weeks. At the start of the journey Daphne bought slices of a big sausage called montadella, which was the only meat available. But when we were told it was made from old mules and donkeys, we decided to eat no more of it.

Bruno's diet was even more important that ours, he bearing the heaviest load. Daphne worked out that he needed three pounds of barley or oats a day, beside as much hay as he could eat in the night's stop. If we could not buy hay, it was vital to find a grassy camping place. Every morning and night Daphne brushed Bruno's coat and anointed his hooves with grease. He became very attached to her and would bray with pleasure when we emerged from our tent at dawn.

The first step would be to remove the mosquito net we had pinned round Bruno the night before. We had bought the net for ourselves, and at several places village women warned us of mosquitoes near the river; but we never suffered from them, so the net went to Bruno who had trouble with horse flies. In most villages each house had DDT painted in big red letters on its face, indicating that it had been treated against malarial mosquitoes.

The first real town we came to was Cosenza and, with the slow pace dictated by my damaged neck, we decided to continue by train to Venice. Although a big town with many smart cars, we did not feel out of place leading the donkey as there were many others in the streets, but none as fine as Bruno. We continued to the edge of the town and found a farm, where the warm-hearted farmer showed keen interest in Bruno and offered 40,000 lira for him, which was about what we paid for him. However we decided that the mule and donkey market was worth seeing and we soon found some gypsies there who wanted him. But Bruno clearly did not like them, so although they offered 50,000 lira, we announced he was not for sale. The gypsies followed us back to the farm, mixing abuse with even higher bids. They turned on the farmer who had to buy them off with a bundle of hay. We were sure, by now, that he was the man to become Bruno's new owner, so settled for the sum he had originally offered.

My damaged neck made slow walking, so it was at Cosenza when we had to sell Bruno. Some gypsies bid high for him but we felt he would be happier with a warm-hearted farmer.

Next day we went by train to Venice, to be met by cousin Nancy, who had a lovely house there. So for a couple of days we combined the beauties of Venice with hospitality which seemed more luxurious than ever compared with life in Calabria. Then re-united with our car, kindly left there by Captain Van der Byl, we drove it back to England just in time for the return of our children for the summer holidays. For me, sadly, it was hospital again.

Word of my adventure training methods had reached the Second Sea Lord in the Admiralty so as a temporary expedient when out of hospital, I was appointed to Dartmouth College, where Captain James Munn had asked that I be lent for two weeks to introduce the system of adventure training. This was followed by a similar visit to *HMS Thunderer*, where Captain Walsham was in charge of training Engineer Officers; next to *HMS Ganges*, where my old friend Robert Franks was in charge of training Boy Sailors for the Navy. So these enthusiastic adventures developed in *Ricasoli* found favour at a high level. Laughingly, Lord Mountbatten wrote to me suggesting that perhaps training for Admirals should include a month on a donkey in Calabria.

Adventure Training for cadets at Royal Naval College Dartmouth.

CHAPTER SIXTEEN

Mid Pacific 1958

W hile in Malta a hint had come to me that my next appointment could be in command of a sloop or frigate; but a broken neck hardly fits in with a job at sea, and the doctors would not give me clearance. When the time came to be called to the Admiralty appointments department, I was surprised to be told that a very senior officer wanted to see me. He told me that there were difficult problems on Christmas Island, mentioning the words 'Mass insubordination', and he felt that I was suited to deal with this, the conditions of living being very tough. Originally the Services had been told to plan for just one H-bomb burst, but this was to develop into a series of tests. Thus, perhaps understandingly, some of the men had reacted adversely to the improvised living quarters, which they could only reasonably have been expected to tolerate for a short time. I was not to mention it to anyone until I had seen it for myself.

So I came to Christmas Island, just about on the equator in mid-Pacific. The appointment was to command *H.M.S. Resolution*, the naval shore base. The flat and largely barren island had been selected to test the H-bomb, likely to prove far more devastating than the atom bomb, which brought the war with Japan to an end. Essentially this was a matter for the scientists who had so recently invented the bomb. But it would need an R.A.F. aircraft to drop, and monitor, the test. Thus an airfield with all the necessary servicing had to be built by the Army, and a port operated by the Navy for unloading all that was needed.

On a 40 mile long flat island, part of which flooded in tropical rains, it was a big task to create a major airfield with all the equipment needed to operate several aircraft; then roads, stores and temporary living accommodation was also a task for the Army. The Navy needed to provide ships and equipment to operate a port through which so much had to be shipped, and to patrol the sea area. That all added up to several thousand men on, or depending upon, the island.

I was flown out to Honolulu in a Comet aircraft, which promised to be a fast trip; but it turned out not to be so due to contrary winds in the Atlantic, so we had to come down for fuel in Iceland. Much the same occurred in the Pacific, where half the passengers and all our luggage had to be left in San Francisco for the next flight.

On Christmas Island my first impressions were terrible. Everyone - except the hamlet of native Gilbertese in huts - lived in tents, many of which were leaking and standing in water. Flies competed with land crabs around the port. A queue of men lined up waiting for the Elsan lavatories. Many were bandaged by a sick berth attendant in his tented sick bay, which he ran single-handed, as the over-worked doctor from the main camp had not been able to visit for several days. At least I had a tent to myself, but was the only man in the port camp who did. There were some 100 Royal Naval personnel, 60 Royal Marines for the landing craft, 70 soldiers, who were mostly Royal Engineer stevedores, and 40 Fiji Royal Naval Volunteer Reserves. Then living in the hamlet beside us were 80 Gilbertese, with most of the men working for the port base.

My predecessor pointed out that as well as taking over from him, I would take on another job from the captain of a ship, then elsewhere. The Air-Vice Marshall was Task Force Commander, in signals called T.F.C, and under him were Commander Task Groups of each service, so I had become for operational signals C.T.G.1, and became responsible for a dozen ships in the area. Captain Weston would hold this responsibility when on Christmas Island, but was normally working in London and only came out for a bomb burst.

A day or two after taking over I was given a splendid lesson in the work of the port. The first cargo ship I handled was nearly unloaded while lying off the port and the army stevedores had done so well that I invited the Army Task Group Commander to fly over by helicopter to the port to congratulate the men. I wanted him to go out to the ship in a small landing craft, as used for the cargo, and it was rough enough to impress the Colonel, who impressed the men by climbing up the rope ladder with the ship rolling heavily. Of course he said all the right things to the men, so it seemed a splendid day and I felt confident that they would quickly complete the unloading that day.

At lunch in the camp the signalman on watch at the port rang with the urgent message that a landing craft coming through the narrow channel to the port was "Taking it terrible." So I rushed down to meet two loaded landing craft which had come in together, manned by their Royal Marine crews. Both coxswains were quite disturbed

"Right across the channel it broke, Sir" they said in unison, then one continued "Quite unsafe, Sir."

My senior Royal Marine Officer was away on an island relief elsewhere, and the Subaltern was out in the ship unloading. So I took the next landing craft out myself. Slow both engines through the narrows, then full ahead port, half astern starboard to swing her round

The narrow channel into the port was shallow and winding through reefs with coral heads. Ships had to anchor outside and unload with landing craft.

the Sandpit. It was only 30 yards across there with a five knot tidal stream at times. Then the channel doubled back after turning through 300 degrees, where the swell was coming in. Full ahead together and after 70 yards a 90 degree turn into the next transit marks. Still well inside the reefs, but there was white water all round as the swell hit the coral heads. Then came the Gauntlet, a deep water channel flanked by reefs, but with marker buoys. It looked quite innocuous among breakers either side, but the coxswain warned me that danger would come with extra large swell waves, perhaps every ten minutes. So I hovered near the inner end to watch, and soon the horizon began to mount up the hull of the nearest cargo ship. There was time to run slowly into the coming surf as the leading wave mounted higher and higher. It was a magnificent sight as it curled over and crashed on the Cochrane rock to starboard, then even more spectacular on the Semple reef to port. Yet still blue water in the channel centre gave the impression of safety. But that was only the leader. No. 2 and 3 waves were even bigger, and even in the channel centre they reached the critical gradient, seemed to hang for a moment, then the wave top crashed down over the trough, right across the channel.

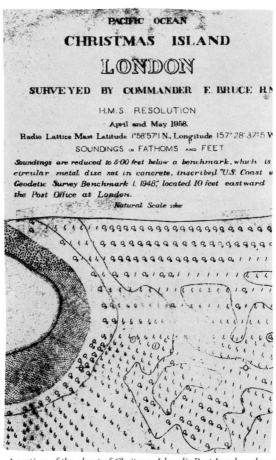

A section of the chart of Chritmas Island's Port London shows
the very narrow entrance for the landing craft bringing
ashore cargo, and often in open ocean seas.

Certainly it was not safe for a loaded landing craft, which coming
in would have to commit itself to the Gauntlet for six minutes when
against a strong ebb tide.

Hell! We could not complete the ship that day after all. But there
was still one more landing craft at the ship, with the stevedores to come
ashore. She had a very good coxswain and also the Royal Marine
subaltern. So when she was ready to start I went out in a craft half
loaded with 15 tons of cement to help stability and passed the incoming
craft just inside the entrance to the Gauntlet. It was then that I saw a

big leader wave coming in, so pointed into it at slow speed; but the other craft was running before it, so I yelled a warning at it, as she was in real danger of being pooped and could broach as well.

That Royal Marine coxswain was up to it; full astern on one engine, full ahead on the other, she spun on her heels. Then I lost sight of her behind the wave. It seemed a long time before she reappeared, right up in sky it looked. Crunch as she plunged, and I could almost feel the cement drums jolting in her hold. Those stevedores crouching amid the cargo below must have hated it. With her safely past danger, I stood on out to sea and boarded a newly arrived cargo ship and piloted her to a safe anchorage, as I was a pilot as well as all else. As she dropped her anchor the radio operator brought a signal to the bridge "Operational immediate C.T.G.1. urgently needed ashore."

With me was David, an Army Captain in charge of the stevedores, who had come out when some of his men were in danger. Already I knew him to be a fine seaman, an Olympic oarsman and 6' 7" tall. He stood in the wheel house looking aft, while I kept my eyes firmly ahead.

"Big one coming" said David quietly.

I promptly put the telegraphs to full ahead and full astern, and the craft easily turned round in time to meet those three big waves head on.

On the pontoon the Yeoman of Signals was jumping up and down.

"I'm afraid I sent that signal, Sir. It's necessary." I asked if he'd told the First Lieutenant.

"No Sir, he is not very well." There was a message from *Messina* saying it was essential that I speak to her Captain as soon as possible.

"You'll have to go to the ops room, up-country, Sir, to get through as she's 400 miles away. Landrover is all ready, as the lagoon road is flooded." It was a delight having a Petty Officer of that calibre.

Messina had been sent to supply an outstation on the Island of Malden, involving a difficult beach landing through the reef. She was commanded by Commander Williams who had done the job several times before, and he had on board my Captain of Marines as beachmaster. Together they made a really strong team.

The radio was not too good, but it was clear enough to show anxiety. One landing craft had been hoisted on board with its ramp torn off, another had been wrecked on the reef. An amphibious craft had picked up the crew, but had then broached and sunk. Twelve men had been washed over the reef and reached shore in unknown state.

"What shall I do?."

"I suggest you lie off for the night, and when the weather improves embark your men with the remaining boats."

"But I can't leave them." Clearly even such a fine seaman as he must have been severely shaken.

"Can't you get here by air to care for those on the beach?"

"There are problems in this weather" I answered, "so I'll send a plane with a doctor, if possible tomorrow morning."

A scrap of paper was pushed in front of my face and glancing round I saw it was from the Group Captain.

"O.K. for plane. Will take off at first light and arrive about 10.00am." I passed this on and added my congratulations that no lives had been lost in such deplorable conditions. I then ordered *Messina* to return to Christmas Island at his discretion.

Driving back to the port I felt inspired by the warm help of the Group Captain, and pondered whether I should not have offered to go myself to Malden. Yet there were several other ships in my area which might have problems, and my First Lieutenant was unwell. Roy Quinton, acting for him, had stayed up to greet me back to my tent with

"You've had a really tough day, Sir. Sleep well." I felt surrounded by really good people.

Next morning the surf was still bad so I kept the port closed until noon. Not only had I seen the day before what the entrance could be like, but a firm memory went back to my first day on the Island when I attended the funeral of one of the four men lost in a surf accident. I felt much better when around noon the RAF brought back from Malden those 12 men, none with serious injuries.

The morale of the Royal Marines manning the boats was excellent, as they had jobs requiring skill and courage. But among those sailors in the camp with hum-drum jobs morale was still poor. Certainly living conditions were difficult, and while soldiers and airmen could expect their turn on the island to last about six months, for the navy it was longer. About the only opportunity for them to relax was the canteen, but things often lacked much peace there. One problem was that the Royal Fleet Auxiliary men, from their ships anchored off the port, also had a drab time, so came ashore to the camp canteen with more pay than the equivalent ranks in the Navy and tended to drink a great deal. Their Masters would not allow them back on board when drunk and we had no spare beds ashore. What is more the Services' police had no authority over them as civilians, so fights were common in the overcrowded canteen.

The High Commissioner for the Western Pacific helped with one part of this by appointing me, with a beautiful Commission and many high sounding words, one of Her Majesty's Deputy Commissioners for the

HIGH COMMISSIONER

COMMISSION

By His Excellency, SIR JOHN GUTCH, Knight Commander of the Most Distinguished Order of Saint Michael and Saint George, Officer of the Most Excellent Order of the British Empire, Her Britannic Majesty's High Commissioner for the Western Pacific

TO COMMANDER ERROLL BRUCE, R.N.

GREETING

In the name and on behalf of Her Majesty the Queen and by virtue of the power and authority in me vested by Her Most Excellent Majesty under the provisions of sub-article (3) of Article 9 of the Pacific Order in Council, 1893, I do hereby by this my Commission under my hand and the official seal of Her Britannic Majesty's High Commissioner for the Western Pacific, appoint you, the said

COMMANDER ERROLL BRUCE, R.N.

to be one of Her Majesty's Deputy Commissioners for the Western Pacific for the particular purpose of implementing the Merchant Shipping Acts with jurisdiction confined to Christmas Island in the Gilbert and Ellice Islands Colony.

Given at Honiara in the British Solomon Islands Protectorate this /ᵗʰⁱʳᵗᵉᵉⁿᵗʰ day of April, 1958, in the seventh year of Her Majesty's Reign.

My formal appointment as one of Her Majesty's Deputy Commissioners for the West Pacific.

West Pacific, which would give me authority over civilians. More important in my mind was making life better for both men of the services and the men of the merchant navy playing a part in the operation.

It was Roy Quentin's idea to give up one of his wooden offices in the port itself. Then I asked for volunteers from the Royal Fleet Auxiliary ships to come ashore and make it into a canteen specially for them. Some of those who came were lags the Masters were delighted to see away, but one sailor proved a leader who made them all into a committee to agree what should be done, paint the place out and work like blazes to finish it. He became my adviser and suggested that a patrol would be helpful to maintain order.

"Marines might sound the obvious choice, as they are trained in unarmed combat, but they might be a challenge to a group of drunks. How about for the opening night, to set the pace, an Officer, a Stoker Petty Officer and a couple of seamen."

Roy agreed to take charge for the first night. He had arranged a rock and roll band from somewhere, then briefly told all what the rules were. So, with tact and firmness, he established a pattern, and from then on things went well with the port canteen, while the camp canteen was far less crowded.

Naturally it was interesting to hear the history of that merchant seaman who had proved a leader. "Disagreed with my father, I fear, Sir", he told me in an educated voice, "and was disinherited of the family place. Joined the navy and liked it, but had a serious slip, so left the country and went to sea." He'd put his heart into starting the canteen, and it gave him a real kick that his efforts had been appreciated.

Another outcome of the canteen operations was that I realised even more fully how effective Roy was as a leader. My First Lieutenant was far from at his best, and now I had a naval doctor who confirmed that these very trying conditions had taken a great deal out of him, and that for his health's sake he should be sent home. So I sent him without waiting for a relief and meantime made Roy my First Lieutenant, although appointing a Supply Branch Officer as Executive Officer was unusual in those days.

Things were moving towards the next H-bomb test, so the Task Force Commander, with many of the planning staff including Captain Guy Weston, arrived on the island. Extra aircraft landed and a couple of destroyers joined as well. On the day of the burst the 80 odd Gilbertese men, women and children from the village beside the port were embarked in a ship and taken well away from the island. Everyone else, except the Task Force Commander and a handful of his staff, gathered in the port.

The bomb would burst high up in the sky, nearly 50 miles from the port. However, the Valiant bomber flew right over our heads, which made some people anxious in case the bomb was dropped too soon. All were seated on the ground, backs to the bomb burst and with clenched fists pressed into the eyes to protect against the brilliant flash. The multitude was divided into pens, each having a pre-arranged leader, while above them on a raised platform I stood in overall command, as they had all come to my port. Some people could get panic-stricken at the vast strength of the burst, so among the pens were medical teams, each of which had a hypodermic syringe ready loaded with a drug which would instantly quieten a disturbed patient.

The explosion of an H bomb seen from nearly 50 miles off.

Away across the island, and very much nearer to the bomb burst, was the Task Force Commander, under a heavy concrete shelter, because he was close enough to need it. In his hand was a switch and by pressing that he could abort the explosion even if a bomb had been dropped. He was in radio contact with the pilot, Squadron Leader Bates, who with his Valiant crew would be the nearest humans to the burst; but as the bomb would have to drop several thousand feet before bursting and the plane was flying very fast, they would be at what scientists calculated would be a safe distance when it exploded.

So it came about exactly as planned. First the flash, then one of the most dramatic man-made explosions the world had even known.

Jubilation was intense and universal throughout the island and area, not only amongst those who had suffered so much discomfort and even danger on and around the island, but also among those who had invented the bomb and planned the operation at home. Special apparatus in widely spread aircraft, in ships patrolling the area, and in many shore posts on Christmas and other islands, recorded the radiation and many other scientific factors. These would be secret, but we were confident that it had been a successful bomb burst. The politically minded even forecast hopefully that it would be the end of all major wars.

There were parties all round, with much profit to the wine and spirit trade, but I had a party which surely had the most fun of all. It was aboard my name ship *Resolution*, a motor fishing vessel, whose working task was to check for radiation in fish but on non-working days could be used for my preferred recreation which was fishing for sport. For that party we gathered well before dawn; there was John Grandy, the Task Force Commander and his deputy, Air Marshal Sir Geoffrey Tuttle, the Deputy Chief of Air Staff, then a visitor from London, and finally my Royal Naval Volunteer Reserve Midshipman Halliwell. The midshipman made the breakfast of coffee and scrambled eggs, while Sir Geoffrey steered and I took the engine room. It was still dark when Sir Geoffrey sighted a dim light to seawards, which promptly disappeared.

"Intruder, no doubt", shouted Sir Geoffrey, "or a Russian sub. Can I turn towards?" I jumped on deck and sent the midshipman to the engine room.

"I'd like you to investigate, Erroll" said the Task Force Commander, who like the Deputy Chief of Air Staff was clearly hoping that we would have a dawn naval action.

"What about an enemy report?", suggested the Air Commodore. "After all we've only got the fishing rods and two gaffs." He was a keen fisherman and resented any deviation from the object, so he went to the lee side of the wheelhouse where I could hear him, but he thought the others could not. "We'll be late for those bloody tuna. Can't you stop this silly play with bows and arrows. There are aeroplanes these days, you know, Erroll" implored the Air Commodore.

"*Resolution*, pass a signal please" said the Task Force Commander, "Operational Immediate. Unknown craft ten miles west of the island. Scramble Shackleton earliest. Am proceeding to investigate by sea."

The Air Commodore had given up trying to fish, so was lookout with the only pair of binoculars. "Bloody something over there" he shouted suddenly.

"Please give your reports correctly, Sir" I objected, "You mean green nine-oh."

"All right then object green nine-oh, skipper - I mean Sir"

"Hard a-starboard, Sir" I ordered the Air Marshall at the wheel,

"Hard a starboard, Sir" he replied.

"I don't want to interfere with running your ship, Erroll", suggested the Task Force Commander, "but we all seemed to be Sir to everyone else; couldn't we drop that until the party is over?"

"It's a conning tower" spoke the lookout. I took the glasses from him and soon we were close enough to recognise a warship's boat out with a fishing expedition like ourselves

"Friendly, Sir", I reported to the Task Force Commander.

"Oh well, it was fun while it lasted, Erroll. Would you signal cancelling the aircraft scramble - operational immediate."

"We won't get any ruddy fish after that" complained Jack Roulston, and he was right.

However, Sir Geoffrey, who like John Grandy was an experienced yachtsman, got something he enjoyed even more when we reached the port entrance, as for once there was no swell. I invited him to steer the craft up the channel, which was marked by a series of buoys and four transit beacons. We just momentarily touched bottom at the 130 degree turn in the tide rip, then went on to berth alongside the wharf perfectly.

"A naval night action, and then this" said Sir Geoffrey, "Why it's the finest fishing expedition I've ever dreamt of."

"You're very honoured, Sir" suggested the Task Force Commander. "I've been out with Erroll half a dozen times, but he's never let me take his ship into the harbour."

The next visit to the port by the Task Force Commander was a formal inspection, which was conducted from a DUWK, an amphibious vehicle that was as happy afloat as ashore, and thus particularly suitable

Air Vice Marshal John Grandy R.A.F. gave an example of superb leadership, showing interest in the work of all those in his Task Force.

for moving between sailors, soldiers and airmen. Once more I was deeply impressed with John Grandy's technique, as he spoke to each man and left him feeling that his job was important, including those with less interesting tasks.

Next came our regatta, organised by a committee with the army and navy about equally represented and a Royal Marine in the chair. It would hardly have been recognised at Cowes or Henley, yet the signal and paymaster team organising the tote would have been at home on any race course. On seeing the programme, Guy Weston rang me saying that the regatta was dangerous and should be cancelled. But it was saved by the Deputy Task Force Commander saying that of course he would attend.

Certainly the regatta was unconventional by strict naval standards. It was designed to give as much fun as possible for everyone. Each type of boat had a different course, but all started and finished on the same line. Ten landing craft were lined up for a standing start, but 15 sailing dinghies were approaching their finish so the starter shouted "wait" to the landing craft. Yet with their engines running fast, some did not hear so shot off, while the rest waited, but the starter waved them on, and no-one even protested. There were races in every type of boat in the port, including native craft. Propulsion in different races was by power, rowing or sailing. The competitors were sailors, soldiers, airman and Gilbertese.

That evening Guy Weston gave a formal dinner party aboard the destroyer *Ulysses*, inviting top scientists and senior officers of the Services. It was near midnight when we guests got back ashore with the Task Force Commander steering my Motor Fishing Boat. We were met by my First Lieutenant, and John Grandy waited to listen when I anxiously asked whether there had been any troubles in the canteens as it was regatta night.

"Not really, Sir", answered Roy, "There were 400 men ashore, and at one time there seemed a bit of a bother as the New Zealanders, Fijians and Far East Station were ganging up against the rest. But I called in David", (the very tall stevedore Captain) "to help. So it never came to anything, Sir. Just a party." Christmas Island was indeed a practice ground for leadership training. Before long a relief First Lieutenant had arrived, so Roy could go back full time to his job as Supply Officer. He had just about saved my life, or at least my reputation in command, a dozen times when acting as Executive Officer.

When the top people had returned to England, I felt it was time to re-survey the harbour as our only chart came from a survey done by Captain Cook aboard another *Resolution* in 1778, before he was murdered by natives. My results were duly sent to the Hydrographer of the Navy, and in time a new chart was headed "Christmas Island, London. Surveyed by Commander E. Bruce RN *HMS Resolution*" Fortunately this surveyor was not murdered by the natives.

The next H-bomb test was not due for a couple of months, so when visiting the island of Fanning in *Narvik* I was delighted to receive a signal from the Deputy Task Force Commander, my fishing friend Jack Roulston, that he needed me as a naval adviser on a visit to Raratonga in the Cook Islands. Back in Christmas Island he told me that after so many months and trials, he felt that we and the Colonel were due for some relief. We went in a Shackleton, whose normal job was weather flying, so he said that after playing with rough weather in small boats I should see what real rough weather was like in a plane. We were together in the bomb aimer's position with a wide view, and we could also hear what was going on in the cockpit above us. Whenever a black cloud showed during that 1,400 mile flight, the pilot was sent into it, and quite an experience it was for a simple sailor.

After living on the flattest island possible, with nothing green bar the odd coconut leaf, the sight of Raratonga was startlingly glamorous, with its jagged peaks, then when closer was the lush colours of flowers, besides the feast of fruit. Yet our main curiosity was the Polynesians who lived there, no doubt very different from the Melanesians we had got to know.

On landing everything was very formal, with the reception committee in long trousers and ties. Then the three of us were borne off to the Residency in cars with crowns instead of number plates. It was New Zealand administered and our host, the High Commissioner, told us that after dinner he had invited the leading officials to meet us. It was still very formal as we saw their cars parked so that at the precise moment each could reach the door in order of precedence.

Then the fun started as the Air Commodore whispered to me "Keep close formation, Erroll" because many of the wives of the officials turned out to be devastatingly lovely Polynesians. There was also the local native Queen, a superb looking woman with white hair but still as straight as a guardsman, who told me about her visit to Buckingham Palace. She introduced me to a girl who was an absolute stunner, and stood well above her husky New Zealand husband. The party passed quickly and when this girl suggested that we went to her house, I remembered that our host had mentioned some arrangements afterwards, so I asked him.

"Oh, that's all right" he answered, "what I had in mind for you was just the lady you were talking to. The Air Commodore met Mary, as I hoped, and the two girls are close friends, so you will be keeping together. The Colonel is not quite acclimatised yet so I don't expect the white matron he is talking to will take him dancing. By the way, the doors are open all night."

What a party it proved to be, the Polynesian girls never stopped laughing and singing. They tried to persuade me to try the hula. "It is indecent the way you do it", I protested "Most suggestive and distinctly sexual."

"Not indecent" she answered "but perhaps the other things. You white people kiss before you make love, we hula and it suggests things perhaps."

"Well what would it suggest if you hula with me?" I asked. "Anything you like to think, Erroll," she replied.

"Even your seven year old daughter would know what I think when you look like that" I replied, "But you are teasing me as your husband is sitting over there drinking."

"That does not matter" she insisted. "To us in Raratonga jealousy is a sin."

"That might mean that you are not faithful to each other" I said. "Of course we are" she answered, bursting into peals of laughter, "We always make love with each other when the other wants to, and I will always love my husband. But it would be silly not to make love with other people you like as well."

Eventually I said that I could not hula with one girl alone, but with safety in numbers, I would not mind trying with two. Peals of laughter again, and soon a gaggle of girls gathered round saying "You must be strong if you want two girls at once."

Jack Roulston and I kept close formation when the time came to go home. At breakfast the next morning our host was thoroughly interesting about it all. His own wife was a New Zealander and away at the time. He said that most of the New Zealand officials there married local girls. He suggested that the Polynesian way of life was reasonable, and they were very happy. They brought up their children well and were usually free from jealousy. He said that when New Zealanders returned to their country taking Polynesian wives, all seemed to go well, as then both conformed to the customs of the country they were in. He pointed out that it was one thing in an island where tourists were almost unknown and outside visitors strictly controlled, but it might not be so virtuous in places where Polynesian customs tended to be commercialised, and sexual diseases spread.

That day, after the business the Air Commodore had come for, the various husbands looked after us, showing us around. At one place I was talking and holding hands with a group of seven year old children, when the doctor appeared.

"Do you know why these children are not in an ordinary school?"

"No" I answered. "Well, they are all lepers," he said.

"But I've been picking them up" I explained, rather shaken. He assured me that I would be O.K. He told me that it was not as bad as elephantiasis for which this was the worst island in the South Pacific, while T.B. was an even bigger menace.

That evening there was a moonlight bathing party. The girls greeted me with "Hello Daddy."

"Certainly I have several children at home, but why do you call me Daddy?"

"The only man we know, who let's us kiss him, but will not make love with us, is our Daddy."

"If he's Daddy, can I be uncle?" asked Jack.

"Oh yes, Uncles often make love with us."

The farewell the next day was an epic in itself. It seemed that the whole island had come along for the event, perhaps mainly because at that time planes only went to the island infrequently. We got out of the official car in front of a line, headed by the Judge. At once the Air Commodore noticed something wrong. From the corner of his mouth he whispered to me, "Three short in the crew muster. Keep talking Erroll, lay it on."

That was not too easy because the officials stood stiffly to attention, expecting the plane to take off at once. Some girls that we had met carried garlands of flowers, but one who had been to a boarding school in New Zealand told them that those actually wearing Her Majesty's uniform should not be decorated with flowers.

Then came a stir among the crowd as an old converted lorry came trundling along to stop beside the plane. Out jumped a bevy of Polynesian girls, followed by three very sad faced airmen, then two children and a dog. The atmosphere was tense and the crowd was loving the drama. The Air Commodore looked grim; the Judge looked judicial; the High Commissioner pretended not to notice, while the late coming crew members hid their faces.

The Polynesian leader of the lorry party took it all in with a glance, swept up to the Air Commodore to throw a garland of flowers round his neck saying "You will be kind to the boys" and of course the whole crowd cheered.

The flight back had no instructional weather deviations, and offered excellent conditions to record every detail of the visit in my diary, besides full letters to Daphne and my good friend Robert Franks. On arrival there was time only to give sincere thanks to Jack Roulston before he was told that he must leave next day for a conference in England. The Colonel would go with him as a War Office message told of his promotion and the need for him to get back at once.

For me Christmas Island was quieter than ever before. Most of the original problems had been solved. Sometimes attached ships visited Honolulu, a thousand miles away but our nearest shopping town. There, facilities were arranged by an American Admiral in charge of the base, who signalled that he would like to visit Christmas Island over some small matters. At the airfield I met him and was surprised by his greeting "Good to be back were I was born."

Surely his geography must be wrong, I thought, as the Island had been uninhabited until long after he was born. Later he explained that his father had been a US Navy Chaplain and was travelling with his wife in *SS Aeon*, when the ship was wrecked, as many others had been, on a stretch of the coast known as the Bay of Wrecks. His mother gave birth on the beach but it was many days before they were rescued. I knew that ship's name well as some dogs were said to descended from survivors from her. For many decades the pack had survived from what they could catch, but the arrival of the H-bomb men gave them an easier catch with the scraps from the port camp galley. Yet on Sundays the cooks rose late, so the dogs went back to their old habits. I only discovered this when a visiting chaplain came to take an early communion service in a tent. I was distracted by much barking in a lagoon nearby, and then saw that the younger dogs were swimming and wading to drive fish towards a neck of shallow water where the older dogs kept guard and snapped up the driven fish to throw them onto the bank.

Around this time news reached the Admiralty from the Headquarters of the International Geophysical Year on Fanning Island, that it was anxious about its observer on the Island of Jervis, some 200 miles from Christmas on the equator. I was told to go and investigate. So in *Narvik*, I set out at once taking a naval doctor, Surgeon Lieutenant David Reed with me. The Geophysical base told me that their observer was an American aged 50, nicknamed Otto the Hermit. This was because he had been living on Jervis alone for nearly a year; however more recently a Gilbertese couple had been sent to help look after him. It was believed that he had collapsed at his radio transmitter, and was probably very ill.

Approaching the island we saw a black skirt fluttering from the flag pole beneath the Stars and Stripes. From a calm sea the doctor and I landed in a ship's boat on a sandy beach. We were met by the Gilbertese couple who led us to a roofless hut where the doctor quickly confirmed that the man had been dead for several days.

Standing on a sand bank nearby I signalled in semaphore, telling of the death, then asking for a party with spades, and also a prayer book. Meanwhile, the doctor, helped by the Gilbertese, wrapped the corpse in a sail. The ship's bosun and his men came back in the boat and set about digging a grave beside the American ensign. When all was ready, we buried the body and I read a brief funeral service. After that I put on my cap, the only person there to have one or even a shirt, with the rest of the naval party wearing just shorts. Yet as I saluted they all came to attention in spirit as smartly as at a Cenotaph parade. The life of Otto Horung had been truly honoured.

Over the next few months there were further H-bomb bursts. It seemed to me, however, that none of them had quite the violence of that first one I experienced. That may have been an emotional judgement as hearing an H-bomb explode for the first time is quite staggering.

A grave was dug for Otto the Hermit and a brief funeral service to his honour.

By then I had more officers, the tents no longer leaked and morale all round was good. During a quiet few days the RAF kindly took me to Fiji for a visit as there were Fijians working in my port. It was not quite the hula dancing of Raratonga, but it was still most interesting, with fire dancers and much else besides.

It was coming to the end of my time on Christmas Island, and that year on the island had been truly valuable to me as a student of leadership. In all three Services there had been fine examples of leading at all levels, and the one who got the highest marks under my theories was appropriately the Task Force Commander, who had taken over when morale was generally very poor and even the expression 'mass insubordination' had been true. There had been many examples of the parade ground style of command proving inadequate on a desert island where we had a demanding task to achieve in extremely difficult conditions.

A letter from the appointments department of the Admiralty said that there had been a slight delay in finding the right officer to relieve me, but I had not been forgotten. Then, apparently, a question was asked in the House of Commons about the health of Service men on Christmas Island, in case they should be affected by radiation. In answering, the Minister stated that no-one was ever left out there for so much as a day more than a year. This had been so, yet those responsible suddenly realised that I might become an exception to embarrass the Minister. So an urgent signal came through that I was to be off the island by midnight on a certain date, and if my relief had not arrived I was to wait in Honolulu.

I probably served as long as anyone on that island of nuclear tests. Yet 35 years later, I can confirm that I have had no sign of radiation sickness, but many very interesting memories. I like to think that the discovery and proving of those devastating Hydrogen bombs have played a part in preventing another major war.

CHAPTER SEVENTEEN

Sea Cadets and Sailing 1959-1962

I arrived back home just too late for the children's Christmas holiday in Dorset, where the family had been staying with Daphne's mother in the delightful village of Nettlecombe. After a year on the equator and two and a half years in Mediterranean sunshine, a cold winter was a major change. Christmas Island duties had been also been demanding and had cumulatively taken a heavy toll on my physical state. The result on my return was a succession of colds, with a long bout of influenza leading to yet another stay in hospital. I was not too surprised when the verdict came from the Naval Office that I was quite unfit for an appointment at sea. It was ten years since I had served, other than temporarily, in England. The Admiralty Officer handling my appointment suggested, therefore, I had earned a job at home, to be with my wife and four children. He mentioned that I had done well in training jobs, so another such appointment would be appropriate. Thus

Sea Cadets trained lads with an interest in a naval career.As Southern area Commander I inspected and gave some instruction to 50 units

I was appointed to the staff of the Admiral Commanding Reserves, Rear Admiral Alastair Ewing, for duty with Sea Cadets.

Sea Cadet units all over Britain were important for training lads with an interest in a naval career. Half a dozen serving Commanders, each with another officer as assistant, were working on this, every pair caring for a regional area. Mine was to be the Southern Area, with some 50 units. The pair of us, with a secretary, needed a centrally located office, so Daphne and I decided to make our home Lymington, where we bought a house big enough to house an office as well.

Each unit required a formal inspection once a year, and that was one of my tasks. They all had special events, such as a regatta or sports, when help was welcome - I usually assisted with any boating activities. It was an interesting job, dealing with people young and old. The Sea Cadet unit officers gave voluntary service to lead the boys, similar to the Boy Scout movement, except that Sea Cadets joined aiming for a sea career. There was far less pressure than in any of my previous jobs. Sea Scout activities could normally begin only after school hours, so apart from taking the boys sailing in holidays, there was ample scope for me to go ocean

Adlard Coles, with whom I often went ocean racing as navigator.

racing. I often went as navigator with some friend who owned a yacht; usually Adlard Coles. Later other owners, new to ocean racing, invited me to skipper their yachts on an amateur basis.

As a committee member of the Royal Naval Sailing Association, I got to know many members, including a number who had previously served in the Royal Navy and thus had the right to retain their membership of this club. Among these was a Hampshire farmer, Tommy Steele, who had been successful in many ocean races, and had done well in the Bermuda race of 1958. He was keen to enter the next one of the series, and the Trans-Atlantic race following it. Yet when the time approached he was unable to get away from his farm, so very generously offered his yacht *Belmore* to the R.N.S.A. One of the Flag Officers suggested that having skippered a yacht in two previous Bermuda and Trans-Atlantic races, I should skipper her. However, I felt that an absence of three months would interfere too much with my Sea Cadet duties. Admiral Ewing, as my boss, did not agree, and said firmly that if I was selected, any success would do more for the Navy and the Sea Cadets than my normal work, for which he could easily find a member of his staff on a temporary basis.

That year, 1960, the Trans-Atlantic race was to be much longer, going north of Scotland to finish in Sweden. I had recovered from the strain of Christmas Island, but was approaching my fiftieth year. Thus I had some doubts whether I was the right person for a really intensive series of races, representing my country as well as the RNSA. When the subject came up for discussion by the club's main committee, although I was chairman of the ocean racing sub-main committee, I was asked to leave the room. When called back, Admiral Sir Manley Power, the Commodore, stated that I had been elected unanimously as skipper for the venture. Soon afterwards a formal letter from the Secretary of the Admiralty stated that Their Lordships had approved special leave for me as skipper of the yacht *Belmore*. Thus again, the decision was made for me.

The Commodore gave a clear directive, stating that my objects were to win the Bermuda and Trans-Atlantic races, using every endeavour within the rules, guided by standards of seasmanship and sportsmanship traditionally set by the R.N.S.A. To achieve this his directive gave me wide discretion, with the right to enter the waters of any country necessary. The crew was selected by the Association from a large number of volunteers. Mate was Captain George Wheatley, an instructor at the Royal Marine Infantry Training Centre. Particularly vital as navigator and tactician was Lieutenant Peter Pafford, of the submarine service; then came Petty Officer Roy Mullender of the Navy's air arm, and Lieutenant

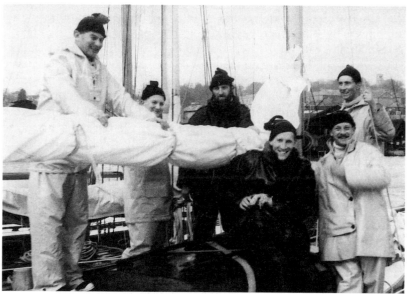

Crew selected by the Royal Naval Sailing Association to race yacht Belmore lent by Tommy Steele for the Bermuda and Trans-Atlantic races 1960. Each contributed a portion of his naval pay towards the cost of this club entry.

Tim Sex, serving in destroyers. Each of the crew was not only an amateur but also a partner, contributing to the cost according to his naval pay.

Once more the Royal Mail Line generously agreed that we should sign on as deck hands, and no charge would be made for the yacht's carriage to Bermuda. Time allowed us to sail the yacht round from Portsmouth to the London docks. The Thames River gave excellent sailing practice as the yacht had no auxiliary engine. The Director of Naval Information was delighted that press photos of the yacht sailing under Tower Bridge had been widely used, which would benefit naval recruiting.

As with *Samuel Pepys*, I made the 600 mile voyage from Bermuda to Long Island Sound in America. This was an important part of training, mainly as it passed through an area where gales were likely at that date. The Bermuda airport misunderstood my question about gale chances, saying the matter was secret. But there happened to be an American warship in Bermuda, so I asked her Captain if he could get a special forecast towards finding a gale, mentioning that the airport said it was secret. He looked down at *Belmore's* 36 foot length and said "Of course the gales should be secret if you are going in something that small." However the report he gave us proved sound, and sure enough an excellent gale made rendezvous with us and gave us such good practice that I felt we had not only got a really good boat for the purpose, but an extremely strong crew. Winning the Bermuda race seemed a possibility if a gale hit the fleet during the race. Sadly enough I had not yet seen all the effects. The next day Peter Pafford had to be relieved from watch in real pain; he was our amateur medical man, so it was left to me to select the pain killer. We encountered fog when approaching America, which offered good exercise in navigation, but Peter was our navigator and it was his persisting pain that made our quick arrival so vital. Thus I had to take on as navigator as well as skipper and coach.

On arrival at Newport it was particularly suitable that we were met in a boat by two submarine officers because Peter was a submarine man, and felt happy in their charge as they took him to the hospital ashore. The verdict on his health came only 4 days before the start of the race; he was quite unfit to sail. There were many young Americans waiting at Newport for such a chance to sail in the famous Bermuda race, but clearly the RNSA would expect a crew of its members. Even at such short notice we had to try to replace Peter. The crew voted for a Petty Officer we had met sailing in a sister yacht of *Belmore*. It would need a miracle to get him on board in time, but our Commodore had practice in miracles, and Petty Officer Barry Barrett arrived from England just before the start of the race.

By then I had decided that, without Peter, I must take over the navigation myself. My absence from full time skipper would put a good deal more pressure on the mates of watches. Several American skippers had given us help in various ways, especially Carleton Mitchell, whose yacht *Finisterre* was the favourite, having won the last Bermuda race. With such a splendid crew it was a superb race for us, and the weather seemed to fit in with all my hopes. The weakest link in the chain however, was me - the intense strain of navigation and skipper proved too much. By the third day I badly needed a few hours of sleep. Even then we were fortunate; the next gale, upon which my plans depended, waited until I woke, and served us truly well.

Then it was flat out for the rest of the race, with no question of sleep for navigator, tactician or skipper. The weather was quiet as we approached Bermuda and those last five miles at slow pace were the toughest of all. As we came up beside the British warship marking the finish came the cry, "*Finisterre* beat you by 25 minutes by our calculations." "What about the others?" shouted George, manning the tiller as the finishing gun fired. "There aren't any others", came the reply, "You are second in the fleet. Congratulations." Their calculations proved correct, and it was confirmed that *Belmore* was second in the fleet of 135 fine ocean racers. It was the first time in the history of the Bermuda race that any yacht foreign to the United States had come so close to winning.

With a week to prepare for the Trans-Atlantic race to Sweden, there was much to be done, but mostly for us to recover full energy. I was staying ashore at Government House. I heard full details of the Governor of Bermuda, General Gasgoigne's, experiences in the race; he had been racing in a large yacht which was dismasted in the gale that had proved so helpful to us. Lady Gasgoigne helped me to rest and advised me to get medical advice, which was that I should take things easy. George and some of the others also felt low following the excitement of doing so well, and faced with the thoughts of greater trials in the much longer race ahead. It was a woman's touch that helped them too. Mr and Mrs Robins had travelled to Bermuda from England in the same ship as we had, so met *Belmore* on arrival from the race, took off some of the soaked and exhausted crew, then sorted our jagged nerves in that delightful feminine way that makes men feel it is all their own work.

In the quiet of Government House I was working with slide rule and note book on how best to cope in the coming race. Certainly I had done this twice before in *Samuel Pepys*, but this time the race to Sweden was much longer, the competition was stronger, and also I was eight years older. We had few of the electronic aids to navigation which became commonplace a few years later. Thus ocean navigation depended mainly upon the hand sextant, measuring the angle above the horizon of sun, moon or stars; best of all stars to give several position lines. Yet that meant the navigator had to be able to see both the stars and the horizon, which was possible for just a few minutes at dusk or dawn if the sky was clear. Dawn was best because then the hour or so of calculations could be done by daylight, while dusk would need electric lights for the calculations, and with no engine to generate electricity, our batteries were limited. I worked out the degree of accuracy required at different times, so that with less need for sights, I could spend time on the skipper's task of being awake and dressed throughout the hours of darkness. I considered giving Tim Sex intensive practice on my sextant, but it was a really old instrument, which had navigated my uncle Captain Scott on his expedition to the South Pole, so it was best for me to keep up this task. In any case Tim had another vital task in the preparations, organising the provisions for five weeks to feed six hungry men. We had no refrigeration, so this was no mean feat. As Peter was no longer with us, Tim was also responsible for seeing that we had the vital medical equipment necessary, and that we knew how to use it in case of accident.

So the day for the start came, and with the mainsail already hoisted and everything ready to set off, a call came that I was wanted on the telephone. "Unless its something to do with the race, tell them to put it through to Sweden in five weeks", I answered rather impatiently. Told that it was urgent, I clambered ashore with pad and pencil expecting an alteration to the race instructions. In fact it was a message from Buckingham Palace: "To yacht *Belmore*. Many congratulations on your fine performance. Philip." That certainly affected the next race, as it gave our morale a splendid boost.

With the starting gun, things settled down really well on board, and very soon no other vessel was in sight. Later came several days of cloud and rain to let me out from sights, but it did not matter as there was no land or shore for thousands of miles in the direction we were going. Yet it did not help scratches to heal and Tim looked quite unwell with an arm badly swollen, in spite of a hot lint poultice. When he came below from his watch he said "I'd like to try penicillin, if anyone feels he could handle a needle." "As an engineer I'm used to spanners" said Mike, and so Peter had to make do with this. Anyway, however roughly the medicine was administered, it worked and by next morning the swelling was under control.

The area of maximum gale frequency lived up to my prayers, and was recorded by the Met. Office as a severe gale.

190

By mid-July we had reached the area of maximum gale frequency. We were about 400 miles short of Rockall and some 500 miles beyond Iceland, so well placed to fight a gale in the wastes of the North Atlantic, with no hazards of land. It was just where my race plan hoped for a gale, which I felt we were better trained to deal with than any of our rivals. Not only did it come then but, unusually for the month and position, it was recorded by the Met. Office as a severe gale, so gave us a magnificent display of angry seas. It was so stimulating that I climbed half way up the mast to glory in it. Actually it was more like climbing along, more than up the mast, the yacht being heeled well over, even with only a tiny scrap of sail set.

As soon as I sensed easing of the gale, it was time to keep up the offensive by setting just a few more feet of canvas; but something jammed so most of my crew gathered round the mast, safety harnesses hooked on, taking violent steps to free the halyard round a split winch barrel. This was real fighting. It was an hour or so before the rain ceased, and the whistle in the rigging changed its tune. At 2.30am Mike and Tim took over the watch on deck. They proved to be a very strong pair in rough weather. There was no chance of a sextant sight so I remained on deck too.

Gradually conditions improved and I was confident that we would have done well from the gale compared with our class rivals, but the bigger yachts might be well ahead of the gale which was tracking to the northwards. The sight of two trawlers hove-to showed that we were approaching Rockall Bank, with wind and sea easing. Without knowing it at the time, we had also passed fairly close to overtake a larger rival, which still had no sails set, so would not have shown up well in the darkness.

The excitement of the gale at its height was over, yet still in brisk winds, some of the crew felt they had been through enough, so suggested heaving-to for a rest; but not Mike and Tim, who stayed on watch well beyond their time. Indeed I worried that Mike might drive himself too far, so when he came below I put a sleeping pill in his tea. He woke from it indignant at the treatment, but certainly rested.

Next night the sky was clear, so I was preparing for a dawn sextant sight when a cry came from Tim, "There's a ruddy great something on the lee bow, about five miles away. Must be land." Sighting land put us 12 miles ahead of our estimated position, having had no sextant sights for several days. We only found out later that the large class yachts were approaching the finish and saw nothing of our main gale. In Belmore we felt much better after that landfall, following 2,780 miles of open ocean with some really hard racing. There was still 600 miles to go, but

I prayed for good visibility and enough wind for the strong tidal waters around Orkney, scene of so many wrecks. My prayers were answered, but I was not so pleased that the winds remained light for the North Sea crossing, assuming that the bigger yachts would have already finished. Actually this was a bonus, as those waters of Denmark and Sweden were not known to me, so it would have been dubious seamanship to make the approach as exhausted as I had been at the finish of my last two Trans-Atlantic races.

"You are the winners", was the hail as we passed the finishing line at the Skaw Light Vessel. In fact we were the winners of our class; overall winner was the fine American yacht *Figaro* of a bigger class. It was a royal prize-giving in Sweden, and the King of Norway, who had competed in a shorter race, commented to me that for the Atlantic race it was appropriate that the biggest cup went to the smallest yacht.

We had a quiet sail back across the North Sea, and on 5th August we crept into the Solent to be escorted by many ships into Portsmouth. Clearly the Royal Navy was pleased. Among those waiting ashore was Tommy Steele, whose generosity in lending *Belmore* to the RNSA had given the six of us such an intriguing adventure. He had asked for her back by 15th August, so there were ten days to ensure everything was in good order. Then from play back to our work, and for me it was the Sea Cadets, with much of interest waiting to be done.

Chief of Naval Information borrowed Belmore from Tommy Steele for the Naval stand at the London Boat Show with her Trans-Atlantic crew and some Sea Cadets.

A month or so later, Admiral Alastair Ewing told me light-heartedly that our exploit had achieved more press coverage than the rest of the Navy put together, so the Chief of Naval Information wanted to borrow my services to organise the naval stand at the Boat Show. I was to report to him straight away for a meeting to discuss this. The purpose of the naval stand was to encourage interest in a naval career among adventurous young people. We quickly agreed that a fine yacht manned by suitable people would do this best, and that if her owner would agree Belmore would be particularly suitable. Once more Tommy Steele was generous for the sake of the Royal Navy. As for those to man the stand I was told that I should arrange it, so I got some of her Trans-Atlantic crew and a few Sea Cadets. This certainly worked, as the very full coverage of the Boat Show in the National and Provincial papers gave more attention to that stand than to any other. It also unexpectedly changed my life.

An Admiral I had once served under, sought me out on the stand and introduced me to a director of a publishing company, who invited us both to lunch. There he told me that he was looking for a new editor of a yachting magazine and felt that I might be the right person. The Navy had provided me with an excellent career, even if limited by injuries and illness. I was then about 50 and could expect a few more years before retiring. I certainly did not expect any promotion, with my medical history. My new acquaintance said that I should give careful consideration to a job which could go on longer and give me more scope. He had read books and articles by me, and said I was well known in yachting circles. I could have a fairly free hand as editor of the yachting magazine. My Admiral friend flattered my talents and asked what he would pay me to come. A figure was named and the Admiral said "That's what a Rear-Admiral gets now, - not bad." I discussed this proposition with Daphne, as her life was involved as much as mine. There was no further prospect of a naval command at sea, yet the likelihood of a shore appointment overseas, perhaps separating me from my family again for a longish time. Assured that the job was mine if I wanted it, I formally told my Admiral that I wished to resign, and this was handed on to the Admiralty, which at that time was faced with having to make reductions of officers at my rank.

Thus ended 35 years of naval career, since joining Dartmouth College. I got no further than middle rank, but had enjoyed a wide variety of experiences. Certainly I could not claim that any talents achieved had gone unnoticed by those on high, as shown by the personal letters I still have from five First Sea Lords and many other very senior officers.

Unfortunately top medical officers knew me well too. Once over a glass of beer in a yacht club bar, a former Medical Director General of the Navy explained with an athletic simile, "Your trouble is that you try to keep up a 100 yard sprint through the equivalent of a Marathon race, so flog your unfortunate body." Certainly the Navy treated me fairly, and I trust it got a reasonable return.

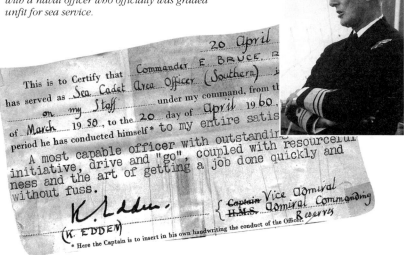

Vice Admiral Sir Kaye Edden seemed satisfied with a naval officer who officially was graded unfit for sea service.

CHAPTER EIGHTEEN

Magazine Editor 1962-1967

It was February 1962 that in the City of London I found my way to Temple Press, a company which printed and published a group of magazines. There I met Frank Snoxell, who for several years had been editor of *Motor Boat*, which had a monthly circulation of some 20,000 copies. He was the only main yachting magazine editor I did not know, and I felt he might not be too happy to be relived by someone more associated with sails than with motors. I was quite wrong. It was soon clear that it was he who had suggested my name to his Board. He agreed that with a new editor known as an ocean racing yachtsman, a member of the Royal Yachting Association Council and author of various yachting books, it would be sound to re-name the journal *Motor Boat and Yachting*. Frank Snoxell remained as adviser for a time, and was particularly valuable to me with his knowledge of the boat industry; for instance he introduced me to the Ship and Boatbuilders National Federation, a trade group which represented the industry. I was already in touch with yachtsmen through the Royal Yachting Association, and as chairman of its increased scope committee introduced power boating to its activities, after which I was elected a member of the RYA Powerboating Committee.

The new title and increased scope of the magazine quickly helped circulation, and there were signs from the sport and industry that more frequent publication would be welcome. So the next stage was to publish fortnightly. Although the number of staff was increased, I still enjoyed a good proportion of the actual reporting.

When I was working in London for the Admiralty years before we made our family home in the suburbs at Holmwood. However for this job, often with late hours, Daphne and I decided that it would be better to live in London and, with memories of her art college in Chelsea, we found a pleasant house close to the River Thames. By then Peregrine was in the Army, Peter in the Royal Navy, Rosamund was working in London and shortly to marry in Chelsea Old Church. Brackens in Lymington remained our main home, and we often returned there for weekends, while Daphne remained there for the school holidays of our younger daughter Errollyn.

A yacht of my own would tend to limit activities, but I was fortunate enough to sail often in other people's boats Thus a challenge for the America's cup was due, and several yachtsmen were interested. One was Lord Craigmyle, who bought a 12-metre yacht as a testing vessel towards perhaps building a new one to challenge. *Norsaga* was also intended for crew training, so I was invited for this. Five 12-metre yachts were racing in Britain with the plan to select one from them for the challenge in America the following year. Over the 10 days of 'Cowes week', these five raced daily. On the first day Eric Maxwell's *Sceptre* won sailed by Prince Philip, and from then on Peter Scott sailed her to six wins. Bobbie Lowein, who had raced against me in a Trans-Atlantic race, shared the helm of *Norsaga* with me, and we gained a couple of wins. Yet it was quite clear that *Sceptre*, with Peter Scott at the helm, should be the challenger, and indeed she was.

Then followed the Fastnet offshore race, in which Harold Rapp invited me to skipper his *Rapparee*, when a hundred yachts faced a severe gale near the Fastnet rock itself. We got round the course, but not among the prize winners. I was also skippering the same yacht against hundreds of competitors in the Round the Isle of Wight race, and indeed was able to enjoy a good deal of sailing, which put me in a strong position to report the events in the magazine.

Powerboat racing was new to me at first, but offered much interest, especially getting to know the people involved. Sport is a matter of competition between people, so whatever the technicalities of sail or power, it is the people who matter most. Indeed the book I wrote of that thrilling Trans-Atlantic venture in *Belmore* was titled "When the Crew Matter Most", and I reckoned we did.

Cruising afloat is as popular as racing, and this covers inland waters, such as the Norfolk Broads and the canals and rivers. So I gave full cover in the magazine towards these waters, perhaps as much as the open ocean epics, which were more favoured by the other yachting journals.

The London Boat Show required all the staff for reporting, and answering questions on our own stand. There were other boat shows in Britain, Holland, Germany, France and Italy, and I usually visited each one of them, with an occasional visit to the New York Boat Show. Perhaps I was most interested in meeting people, so for reports upon boats I normally depended on those with knowledge of design and construction.

All in all a yachting magazine editor could have a very busy and interesting time. My satisfaction was improved further seeing the magazine sales increasing well. Based in London one was readily available to sit on committees. Thus the Board of Trade appointed me to one on yacht safety and another on training; the British Standards Institute appointed me chairman of a 24 man committee. There was also the Royal Yachting Association, of which I was Vice-Chairman of the General Purposes and Powerboat committees, chairman of the Increased Scope committee, and a member of the Training Committee also, Publications, besides the Finance and Administration committees. In Europe I was appointed as a delegate to the Union of International Motor Boating and was still a member of the Royal Naval Sailing Association committee and various other club committees. The International Publishing Company, which owned my magazine and many others, decided that yachting as a sport interested many of those in the company, so instructed me to form what we called the I.P.C. Yacht Club, with the company chairman as Commodore, while I was elected Rear-Commodore. Certainly I was in close touch with the human aspect of the sport.

Back from committees to sport itself, the Royal Ocean Racing Club started a competition between national teams of three yachts for the Admiral's Cup. It involved competing in the Fastnet and some other races. An American friend, Bill Snaith, had contacted me to say he wanted to come, but felt he should have someone experienced in those waters as navigator. So I agreed to sail in his *Figaro* as part of the American team. That was 1963 and the Fastnet race had a record number of starters; some were dismasted and the smaller class had some tough weather, although our conditions for the biggest class were about average. Certainly we in *Figaro* were delighted to be the winners of her class of 35 yachts. As a result, Bill Snaith invited me to navigate his *Figaro* in each of the next two Admiral's Cup series. In the 1965 Fastnet, with another record entry, we won second place in our class, then in 1967 it was the same again.

In another big race I reported for my magazine from an American craft. She was *Bolero* sailing in a Trans-Atlantic race from Newport to Plymouth, and as a very big yacht it seemed likely to involve only a couple of weeks absence from my office. I had accepted the invitation of Sally Langmuir, the owner, to navigate, and this was my fourth race across the Atlantic, but it drove me to the opinion that for such courses small yachts were safer. The wind had moderated after a blow which split our mainsail, and I was on deck glued to my sextant when something parted, so the main boom give me a real bang on the head. I came to in my bunk with a nasty headache, but much worse was that, when next I took out the sextant, a sight was impossible due to double vision. It happened that none others of the large crew could take a

Bolero's large crew would have needed much training to win a Trans-Atlantic race but had a moderate passage.

sight. Fortunately the weather remained friendly, so we found the way and made quite a good time to the finish. Indeed we got there first to the owner's delight, although not in the prize list on handicap. But I was unable to join her celebration, as my skull had been cracked, so hospital treatment was needed.

An important part of the editor's function is to get the best contributors, and I was fortunate to know great sailors who were also good writers. Among these were Francis Chichester, who I had met as a boy, but began to see more of after he won the first solo trans-Atlantic race. This was in 1960, the year I won the fully-manned race in *Belmore*. Thus we had many discussions when he was preparing his *Gypsy Moth IV* to sail single-handed round the world. Indeed I sailed with him down the English Channel before he set off from Plymouth, and sometimes we had contact by radio after that.

Coming back off the Spanish coast he told me by radio his annoyance to be woken by a reporter who had actually boarded his yacht in the open ocean without permission. I stressed to him how much interest his voyage was creating, and as an example told him that a television network had offered to pay me a substantial sum to go out in a small ship and report live his approach to the English Channel. "Did you accept?" he asked and I answered that seemed hardly the thing as we were friends. "Well, please accept, and between us we'll see that the other TV network, whose man boarded me, does not benefit." So I found myself in a Dutch coaster somewhere off Ushant when we sighted *Gypsy Moth IV* sailing over a very quiet sea. He agreed on the radio that I should come over in a rubber dinghy to lie nearby for a talk, but not, of course, to board his yacht. An R.A.F. plane flew over, so his position would be known, and Francis was concerned that he might be disturbed by "press hooligans" in the night. So he told me that once it was dark he would make a big alteration of course to avoid disturbance. Finally he assured me that he was well up with his report for my magazine. We saw a British warship approaching, so Francis asked me to let it know his plan. I went aboard her from the dinghy to find that I knew her Captain, who had been sent out to escort *Gypsy Moth IV*. This relieved me of the escort job, so back in the coaster we could put through the interview for ITV news.

Next morning was his final day, so many craft came up to cheer. Most impressive was a great aircraft carrier, whose company of perhaps a thousand men lined her flight deck to give formal three cheers. There was a big reception at Plymouth but Francis, with Sheila Chichester beside him, had time to speak to me. From Sydney he had asked me to sail with him, Sheila and their son Giles, on the trip to London, but he had to tell me that this must be postponed; indeed it was obvious that he was in a great deal of pain.

A week or two beforehand Commander Parmiter, Harbourmaster of the Port of London, had given me a practice run over the course of the Thames River, as *Gypsy Moth* would need to be precise in her time of arrival at Greenwich Pier. I visited Francis more than once in the naval hospital at Plymouth, and at one stage his doctor said he would only be fit enough to join the yacht at *Tilbury*. Francis would have none of that, insisting that I would be in charge of the yacht, with him a passenger down below. Indeed that is how we started off, and when the Press questioned the arrangement, he said that I was Sailing Master, which was about it, as he was on deck for the departure from Plymouth but I was handling the vessel.

It was not to be the quiet family cruise we had expected, but instead a ceremonial parade much of the way. I paused for a night in Newhaven, but had to shift berth in the Cresta Marina, as the size of the crowd threatened to capsize the pontoons. However the sea was doing Francis more good than the hospital, and he was happy to be on deck to wave back, but really tired after doing it. The weather continued perfect for us, so I anchored for a quiet night under North Foreland. The plan arranged with the Port of London Harbourmaster was to

Aboard Gypsy Moth IV it was a quiet family cruise with Sheila, Giles and Francis Chichester, besides me as Sailing Master, so long as we remained at sea, but a ceremonial parade in every harbour and a royal ceremony on reaching Greenwich Palace for the knighting.

rendezvous at No 1 Sea Reach buoy at 09.00, so when I told Francis he instructed me "Let's be exact." Yet before that critical moment the Harbourmaster approached in his official barge *Nore* and indicated that he was all ready to go ahead. Thus I passed the buoy two minutes early; so when Francis came on deck precisely on time, he was far from pleased at such slapdash navigation, and told me to complete the washing up while Giles steered for the next 15 minutes.

Again the weather favoured us and a light easterly breeze took us well up the Thames with an armada of craft joining the procession to Gravesend. There the Harbourmaster asked me to sail with him and take a tow for the safety of shipping. Then arrived an official looking craft and a member of the Royal Household came on board. "It's a lovely day," he told me, "so there's to be a change in plans." It had been arranged that after berthing at the pier of Greenwich Palace, the

Chichesters would go to the Admiral's quarters for a quiet ceremony of the knighting. Indeed Sheila had sent her suitable clothes there, convenient for changing while Francis smartened up. However Sir John told me that the knighting ceremony was to be in front of the public, television and all, as Sir Francis came ashore. I told him about the preparations to which he replied, "It is Her Majesty's wish that Sir Francis should be honoured as he comes ashore from his yacht at the end of his historic voyage, and what more suitable than that Lady Chichester should also be dressed for sailing as she comes ashore."

He went below to speak with the family, and I heard some fairly strong feelings expressed about clothes. Francis mentioned that he was not well, and how embarrassing it would be for the Queen if he fainted in front of her. "Commander Bruce will give you a sip of brandy beforehand," he instructed, but Francis protested that he would not breathe brandy at the Queen. At Greenwich Palace Pier there could be no more slapdash navigation, so after slipping the tow we came alongside to split second timing. So did her Majesty in her beautiful car, accompanied by His Royal Highness the Duke of Edinburgh. Francis was led to a position in front of a dais, while Sheila, Giles and I were beckoned to stand with Prince Philip in a supporting quartet. It was Sir Francis Drake's sword that Her Majesty used for the knighting.

The ceremony over, every item as precise as the Royal Household always makes such affairs, Sir Francis invited the Royal couple to visit *Gypsy Moth*, and he told me to dig out the bottle of champagne that had sailed round the world with him. When I struggled to open it, Prince Philip, who knew me quite well, relaxed the atmosphere by warning me "Look out, Erroll, you will squirt champagne at Her Majesty", and he duly earned a wifely reprimand. That great occasion over, I took the yacht off from Greenwich Palace Pier, then under Tower Bridge to berth on Tower Pier, where Sir Francis was welcomed by the Lord Major of London as a formal ending of a Londoner's voyage. Could ever a journalist been better placed for reporting such events as I'd seen that day?

Soon after I became Editor of my magazine, the Royal Naval Sailing Association in association with Whitbread, founded the Round the World Race, and I was made a member of the organising committee. With my new profession to assimilate I could not take a very major part with this; however its success led to another race round the world four years later, and by 1977 I could do much more. Indeed one of my voluntary tasks was assisting our Commodore, Rear-Admiral Otto Steiner, to receive the 15 competitors at Auckland, and then start them off again for their leg round Cape Horn. It also gave me the opportunity to cruise for a few days in New Zealand waters, followed by a visit to Australia. This race proved another success and I had been asked to write a book as the official account. His Royal Highness the Duke of Edinburgh, in a foreword to my book, wrote that it made clear that if people went into the race for adventure they certainly got it. His Excellency the Governor General of New Zealand, Sir Keith Holyoake, also wrote a message for the book telling of the stirring tales of adventure at sea he had heard from the competitors.

Another thoroughly interesting task on behalf of my magazine involved a series of visits afloat in lifeboats throughout Britain. The Royal National Lifeboat Institution had published records to show that in 1966 nearly half the calls for its rescue craft were from yachts, dinghies, small boats and other types of pleasure craft. Captain Wyndham-Quin, then Chairman of the R.N.L.I., agreed that the Institution would inform me in which areas the calls for help had been greatest, and then let me go out in those lifeboats to hear, actually on the water, the positions and conditions in which they had given rescue services. Obviously arrangements for each visit had to be made well in

Actually afloat, sometimes in rough seas, proved the best background for the coxswains of 18 R.N.L.I. lifeboats to describe to me how small craft had needed rescue in their area around Britain.

advance, so we had to accept whatever weather there was that day. Thus some of the outings were in typical lifeboat weather and others chanced to be quiet. Cape Clear at the south-west corner of Ireland was one where craft navigating round from the south to Bantry Bay would be fully exposed to Atlantic seas with plenty of rocks and shoals. Coxswain Jim Fitzgerald told that many of his calls were from local craft; the largest number of yachts came to the area with the Fastnet race, "But they had been pre-tested on their way here." For the Mull of Galloway there was the Kirkudbright lifeboat, where Coxswain George Davidson B.E.M. explained the dangers of the strong tides. Obviously there had been many rescue calls in the English Channel, as so many yachts sailed there. I was also invited out in lifeboats on the Yorkshire coast, in Welsh waters and the Wash. After launches in no less than 18 lifeboats, the overriding impression was respect for the courage and skill of these R.N.L.I. crews.

There was always much to be done in the office, but 1967 was a real treat for someone who enjoyed the practical side of sailing. With the Admiral's Cup series, Sir Francis Chichester's arrival, a recent visit to Corsica, a few days in the Bahamas, besides New York, the six hour motor boat race in Paris, then competing as navigator in the Cowes-Torquay Offshore Powerboat Race, it had been a lively year. I was surprised when the company's Managing Director walked into my office. He congratulated me on the excellent performance of the magazine then, shutting the door, said that the time had come for me to move to higher responsibilities.

Naturally I was flattered. Yet further consideration over the next day or two suggested that this would inevitably mean management with very little time for getting out afloat. If I was considered fit for such work, then it would be better to start my own company, based on the coast. So the next meeting with my Managing Director was in his office, when I tendered my resignation, coupled with a recommendation that John Liley should succeed me as editor. By then the magazine had become part of the International Publishing Company, whose chairman Hugh Cudlipp arranged that I should remain a part-time consultant concerned with founding a new international magazine. This was a help until I got established in a new career.

CHAPTER NINETEEN

Nautical Publishing 1967-1983

There were other reasons why I resigned. The main one was family. Our youngest daughter Chloe was two years old, and we had little doubt that it would suit her best to live in the country. We had an excellent house in Lymington, which would suit us both as a family home and a base to start a business venture. Indeed Daphne had already moved there so, with a large number of absences travelling for the magazine, I had moved to my club in London, hoping to get home in Lymington most weekends. By then I had written several books, and thus developed an interest in book publishing. Also I was in contact with many people whose knowledge or experiences would justify a book. Some years before that Adlard Coles had told me that there was a job with him if I wanted it; but I was intrigued by the idea of starting my own business. Yet Adlard was a very good friend, and as his was the name of the leading book publisher in that field, I did not want to set up in opposition without first discussing it with him.

Chloe, on the right, with three of our grandchildren, Tabitha, Polly and Ben in the garden made one reason to change my work from London to Lymington, following a life of adventures the world over.

At our meeting in his Bursledon home he warmly supported my idea and, to my surprise, said he would like to join me, although it would mean him moving to Lymington. I had not realised that he had sold his company, so was Editorial Director under new management. We agreed at once to a partnership which he suggested that we call Bruce and Coles. However our solicitor said that he had sold his name as well as his company, so instead we settled on the name Nautical Publishing Company. On Adlard's resignation from his old company, his place as Editorial Director was taken by Richard Creagh-Osborne, a friend of us both.

The new partnership was formally established in October 1967, the day after resignation from my previous company became effective. It was a great benefit to have Adlard as a partner; he was well known as an author and yachtsman, who had already built up another successful publishing business, and he was a chartered accountant. Twelve years older than me, he told me that at 65 he reckoned he was good for at least another 3 years. of work. Perhaps my asset was knowing so many people in the sport, management and industry of boating, both sail and power. Indeed the first book we formally accepted was my "Who's Who in Yachting." Several other books were accepted the same day, two of them by well known authors. We decided that our strength lay in finding authors, besides editing and production. We would not take on staff for selling to the Book Trade, and two London publishers approached us for this. An agreement was signed with George Harrap and Co., but we kept the rights for selling to the Marine Trade, such as chandlers, besides direct selling to individuals. I was determined to keep foreign rights, although Adlard had not handled these in his former company.

An early breakthrough came with the single-handed sail round the world by Alec Rose, a greengrocer and former market gardener. Although so soon after Francis Chichester's great voyage, this one appealed to a wide public, as it was sailed by what was heralded as a simple man with no previous major achievements. Unlike Sir Francis's string of excellent books on various subjects, Sir Alec, (he was also knighted) had never before written for publication. Yet we were determined that he not only had a really good story, but could write it himself.

And write it he did, largely sitting under the apple tree in the garden of Adlard Cole's house, free from disturbance throughout the week. Then he returned to his shop and home for the weekends. It proved an excellent story, well told, but Adlard felt there was more to develop the theme so added a second part to the book written by half a dozen

Sir Alec Rose was an early breakthrough with several editions in different languages.

known authors. With Alec Rose's story simply written and Adlard Coles' skill in presenting it, that book became a real success, not only with several of our own editions or impressions, but also we sold foreign rights to six other countries, which led the way to foreign rights sales for many of our books which followed. Indeed five years later we sold publishing rights to one of our books in 13 different countries.

Nautical Publishing Company got going much quicker than either of us expected. After one year Adlard sent me a note stating that by then we had more books in hand than had his very well established publishing company when he left it. Living beside the sea it was reasonable for me to own a boat of my own, so I bought a 28 foot overall length Twister class sloop, which Daphne and I named *Dayspring*, bringing back the name of the old converted trawler which had been our family home nearly 30 years earlier. This easily handled yacht was intended mostly for the use of our five children, of which all except Chloe were adults. Time was a big factor for me, so I began to develop the habit of a short sail before breakfast to steady me for the intensity of a day's work.

The pressure was eased to some extent when Richard Creagh-Osborne, who had taken over from Adlard Coles as Editorial Director of Adlard Coles Ltd. left that firm and joined us at Nautical. He had written several successful books, had three times been in British Olympic teams, and was a very live wire. While Adlard and I were mostly concerned with ocean racing and yacht cruising, Richard was a world authority on dinghy racing. About then we ceased to trade as a partnership and became a Limited Company, with each of the three directors holding equal shares. Richard Creagh-Osborne was also a director of another company, which sold specialised boat equipment and also books. By then I too was involved elsewhere as Founder Chairman of Sea Sailors Ltd. This had been started as the Lymington Seamanship and Navigation Centre by Philip Harley and Captain James Crawford R. N, who took students out in their two yachts, normally for a week's training cruise. They also gave instructional courses in the centre. When the time came to establish it as a limited company, they invited me to join as Company Chairman. In its early days I was sometimes called upon to help teaching afloat and once, in an emergency, shot off to take over one of their yachts in Weymouth, owing to some domestic emergency. That certainly showed me that the instructors earned their pay, as these mature students were a long way behind the standard of the Sea Cadets I had been instructing afloat.

Voluntary work for the Royal Yachting Association also increased as I became Deputy Chairman of the Council, as well as the previous responsibilities in various of its committees. Then came pressure to start a R.Y.A. magazine, and with past experience of this field it was difficult for me to argue against becoming honorary founder editor, when pressed to do so. Prince Philip sent a letter from Buckingham Palace to use as an introduction to the magazine and after a year a permanent editor was found.

By 1970 things were going well with Nautical Publishing; it was our third year and in it we published 13 books, every one of which was to make a profit. "Winning" by John Oakley was a best seller with seven foreign book rights sold. Another book, also brought in by Richard Creagh-Osborne, was "Elvstrom Speaks" by the Danish world champion sailor Paul Elvstrom. Certainly we had developed much faster than expected, and Adlard found the strain heavy, so it was perfectly reasonable for him to ease down. We mutually agreed that the best way would be for him to hand over his directorship, but remain a consultant. One of the books he had handled the previous year was "Ocean Racing and Offshore Yachts", and Adlard got to know well its author, Peter Johnson, who had made his mark in small ocean racers and also writing in yachting journals. So Adlard suggested that Peter Johnson take over from him as a director.

The work load had been heavy for me also: as Chairman I had undertaken much of the general management, as well as handling more than half the books we published. So practical sailing, except for early morning local outings, had to take a low priority. However by 1971, with things becoming less hectic, it seemed reasonable to take part in the races for the Admiral's Cup series, sailing as navigator in Shorty Trimingham's *Wizard* of the Bermuda team.

An extraordinary story came to light with the news that a man and his wife had been picked up in the Pacific Ocean after nearly four months adrift in their life raft. I knew Maurice Bailey, as he had worked at Camelot Press, which had printed some of our books. So I cabled to Hawaii congratulations on their survival, with the offer to publish a book. Maurice said later that half a dozen publishers had also made contact, but knowing me personally decided them to come to us. They had started to write their story on board the rescue ship, and Marilyn had kept a diary in the life raft, besides Maurice's log book. On flying back to England they came to stay with Daphne and I in our home near Lymington, and made writing the book their full time occupation. Maurice's work had involved dealing with book production, which was a help even if neither of them had previously written for publication. It was fun for Daphne and I, as each of the couple wrote their accounts in separate rooms, then in the evening we all discussed the progress together. Birds and fishes were a big part of their life adrift, so my cousin, Sir Peter Scott, gave advice on this aspect as he was familiar with the marine life of the Galapagos area, where they had been adrift. He also wrote a foreword to the book.

They had actually been adrift for 119 days after their yacht had been sunk by a whale. However the initial news reports had named the adventure "117 Days Adrift", due to misreading Marilyn's diary; so they kept this as the title of their book to avoid any suggestion of exaggeration. The book was an enormous success, with foreign book rights taken up in 13 countries, besides film and radio rights. Much of the money came in quickly and this, coupled with the success of "My Lively Lady" by Sir Alec Rose, was a very great help to a company which had set off with very little capital.

It was pleasing that several well known authors came to us and often became family friends. Thus Bill Tilman, the famous mountaineer who led an Everest Expedition and had written 14 books, came to us for his

15th, and also became a welcome guest at our house. Miles Smeeton, another Himalayan mountaineer had, with his wife Beryl, twice been capsized in their yacht off Cape Horn. He had written five previous books, but came to Nautical for his sixth, and became a welcome family friend. Another fine yachtsman who had experienced the capsize of his yacht in the Southern Ocean was Bill King, and he had written an excellent book. He came to Nautical for his book "Capsize", and he too became a family guest whose company we greatly enjoyed. John Illingworth, twice winner of the Fastnet race, winner of the Sydney-Hobart race, and well known as a yacht designer, was the author of four books, but he came to Nautical for his next one "The Malham Story."

Our books had become well established in many countries, so I looked very carefully into the possibility of forming an international company, perhaps jointly with companies in our field from other countries. Konrad-Wilhelm of Germany showed interest, and we were advised that it would be best to form such a company in Switzerland. So I went there to make enquiries, suggesting the name International Nautical Publishing Company. A helpful and distinctly charming woman told me that if the word International came into the title, a large capital

Richard Creagh-Osborne and I discuss with Herr Delius forming United Nautical Publishers, adding Unieboek of Holland and Ugo Mursia of Italy

was necessary. I told her jokingly that I had needed to borrow a few coins even to buy a stick of shaving soap, but she insisted that borrowing a million francs would be easier. That did not appeal to me, so it came out that the word United instead of International would make it more within our likely means.

The company was duly formed as United Nautical Publishers, and the shares were held by Nautical Publishing of England, Delius Klasing of Germany, Unieboek of Holland and Ugo Mursia of Italy. The first meeting, with the chairmen of the four companies attending, was held at Lymington when I took the chair. It was agreed that administrative board meetings should normally be held in the home offices of the President, which each company would take in term for two years. The first was Herr Delius, who got agreement that the next meeting would be held in Lymington, perhaps because after the meeting was over we could go out in my yacht.

United Nautical Publishers came to be known as UNP, and the first title we published was written by Richard Creagh-Osborne, edited in Lymington and called "This is Sailing." It was not only an outstanding success but also founded a series of "This is...." volumes with colour illustrations. Book rights of "This is Sailing" were sold in 13 countries and sales after 10 years were well over 400,000, with a revised edition being prepared. This thoroughly valuable book was followed with many more in the same series. My own contribution was "This is Rough Weather Sailing", which was published in nine languages and after two years over 100,000 copies had been sold.

Of course it was pleasant to receive royalty cheques, but I found one of the greatest joys from writing a book came from letters of comment when it was published. Normally they were personal letters from people I knew, or perhaps had known many years before. But there were also letters from unexpected quarters. For instance one came from Parkhurst Prison asking for advice on a sailing problem; apparently that long term prisoner helped to pass his time inside by dreaming of the time when he could go sailing.

Managing a company certainly has human factors, and so much of our success depended on the people of all ranks that worked for the company. In Nautical Publishing 15 people, other than directors, worked for us and from the quality and quantity of their work, they must have enjoyed it. For the first two years the business ran from a section of our house in Captain's Row, Lymington. Then the office shifted to a nearby house, as Daphne and I moved our home a couple of miles out into the country in Pennington, where we could look over a few fields to the Solent and the Isle of Wight. From my bed the red flash of Needles Lighthouse was visible, and sometimes I could also see the lights of a ship in the English Channel, making for the western entrance to the Solent.

By then things had settled enough to be able to take a week or two off from work and three times more I was able to sail in the Admiral's Cup series. My own small sailing cruiser enjoyed more sailing, with family visits across to the Channel Islands and Brittany. By the end of 1980, thirteen years after the partnership was formed, we had published 154 books, besides some films. The age of 70 was in sight, so it was time to think of the company's future. The obvious thing seemed to me that Richard Creagh-Osborne should become Managing Director and Chairman, while I could become a consultant. When I mentioned this to him, he surprised me by saying that his health was worrying him and he did not feel like taking on more responsibility, although only just past 50 years old. I was shocked when he told me he was suffering from cancer. I had not got over this shock when not very long afterwards he died. We were all very distressed and sad to lose a good friend and colleague.

My capital was nearly all in my house, my yacht and my share of the company, so I could not buy Richard's share. The answer was to sell Nautical with its share of United Nautical, and two London publishers at once showed interest. Negotiations proved that the distinguished company of Macmillan would be best, particularly for Richard's share, which would go to his widow. The sale naturally required that Peter, who had by then inherited a baronetcy so had become Sir Peter Johnson, and myself should sell our shares. However the new directors appointed by Macmillan willingly took on Peter as Editorial Manager. For myself Macmillan contracted to engage me as consultant for three years. A Board of Management was appointed with the Right Hon. Maurice Macmillan M.P. as chairman, and myself as Deputy Chairman. Thus still working from Lymington I had ample opportunity to look for new books, to edit publishing projects, and to promote Nautical. In effect Julian Ashby, a Macmillan director, acted as Managing Director, while Richard Hartgill, Macmillan's Assistant Management Accountant, took on all the accounting which had previously been my responsibility. Thus I was free for far more activities out of the office.

Adlard Coles' classic "Channel Harbours and Anchorages" had been first published some 25 year earlier, so was due for major revision, which Macmillans invited me to undertake. Many of the small French harbours dried out at low tide, so it was convenient to use a twin keel yacht which would remain upright. I was due for a new family yacht, so selected a Westerly Griffon class boat, which had twin keels, and transferred the name *Dayspring* to her. Many a weekend and more of the following summer was spent in *Dayspring* visiting delightful little harbours and anchorages on the French north coast from Barfleur to St Malo, besides the Channel Islands. I was normally accompanied for this book revision by Peter Moens and Hugo Walford, both experienced yacht skippers, while sometimes Daphne was able to come too.

This *Dayspring* was very much a cruising boat, so never went racing. Yet I kept some

Dayspring was just right as a family cruising boat.

interest in racing when invited to join protest committees, as in the sport of yacht racing the rules are mainly enforced by skippers protesting against other competitors. Such protests come before a committee which hears evidence from both sides, and then acts as a jury to decide the case. My records show 200 protest committees in which I served as chairman, and a few more when the chair was taken by very experienced authorities on the racing rules, especially Mary Pera, who under her maiden name of Blewitt had navigated a Fastnet race winner, besides a yacht crossing the Atlantic both ways. She had also written several books and I considered her the leading authority on yacht racing rules.

The sport of ocean racing owed much to the handicap system so that yachts of many sizes, types and rigs could race against each other. At that time the rating system of the Royal Ocean Racing Club was widely used, although not in America. Under any system, each potential competitor had to be measured by someone specially qualified to do this, and the handicaps were then calculated by a technical office. At that time this office was established in Lymington, and as I lived nearby the Royal Ocean Racing Club appointed me as the committee member to keep an eye on this office, as it was far from the main office in London.

Macmillan meetings normally only required visits to London every few months, so I cut down honorary work in London so far as possible. This included no longer standing for election to the Royal Yachting Association Council, besides resigning from its various committees. Those who were not approaching 70 years old could do these things better. Yet I doubt if many of them could enjoy quiet cruising any more than I did.

In winter I could travel further afield for lecturing, which meant visiting Scotland and Eire. Such visits were very enjoyable, meeting so many delightful people. As well as lectures to yacht clubs, there were schools training establishments. I even lectured to prisons, which were flattering as the inmates always wanted to keep out of their cells so they tried to prolong my lecture as long as possible and they specially relished question time with the freedom to express their own views.

CHAPTER TWENTY

Septuagenarian and Beyond 1983-

The end of 1983 meant reaching my seventies, and the contract with Macmillans had run its course. All five of our children were beyond school age and, by then, we had ten grandchildren. We built on to our house in Lower Pennington, a mile or so outside Lymington. Daphne's twin brother David retired from the Army and, as a bachelor, has a section of the house as his own. He could use the two acres of paddocks and part of the stables for his polo ponies.

Yet we could still have the whole family bunch to stay. Some could camp in our small woodlet and some sleep in a tree house which David had built in a large oak tree. Part of the house extension is a studio for Daphne. She enjoys painting, and her work is well regarded, especially her seascapes. While she works creating pictures, I was often typing in my study, from which I can see the Solent when the leaves are off the trees. A few articles, usually associated with the sea, covered the costs, at

The new wing built onto our house near Lymington gave more space for visits by the fast increasing family.

214

least, of my boat. Daphne designs, manages and mainly works the flower garden, while I look after the kitchen garden. This is a pleasure especially because Daphne became a vegetarian some years ago, and finds the flavour of our own fruit and vegetables better than any from the shops.

When the weather was good, we often sailed off for picnics in the Solent, especially favouring Newtown River in the Isle of Wight and Keyhaven on the Hampshire side. We sometime entered through Hawker's Lake, named after one of Daphne's ancestors Colonel Hawker. Occasionally we sailed across to France or the Channel Islands, but for cruising further in more comfort than my small boat can offer, we were fortunate as my cousins Alan and Rosemary Burroughs had a very much bigger Westerly sloop called *Brilliance* and would often take us sailing. Indeed, throughout my early seventies the pattern was an early summer cruise to Brittany, the weather being better in the Bay of Biscay than in the English Channel. Often Daphne could not come, but each year I went as navigator; another regular member of the crew was Johnie Everett, who like Alan had been a keen oar in his younger days. Alan had rowed in the Cambridge crew more than once against Oxford, and even after losing a leg in the war, could row a boat better than most. So suitably, he lived on the River Thames at Henley, and sometimes we were guests in their house for the Henley Regatta. The Burroughs also have a house in Jersey, where Rosemary's grandfather Lord Trent, who had founded the famous chemists firm of Boots, had lived when Rosemary was a child. The Burroughs' Jersey house was usually on the track coming back from Brittany.

On one particular cruise in *Brilliance* we visited the Normandy harbour of St Vaast, where nearby was the old chateau of Baron Brix. He welcomed us warmly, saying that both Rosemary and I were his cousins. Later I got my brother Merlin, a connoisseur of Bruce history, to substantiate this. He confirmed that after the Viking Brusce family had settled in Normandy, Robert the Norman crossed the English Channel in 1066 with William the Conqueror, while his elder brother remained in Normandy. Thus we were cousins, but very long range ones. Many of the Brix family lived in the area, so there was a massive family reunion in a hotel owned by one of them. As the eldest of the British branch of the family present, it was my responsibility to give formal thanks to our hosts, but my French seemed hardly up to this. However one of the Brix family arranged for someone to sit next to me who was familiar with both languages to act as a prompt should I falter. This proved a real bonus, as Stephanie was not only bilingual, but a very attractive girl still studying in Paris.

The sea and a sail were my favourite means of travel, but sometimes other methods had to be used, even for pleasure. Thus one summer my sister Lorema and sister-in-law Joan joined Daphne and I for a camping and walking visit in the central Pyrenees. Another year, it was painting and walking in Southern Spain. Then again it was Florence to enjoy art galleries.

Daphne and I have been very fortunate to have both our sons living within walking distance of us. For over fifteen years Peregrine and his family have lived within five miles of us. After leaving the Army he worked for a time in the yacht industry and then started up his own business nearby. He owns a cruising yacht which is much better than mine, but his two daughters, Rachel and Anna, love ponies much more than boats. When Peter left the Navy as a Commander he also bought a house within a few miles of us. For him, a bachelor, sailing took a very high position, and when racing his various yachts it was rarity for him not to win a place. As an author of pilotage books, he soon took on the reputation that Adlard Coles had enjoyed a generation before, and indeed he was invited to bring up to date some of Adlard's books, including his great work on heavy weather sailing. Peter also set up his own publishing company as I had done.

Our three daughters are much further afield. Rosamund, whose husband Jeremy Holmes is a psychiatric consultant, moved from London to North Devon and became a grandmother in 1986 to make us great grandparents. Errollyn, whose husband Richard Lindley was a university lecturer before turning to the law, lives in West Yorkshire with their three bright children, Sam, Emma and Joe. Chloe has taken over a nearly derelict Scottish croft in Kirkcudbright, working as a herbalist and to make the croft habitable for her three children.

In 1989, all the family gathered at our home for our Golden Wedding Anniversary. Grandchildren and great grandchildren amounted to eighteen, while another was born later that year. We had indeed been blessed. It was another blessing that through my seventies physical health was so good, especially considering that my early days had been rather plagued by injuries and illnesses. However my memory did not age so well, and I am often stuck over the names of close acquaintances, although the name of a casual acquaintance of half a century before will come up clearly. Places also get muddled and, after more than 30 years living in Lymington, I sometimes can not remember which turning to take when shopping. Yet once in a boat my memory seems quite at home.

Thus the boat provides treatment. At least in the winter months, when my mind gets most sleepy, an hour or two of sailing exercises the brain. A regular routine for some years made it a habit to wake with the radio shipping forecast at 5.55 a.m. This told me whether to don seaboots and oilskins while a gale warning for the area advised me to set a modest amount of sail. The forecast of fog meant I probably stayed ashore. Then I got down to the harbour and climbed aboard at pontoon moorings. I know the boat so well that even in the dark it needs no more than five minutes preparation before hauling clear. Rigged with furling sails it is so simple to set the amount required, and I could confidently expect to sail out from the line of moored yachts by 6.30 a.m. In December and January it is still completely dark then, unless the moon is up. With a reasonable amount of wind the boat can be out in the Solent by 7.00a.m., and on a clear night the first signs of dawn will be showing in the East, while the flash of the Needles Lighthouse will still be visible to the West. So often the best weather of the day is around dawn, and even a few tacks in the Solent is surely enough to make anyone cheerful for the rest of the day.

Coming back up the river there are often some fishing boats outward bound to exchange waves with, and the Isle of Wight ferry to avoid, as it has the right of way. At low tide, if still fairly dark on a cloudy morning, the Brent geese usually tell me if I am getting into the shallows, and by the time they set off back to Siberia, the early mornings are light. In mid-winter sometimes I get back to my moorings as the top rim of the sun rises above the Isle of Wight. Life then feels very good.

One January morning was not so good. It was freezing hard, but I had donned masses of clothing, so all seemed well enough as I returned to the boat's regular mooring and secured her forward and aft. Then leaning over to pick up a fender, the icy boathook slipped out of my hands, so I lay down on the deck trying to reach it, but the deck was too icy and a slight wash from a passing motor boat slipped me into the river. They knew nothing about it as it was dark and the motor boat was far off in any case.

I could not reach the deck, and although the yacht has a ladder secured to the stern I could not get to it with the strong tide, yet I could struggle to the pontoon ahead, but that was also too high for me to haul out. So it meant swimming under the pontoon and after a long struggle to remain afloat, to reach the muddy shore following half an hour in the ice cold water. There was still quite a struggle along the mud to a ladder that could take me up the high wall bounding the river. There I lay down on the grass to empty the water from my sea boots and heavy clothing.

It's hardly surprising that I then lost consciousness, but the habit of going to my nearby car on so many dawns took me there and it seems that the car itself well knew the mile back home, as only when I saw Daphne did my consciousness tell me who and where I was. At that point she took over the thinking and quickly undressed me and put me in a warm bath.

In my eighties I know that life has favoured me superbly. Despite rather a large share of accidents and illnesses, I have enjoyed enough sparkling good health to give brilliance to so many intriguing adventures and to enjoy the company of so many interesting people. In professional life - the navy, writing, magazine editing and book publishing, so much has depended upon human relationships. This applies very much also with the sport of sailing and all other forms of recreation. Some naval friends suggested that nearly three years of isolation from anyone I knew, while serving in the Isles of Orkney, would prove a strain; yet there was warm friendship with the people of those islands who were remarkable for helping others. Perhaps in my life family relationships have been the most significant of all. Indeed Daphne and I have been blessed with more than 20 direct descendants - children, grand-children and great-grand-children. Thus I can feel deeply that my greatest fortune was that Daphne agreed to be my wife, and the benefits of our marriage grow year by year.